# Collective Bargaining and Wage Formation

## ETLA – The Research Institute of the Finnish Economy

Series A39 (ISSN 0356-7435)

ETLA

ETLA, The Research Institute of the Finnish Economy, established in 1946, is a private independent non-profit research organisation that produces economic forecasts and carries out research in economics, business administration and social policy. By focussing on topics that are central to Finland's international competitiveness and economic performance, ETLA provides important support to decision-making on key issues of economic and social policy.

Address: ETLA, Lönnrotinkatu 4 B, FIN-00120 Helsinki, Finland
Internet: www.etla.fi

Previous Volumes Published in Association with ETLA, Helsinki

Synnöve Vuori and Pentti Vuorinen (Eds.)
Explaining Technical Change in a Small Country

Rita Asplund (Ed.) Human Capital Creation in an Economic Perspective

Broer Peter and Jukka Lassila (Eds.)
Pension Policies and Public Debt in Dynamic CGE Models

## PT – Labour Institute for Economic Research

Studies 91 (ISSN 1236-7176)

LABOUR INSTITUTE FOR ECONOMIC RESEARCH

The Labour Institute for Economic Research is an independent and non-profit research organisation founded in 1971. The Institute carries out economic research, monitors economic development and publishes macroeconomic forecasts. The aim is to contribute to the economic debate and to provide information for economic policy decision making in Finland.

Address: PT, Pitkänsillanranta 3 A, FIN-00530 Helsinki, Finland
Internet: www.labour.fi

Hannu Piekkola · Kenneth Snellman
(Editors)

# Collective Bargaining and Wage Formation

## Performance and Challenges

With 48 Figures and 28 Tables

Physica-Verlag
A Springer Company

Hannu Piekkola, Ph.D.
ETLA
Lönnrotinkatu 4 B
00120 Helsinki
Finland
hannu.piekkola@etla.fi

Kenneth Snellman, Ph.D.
Labour Institute
for Economic Research
Pitkänsillanranta 3 A
00530 Helsinki
Finland
kenneth.snellman@labour.fi

Cataloging-in-Publication Data
Library of Congress Control Number: 2004111081

ISBN 3-7908-1558-6 Physica-Verlag Heidelberg New York



Physica is a part of Springer Science+Business Media

springeronline.com


Printed in Germany



Cover-Design: Erich Kirchner, Heidelberg

SPIN 11019503 88/3130-5 4 3 2 1 0 – Printed on acid-free paper

## Preface and Acknowledgements

In recent years, new ways to adjust to changes in industrial organisation and the labour market have been tested in the process of collective bargaining. Globalization, EMU, and the increase in (intra-)industrial trade have reshaped wage setting in European countries. Collective bargaining and continuous interplay between employee and employer organisations have faced new challenges.

To study these issues, a project "Rules of the game in the labour market: Industrial relations, the bargaining system and income policies in the 2000s", financed by the Finnish Work Environment Fund and carried out jointly by ETLA (The Research Institute of the Finnish Economy) and the Labour Institute for Economic Research, was initiated in 2001. A seminar on "Collective Bargaining and Wage Formation" was organised by ETLA and the Labour Institute for Economic Research in Helsinki, Finland, on December 15, 2003.

This volume contains refereed versions of these papers. The Finnish contributions were part of the above research project. Financial support from the Finnish Work Environment Fund is gratefully acknowledged.

Helsinki, June 2004

Hannu Piekkola
Kenneth Snellman

# Contents

# Introduction and Summary

Hannu Piekkola and Kenneth Snellman

ETLA, The Research Institute of the Finnish Economy, Helsinki, Finland
The Labour Institute for Economic Research, Helsinki, Finland

## 1 The Basic Issues

Wages have traditionally been agreed on collectively in Europe. The articles in this volume examine the current state of collective bargaining as well as the challenges it is currently facing. The issues examined in these papers have a wide applicability to problems on the European labour markets. Torben M. Andersen and Steinar Holden review challenges from globalisation and inter-industry trade and the adaptation to a low-inflation environment. The other contributions are part of the project investigating collective bargaining in Finland, carried out by ETLA (the Research Institute of the Finnish Economy) and the Labour Institute for Economic Research. Some of them use results from a Finnish survey carried out by the two institutes ETLA and the Labour Institute on the views of employers and employees about labour relations and the labour market negotiation system.

Bargaining systems are complex and their future development depends on their historical evolution, recent and past experiences, and the current situation in the labour market, as well as changes in the international environment. By examining the past functioning of the bargaining system one can observe how different elements in it have interacted with various factors in the environment of the system. We think that the articles analysing the functioning of the Finnish labour market also have important implications for other European countries with similar wage bargaining regimes.

We aim at providing a thorough investigation of the properties, advantages and drawbacks of collective bargaining in different forms. The aim of this publication is also to supply an examination of the most significant current pressures on the collective bargaining system and to examine how it should respond to them. For this purpose one inevitably has to consider the changes occurring in the economy that forms the setting of the wage bargaining.

An issue of much current interest is the implications of a low-inflation environment, anchored by the EMU, for collective bargaining and wage formation in the EU. Entry into the monetary union has implied a radical shift from the times of high inflation in the 1970s and 1980s. The monetary union may have raised the demand for coordination in the labour market to hold pay rises down, as the costs of high pay rises have risen. On the other hand, there may be more need for flexibility in wage setting as inflation and exchange rate adjustments no longer correct possible errors made in setting nominal wages. This constrains the labour markets and reshapes the institutions as the bargaining parties search for more appropriate ways to settle in the new environment.

Besides the obvious change in the expectations concerning inflation and monetary policy, there have been other more subtle changes in the environment of the bargaining system. These include changes in the structure and location of production. Firms have become ever more interdependent, as specialisation has grown and intra-industrial trade has increased. Competition has increased, as it has been possible to buy an ever-larger part of the labour services needed in a firm from outside. Stronger dependence on other firms also means a need to respond more often to changes in their environment. Increasing specialisation has also meant relocations of production to places abroad, and more import of goods and services needed to assemble the final product. Both inexpensive, unskilled labour and, to an ever larger extent, also skilled labour is available from the new member countries of the EU and outside Europe, and this has implied increasing competition for the workers employed in these industries in the old EU.

These changes in the economic environment form the background to the studies on the performance of the labour market and the wage bargaining included in this volume. Because of the complexity of the bargaining systems one has to simplify and focus on a small number of the systems' characteristics. One such simplification is the concept of the degree of centralisation that the bargaining has.

Finland can be considered as an example of a centralised bargaining system. The Finnish labour market is highly organised. Approximately 80 per cent of the salaried employees belong to unions, and the coverage of collective agreements is over 90 per cent. Similarly, most employers are organised in their federations and confederations. Wage bargaining takes place mainly at the sectoral or industry level, and there are usually different collective agreements for workers who are paid on an hourly basis and for salaried employees. The collective agreements usually stipulate the minimum tariff wages at different job-complexity levels and educational levels in a given industry. The wage bargaining usually starts with negotiation between the central organisations of the employees' unions and the employers' confederations. If a central nationwide agreement is reached between them, the employees' unions and employers' federations decide whether it is acceptable or not for the industry and the employee group concerned. If they accept the central framework agreement, the process stops there. On the other hand, if they reject it, they will negotiate their own collective agreement separately from the central agreement. The government has often taken part in these negotiations in an intermediating role, even though there is no formal basis for this.

The centralised bargaining and tripartite system in economic and labour market policies has been seen as a way to keep nominal wage increases and inflation down. However, it has turned out to be difficult to take into account industry- or firm-specific issues in the centralised bargaining. Although union density has been slightly declining in many European countries, collective bargaining of one kind or another is still a central feature of wage formation. Collective bargaining can take many forms from firm-wise via industry-level to economy-wide centralised bargaining; in the future there may even be Europe-wide bargaining. Thus, there is a range of alternative ways of bargaining collectively, and in the countries which have experienced a decentralisation of bargaining there has not been an unequivocal transformation of the bargaining systems towards bargaining only on the level of the firm. What will be the share of local bargaining at the firm level and what will be the role of individual-level bargaining, which is customary for professional, salaried employees? This collection of papers provides a scientific look at these issues in a field with much political interest.

## 2 The Articles in this Volume

*Torben M. Andersen* highlights the increasing importance of trade, especially intra-industry trade, caused by the reduction of trade frictions. About 75% of global trade is intra-industrial. Thereby, the relocation of activities and production has become easier, which clearly affects labour markets, too. Labour demand will become more elastic with respect to wage claims in this globalisation process. The Volkswagen agreement in 2001 was an example of a case where relocation of production shifted the firm's threat point in case a wage agreement was not reached. Another aspect of globalisation is an increase in foreign direct investments (FDI). Jobs are transferred within multinationals to plants in low-wage countries. *Pekka Ilmakunnas*, in his comment on Andersen, emphasises that this will happen, especially in a later stage of the industry life cycle, when production is more standardised. Andersen notes that these wage pressures have caused more flexible wage setting, while centralised elements have remained in the Nordic labour markets, especially in other issues like bargaining on working hours and working conditions.

Andersen uses a stylised partial equilibrium approach, but adheres to his general equilibrium analysis in Andersen and Skaksen (2003). He carefully examines the consequences of the globalisation process, which also has its advantages for the industrial countries. Despite the weakening of their negotiating power, employees may actually be better off, both in terms of employment and wages. However, he also discusses an eventual increase in demand for an insurance mechanism if globalisation brings more risk to one's position in the labour market. Both Anderson and Ilmakunnas also discuss the union's problems in setting wage demands, especially in the timing of the wage demands. Early wage moderation may slow down later relocation, but if it is known that relocation is inevitable, it may be optimal to demand high wages in the beginning.

*Steinar Holden* considers the labour market in a low-inflation environment. He reviews the literature on the effects of low steady-state inflation on wage formation that can be approached from four different viewpoints. The first effect is that, under low inflation, downward nominal wage rigidity may prevent real wage cuts, which would have been achieved with higher inflation. There may be several reasons for this. One reason is that contracts need to be renegotiated as in Holden (1994) and MacLeod and Malcomson (1993). Another reason is fairness considerations and money illusion. The second effect concerns the notion that wages are given by nominal contracts, and that inflation affects both how often wages are adjusted, and to what extent wages are set in a forward-looking manner. The third effect considered concerns the fact that with incomplete contracts firms are forced to raise nominal wages to prevent workers from inflicting costs on the firm. Under low inflation this leads to higher real wage pressures and higher unemployment. Fourth, Holden considers the idea that moderate positive inflation reduces wage pressure when effort depends on wages relative to a reference level, and workers and firms underweight inflation when updating the reference level. Holden then ends the article by discussing to what extent labour markets may adapt to a low-inflation environment. The conclusion is that there are good reasons to believe that moderate inflation increases employment in the long run from what it would be at zero inflation. Economic institutions and expectations may, to some extent, adapt to low inflation, but this is unlikely to eliminate the effect on wage formation and employment. Fixed wage contracts may be good for inducing investments, but this does not always compensate for the reduction in flexibility (Holden 2001). In his comment *Tapio Palokangas* discusses some of the microeconomic foundations of the bargaining process and their role in accomplishing downward nominal wage rigidity. He especially emphasises the role of risk in wage formation.

*Jukka Pekkarinen and Kari E.O. Alho* present results from a unique survey of bargaining agents' perceptions of the Finnish bargaining system. As opposed to earlier surveys like Agell and Lundborg (1995), the survey also covers employees, and the same questionnaire was addressed both to employers and to employees in a sample of firms that cover the private sector in Finland. The questionnaire was also sent – with minimal changes – to the representatives of the unions and employer federations and the representatives of the respective central organisations in the labour market. The survey reveals differences in the opinions on labour market flexibility between employers and employees. Employers view the current labour market flexibility as insufficient and many would like to have the option to offer employment at a somewhat lower wage than the going tariff wages. Employees, on the other hand, oppose flexibility that entails higher wage dispersion on the grounds that it would adversely affect the position of the weakest segment of the labour force. This dispute remains unresolved, not least because of divergent opinions as to what degree greater wage dispersion would actually raise employment.

One topic in which these differences in opinions are reflected is the role of tariff wages, which set a minimum wage for each skill level and industry and thus a minimum wage for all employees. Tariff wages may create a constraint for the recruitment of less productive low-wage workers. According to the survey results, employers partly agree with the view that such contractual wage floors do prevent the creation of low-wage jobs. Employees also consider it very important that tariff wages set a minimum level for the pay, thus affording them security.

Based on the survey results, the general opinion among the labour market actors is fairly positive on both sides of the current wage negotiation system. However, wide support for greater company-level wage bargaining prevails among employers. This does not, however, imply support for atomistic wage setting, because the peace clause included in industry-level agreements is highly valued. Some caution in interpreting the results is also appropriate. First of all, the employee opinions are those of union representatives, i.e. shop stewards in the firm. The expressed opinions may thus not perfectly reflect the opinions of employees in the firms, which may partly explain the relatively low variation in employee responses between firms. One should also note that opinions reflect desires, while the existing level of flexibility in wage setting differs between employees and salaried workers and may vary from one industry to another.

*Kari E.O. Alho* challenges Finnish centralised wage bargaining about the way in which it can produce incentives for a skilled workforce. Alho argues that the Finnish wage bargaining system has rested on the implicit agreement that the labour unions obey, on average, a moderate wage and incomes policy, but at the same time the largest of them have the power to influence the pattern of wage rises over the wage scale in a decisive way. This has led to solidaristic wage formation and excessive rises in the wages at the lower end of the income distribution and in firms and industries with lower-than-average productivity. Alho shows that the wage level in the five lowest-productivity industries relative to average in all industries exceeds the equivalent productivity ratio between low and average productivity industries by 17 percentage points. This is three times as much as in the US. What are the consequences of negotiated wages that are possibly set at too high a level for low-skilled workers in the low productivity industries? He first shows the expected outcome that the wages of skilled workers will be scaled down, as the productivity of the skilled labour is lower in an equilibrium for this type of labour. However, Alho then shows in an efficiency wage framework that the wages of the highly skilled will be adjusted upwards. The intuition behind this is the aim to maintain wage differences in order not to decrease the effort of high-skilled workers too excessively. This can also be explained by considerations of envy, since the effort of highly skilled workers depends, in his model, on the relative wages between high-skilled and low-skilled workers. The relative wages tend to remain unchanged, even though there is a regulation raising the low wages. Overall, Alho is worried about sufficient incentive mechanisms and labour demand in centralised bargaining. As the final item, Alho raises the issue as to what the relationship is between productivity and its reward in wages within a firm. This is an important topic which deserves more attention, as some recent analysis, see Moen and Rosén (2003), suggests that the marginal reward should be rising in terms of productivity, while in practice it seems to be more the case that a reverse relationship holds between productivity and the wage rate.

*Anni Heikkilä and Hannu Piekkola* analyse the opinion of the proper, locally bargained share of contract wages using the unique survey of bargaining agents' perceptions of the Finnish bargaining system. They show that Finnish employers and employees diverge in their desire for local wage bargaining. The employers want the locally bargained wage share to be approximately half of the total wage rise, while the majority of employees prefer this share to be below 25%. Finnish employers thus want the locally bargained wage share to be significantly larger than the locally bargained share in the current centralised wage agreement. However, employers' attitudes towards local bargaining vary a lot with the firm characteristics. It is shown that employers in large firms and in the financial services sector demand the largest locally bargained share of contract wages.

Heikkilä and Piekkola also show that employers are willing to incorporate employees into local bargaining decisions when the firm size is 30–299 employees or when the firm is profitable and operates in the service sector. The divergence of opinions of employees and employers in large firms and the employers' reluctance to incorporate employees in decision-making creates a major challenge to the local wage bargaining.

*Roope Uusitalo* considers the consequences of centralised bargaining for the level of the wage increases in the economy. According to his results, centralised bargaining rounds in Finland have given both lower bargained and lower actual nominal wage increases. The effect remains and even becomes stronger when the negative effect of unemployment on wage changes is taken into account. This indicates that centralised bargaining can be an important method for holding inflation at a low level. However, Uusitalo emphasises that a part of the effects on wage changes may be a result of the fact that the government has often participated in centralised bargaining, changing government policies in a way that has benefited employees. He also points out that the choice to bargain on the industry level is sometimes made as a consequence of the fact that centralised bargaining has failed. The industry-level bargaining that follows may then have a worse starting point.

*Kenneth Snellman* examines wage changes under centralised and industry-level bargaining in Finland and shows that, in addition to the average level of wage changes, the relative wage changes between industries have differed in centralised and industry-level rounds. Parting from a centralised agreement has led to a relative rise in the bargained wage changes in food, saw-milling, and building construction, as well as the hotel and restaurant industries. To some extent, wage drift has compensated for the differences in changes in bargained wages. However, in years with bargaining at the industry level covering all industries food, saw-milling, and building construction industries have not experienced a higher increase in bargained wages relative to the average. Snellman also examines whether the opinions expressed by employees and employers in the survey can explain the observed behaviour in recent decades. However, he concludes that differences in employees' opinions are small across industries and, hence, do not seem to reflect the differences observed in the propensity to participate in centralised agreements.

*Pekka Sauramo* analyses the drastic decline in the labour share of income which took place in Finland during the 1990s. He examines whether the low level of the labour share can be regarded as a new equilibrium level or whether it reflects a macro-economic disequilibrium. In the analysis, he utilises the concept of ELIS (equilibrium labour income share) originally employed by Draper and Huizinga (2000). Within the framework, the ELIS is affected by three major factors: movements in relative prices, changes in technology and alternations in the intensity of competition in the product market. The main conclusion Sauramo draws is that the decline in the labour share cannot be explained as a decline in the ELIS, i.e. it cannot be explained by the three factors. The low labour share is therefore an indication of a macro-economic disequilibrium. Furthermore, the disequilibrium is characterised by abnormally high levels of profitability and unemployment. The equilibrium can therefore be achieved through a process during which the labour share increases and the unemployment rate decreases. Consequently, the increase in the labour share should not automatically be interpreted as a worrisome sign of weakening economic developments. Sauramo argues that this assessment can be taken as a starting point in future negotiations on incomes policy. However, he also emphasises that the labour share, which is too low, should not be restored immediately. As long as the unemployment rate is above the NAIRU, the labour share should be below the ELIS. The openness of the economy and shocks from abroad may also influence future development.

*Jukka Lassila* presents the recent reform of the earnings-related pension system in the private sector in Finland. The reform was heavily influenced by tripartite participation of the employers and the employee organisations and the central government, since all partners had to agree on the reform. Lassila points out the role of the labour market parties, and examines the mechanisms of the pension system as well as the welfare outcomes for citizens. In particular, he analyses the effects on the income of different cohorts in an Auerbach-Kotlikoff type of dynamic general equilibrium model. According to his analyses current young workers lose somewhat because of the reform, while future workers will gain. For current old workers the effect of the reform is small. Because early retirement was punished in the reform, the total effect on income is more positive for those with higher education who generally retire later. Lassila also emphasises that the pension system will interact with wage bargaining as the current wage changes affect capital accumulation, current pensions and thereby the future pensions of the current workers. To raise future pensions the workers may reduce their wage claims somewhat.

The book ends with two general notes by representatives of Finnish employer and employee organisations. *Risto Alanko* is head of the department of Labour Market Policy in The Confederation of Finnish Industry and Employers TT and *Leena Kostiainen* is director at the Finnish Confederation of Salaried Employees STTK. Alanko emphasises that the flexibility of labour market agreements is not necessarily related to the level at which negotiations are made: central or sectoral. Both central and industry levels are centralised levels from the point of view of an individual company. Kostiainen points out the importance of determining the role of local bargaining and how it can be used to attain flexibility.

The articles in this volume clearly indicate challenges for the collective bargaining created by international trade and a new area of collective bargaining under low inflation. The articles analyse many relevant aspects, such as the appropriate labour share in total valued added, the desired locally bargained share of contract wages and flexibility in terms of industry-level or firm-level productivity differences, or the adaptation of collective bargaining in other fields closely related to the labour market, such as the pension system. The volume thus gives new insights into how the labour market has evolved and how labour market institutions have or should adapt to a globalised environment.

## References

Agell, J. and Lundborg, P. (1995): Theories of Pay and Unemployment: Survey Evidence of Swedish Manufacturing Firms. *Scandinavian Journal of Economics 97*, 295–307.

Andersen, T.M. and Skaksen, J.R. (2003): Product Market Integration, Comparative Advantages and Labour Market Performance, IZA Working Paper, No. 698.

Draper, N. and Huizinga, F. (2000): ELIS: Equilibrium Labour Income Share, De Economist, vol. 148, nro5, s. 345–371.

Holden, S. (1994): Wage bargaining and nominal rigidities, *European Economic Review 38*, 1994, 1021–1039.

Holden, S. (2001): Does price stability exacerbate labour market rigidities in the EMU? Empirica 28, 403–418.

Ilmakunnas, P. and Maliranta, M. (2003): "Foreign medicine: A treatment effect analysis of the productivity effects of foreign ownership", mimeo.

MacLeod, W. B. and Malcolmson, J.M. (1993): Investment, hold-up, and the form of market contracts. *American Economic Review, 37*, 343–354.

Moen, E. and Rosén, Å. (2003): "Equilibrium Incentive Contracts", CEPR Discussion paper, No. 3790.

# International Product Market Integration and Wage Bargaining

Torben M. Andersen

Department of Economics, University of Aarhus, Denmark
CEPR, IZA and EPRU

## Abstract

The consequences of further international product market integration for wage bargaining are discussed. It is argued that current changes in international interactions pose new challenges for wage formation. In particular, the scope for appropriating rents may be affected, and it may become more difficult or costly to maintain centralized wage bargaining arrangements with solidaristic elements. At the same time, the demand for insurance mechanisms may increase, which is a particular challenge for the Nordic countries.

## 1 Introduction

It is recurrently questioned whether labour markets will have to adapt to the ongoing process of international integration. In particular, it is debated as to whether centralized systems of wage formation can be maintained, and whether observed trends towards more decentralization in some countries can be attributed to international integration. A related issue is the issue of whether a Europeanization of labour markets is taking place in the sense that the integration process forces national labour markets to become more similar in structure and whether the need for international cooperation increases.

These issues are particularly important for the Nordic countries, since these have historically been characterized by relatively centralized wage formation, which among other things has included more solidaristic wage outcomes (see e.g. Barth et al. (2003)). This is often seen as complementary to the development of an extended welfare state based on universalistic principles, since centralized wage formation, among other things, makes it possible to internalize the public budget and therefore avoid the strong distortionary effects of wage income taxation (Summers et al. (1993), Andersen (2003)).

It is therefore natural to ask why international integration poses new challenges for wage formation in the Nordic countries. These countries are routinely classified as "small and open", reflecting the fact that they have been tightly integrated in international markets for many years. Historically, the Nordic wage bargaining systems have evolved so as to deal with the competitive pressure from international markets. This is most clearly reflected in the so-called Scandinavian model of inflation (also known as the Aukrust or EFO model), which has two main ingredients, namely, i) room for wage increases is determined by the tradeable sector (basically as the sum of productivity increases and foreign price increases) and ii) solidaristic elements in wage formation imply that non-tradeable sectors are entitled to the same wage increase (see e.g. Bruce and Purvis (1985)). Institutionally, this has been accomplished in different ways in the Nordic countries, but the constraint set by the concern for international competitiveness has been present in all countries.

However, wage formation came under pressure in the Nordic countries during the 1980s and 1990s, and important changes have been made which are usually classified as "centralized decentralization". By this it is understood that the systems currently allow much more decentralized leverage over wage formation although some centralized elements remain, in respect to overall issues like pensions, working hours and work conditions. For an elaboration see, for example, Madsen et al. (2001). Figure 1 shows that the coordination index (see Boeri et al. (2001)) that captures the degree of centralization and coordination in wage setting in recent years has fallen for Denmark, Finland and Sweden, while it has remained unchanged for Norway.

**Fig. 1.** Labour Market Coordination Index

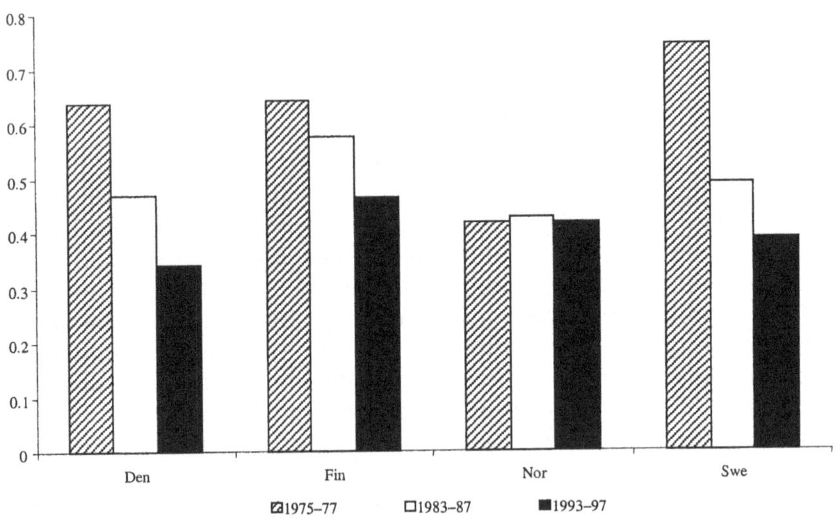


Source: Boeri et al. (2001).

Surprisingly, in an assessment of the future role of unions, Boeri et al. (2001) devote very little attention to the role of international integration and conclude that although trade has shifted from inter- towards intra-industrial trade, "this is consistent with our argument that economic integration in Europe has not so far been necessarily damaging to the prospects for unions' capturing a share of rents generated in (persistently) imperfectly competitive product markets". This conclusion stands in sharp contrast to casual evidence suggesting that a "European" element is playing a larger role in labour markets. Wage setting is often explicitly made with a reference to the "European norm" and the concern to have nominal wage increases to develop in accordance with the overall monetary objective of low and stable inflation, see, for example, the EU Commission (2003). In specific cases it is also quite visible that the improved "exit option" of employers affects labour market bargaining. Restructuring and employment reductions by multinationals like Danone and Marks and Spencer are two examples that have attracted substantial media attention. They were widely interpreted as examples of the Europeanization of labour markets and the flexibility with which firms operating in several European countries can relocate production and thus employment to the advantage of the firm and the disadvantage of the incumbent work force. Another important example is the Volkswagen agreement in 2001, which led to more flexible work conditions and wage moderation. In the latter case it was quite clear that the management explicitly used the argument that production could be relocated if the outcome was not satisfactory for the management.

Recent empirical work on the relation between trade and wages suggests some potential important links. In particular, it has been documented that exporting firms tend to have higher productivity and pay higher wages than comparable non-exporting firms, and the causality runs from productivity to exports, i.e. productive firms become exporters. Export is also associated with an exit of less productive firms and reallocation of resources to more efficient firms (Bernhard and Jensen (1999a, b), Bernhard, Eaton, Jensen and Kotum (2001)). Studies focusing on the import side of trade have found that lower trade barriers tend to decrease wage premia and that import penetration has a negative effect on wages (Nicoletti et al. 2001, Jean and Nicoletti (2001)). This evidence suggests that wage formation is affected by opposite forces running via an export opportunity tending to improve wage and job prospects and an import threat tending to worsen wage and employment prospects.

Accordingly, there is good reason to question whether the ongoing process of international integration changes economic structures in a way which will affect not only wage formation but also the institutional setting in labour markets. This paper provides an overview of some of the possible reasons why international integration may have such effects. The starting point is a brief summary of the trends in product market integration (Section 2) to point out that the level of trade has increased rapidly, but most importantly that the nature of trade has changed such that intra-industrial trade plays the dominant role. The latter is important, since it is a reason why wage bargaining systems which have operated well in the past may have to change. Having dealt with the empirical facts at the outset, the paper turns to the implications that intra-industrial trade has for wage formation, and outlines some basic mechanisms (section 3). An essential part of this process is the way in which integration affects the scope for risk sharing, since many labour market institutions can be interpreted as (implicit) risk-sharing arrangements, and section 4 discusses some of these aspects. Section 5 provides a few concluding remarks.

## 2 Trends in Integration

International trade has been growing rapidly in recent years, and matters significantly more for value added than in the past. Whereas GDP within the OECD area has grown by a factor of 4 since 1960 until today, international trade has grown by a factor of 16.

**Fig. 2.** Total EU-Trade: Cross-Country Average of EU Countries

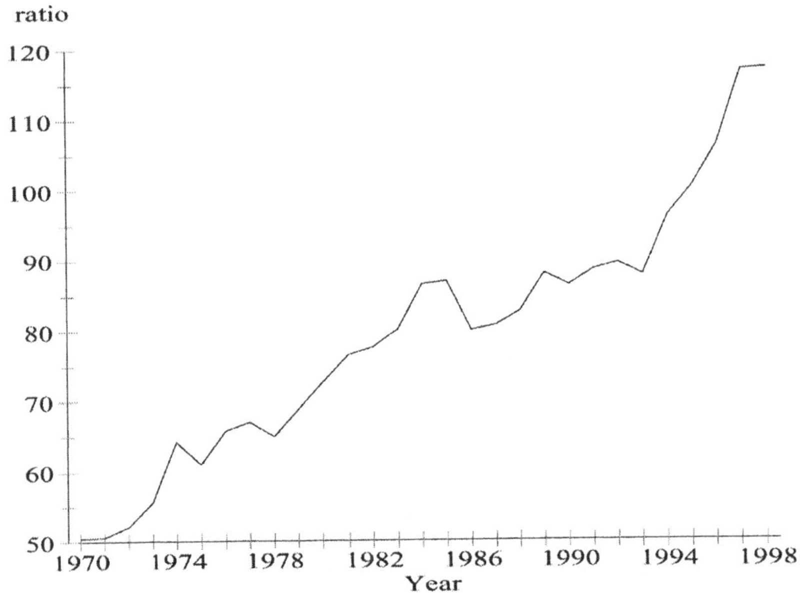


Source: Andersen, Haldrup and Sørensen (2000).

There are a number of important facts underlying this growth, which is of potential importance for labour markets. First, for sectors engaged in international trade, the increase in the relative importance of trade has been substantial. Figure 2 shows the trade share for the manufacturing sector in EU countries and a striking growth is observed. Whereas there has been a global increase in trade, it is noteworthy that trade flows remain concentrated regionally, as seen by Figure 3, showing that the EU is not significantly more open today than it was some three or four decades ago. That is, there has been a tremendous increase in trade, but most of this growth is concentrated on trade between European countries. The immediate implications are that the pressure from international integration primarily arises from countries with similar endowment structures, technologies etc., i.e. European integration.

**Fig. 3.** Extra-EU-Trade as a % of GDP – EU and USA

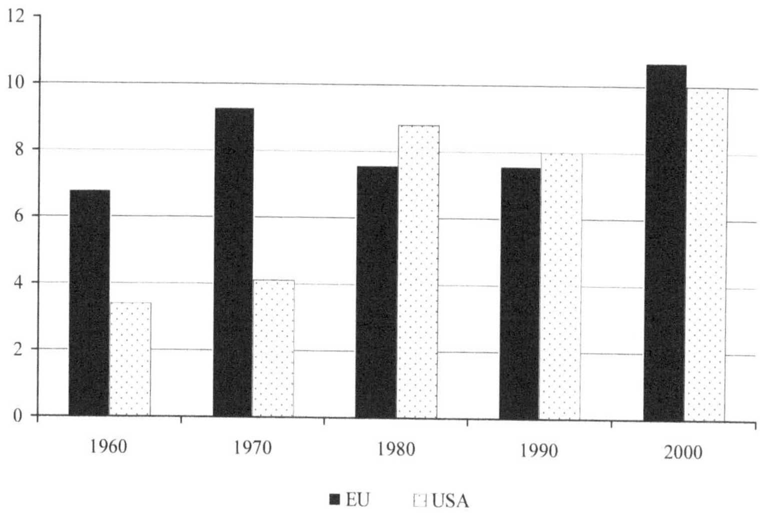


Source: OECD.

**Fig. 4.** Index for Intra-Industrial Trade, EU 1970–1986

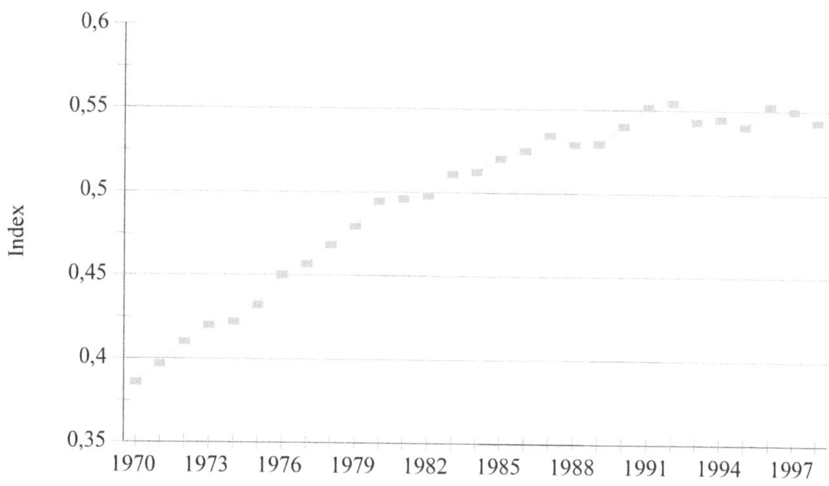


Note: The index for intra-industrial trade is the Grubel-Lloyd index.
Source: Andersen, Haldrup and Sørensen (2000).

A second important fact is that the nature of trade has changed. The major change is from inter-industrial towards intra-industrial trade. Historically, inter-industrial trade has been dominant, but today about 75% of global trade is intra-industrial. Figure 4 shows an index for the development in intra-industrial trade for the EU, and Table 1 gives the development for selected countries. It is seen that there has been a notable increase, especially during the 1980s.

Intra-industrial trade may arise from three sources: horizontal differentiation (e.g. different brands), vertical differentiation (e.g. different qualities) or vertical specialization of the production process (outsourcing of parts of the production process). The important thing about intra-industrial trade as compared with inter-industrial trade is that it tends to imply that production is less dependent on close proximity to natural resources or final consumers. It follows that these activities can more easily be relocated across countries and thus potentially different labour markets.

**Table 1.** Grubel-Lloyd Index of Intra-Industrial Trade: EU Countries

| Country | 1970 | 1980 | 1988–91 | 1992–95 | 1996–2000 |
|---|---|---|---|---|---|
| BEL/LUX | 69 | 76 | 77.6 | 77.7 | 71.4 |
| DEN | 41 | 52 | 61.6 | 63.4 | 64.8 |
| GER | 73 | 78 | 67.1 | 72.0 | 72.0 |
| GRE | 22 | 24 | 42.8 | 39.5 | 36.9 |
| SPA | 35 | 57 | 68.2 | 72.1 | 71.2 |
| FRA | 76 | 83 | 75.9 | 77.6 | 77.5 |
| IRE | 36 | 61 | 58.6 | 57.2 | 54.6 |
| ITA | 63 | 55 | 61.6 | 64.0 | 64.7 |
| NET | 67 | 73 | 69.2 | 70.4 | 68.9 |
| AUT | Na | na | 71.8 | 74.3 | 74.2 |
| POR | 23 | 32 | 52.4 | 56.3 | 61.3 |
| FIN | Na | na | 53.8 | 53.2 | 53.9 |
| SWE | Na | na | 64.2 | 64.6 | 66.6 |
| GBR | 74 | 81 | 70.1 | 73.1 | 73.7 |

Source: 1970 and 1980: EU Commission (1999), 1988–91, 1992–95 and 1996–2000, OECD (2002).

The internationalization of production is also reflected in the fact that foreign direct investments have been increasing, cf. Figure 5. It is seen that there has been a parallel increase in in- and out-flows of foreign direct investments to Europe. It is noteworthy that the development in in- and out-flows is so balanced. Moreover, it is seen that the increase was particularly strong in the 1990s, although the increase was from a low initial level. Cross-border ownership and mergers and acquisitions have thus become more important in recent years.

The increase in the importance of international trade and the scope for production relocation and the change in the nature of trade have potential, important implications for the labour market. As noted above, these changes can be briefly summarized as implying a situation where there is more trade in Europe in commodities and activities, which can easily be relocated across countries and labour markets.

**Fig. 5.** Foreign Direct Investments: Outflows and Inflows as a Share

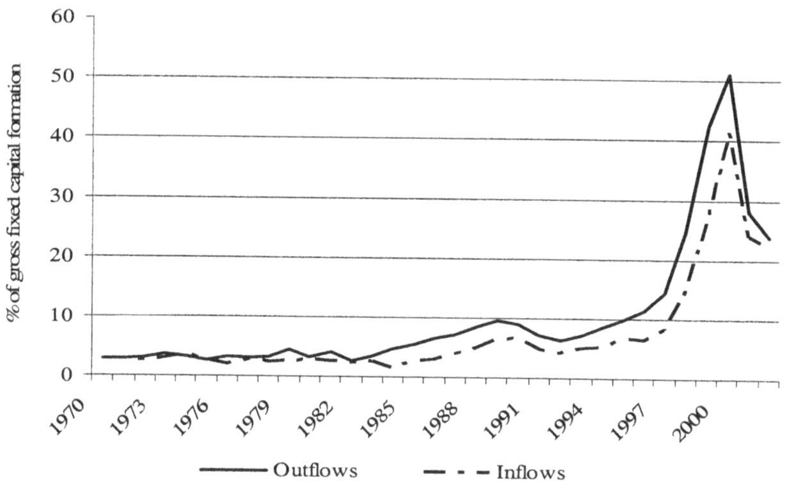


Source: UNCTAD, FDI Database, (www.unctad.org/fdistatistics).

This is so, since close geographical proximity to natural resources or final consumer matters less today than in the past. Since firms are producing for the same market, and have access to the same capital market (and also, for a large part, the same currency) and information and transactions costs have been lowered, it follows that differences in labour market conditions can potentially come to play a more important role than in the past. In short, this can be summarized as implying that the mobility of jobs increases. This mobility can arise via changes in market shares, outsourcing of parts of production or, eventually, international relocation of plants. A consequence of this is that the sensitivity of employment to wages, for example, may change and the threat points or outside options in wage bargaining may be affected.

Most of the existing literature on wage bargaining takes the trade structure for given and usually assumes an exogenously given structure of specialization in production. This is well known from, for example, the Scandinavian model of inflation, which builds on a given split between tradeable and non-tradeable sectors in the economy. While this may be a reasonable approximation to a situation where trade is mainly inter-industrial, and specialization is explained by differences in endowments (natural resources), it captures the current situation to a decreasing degree. The following provides an overview of recent work, which explicitly allows for the phenomena outlined above, and considers the implications for wage bargaining.

## 3 Intra-Industrial Trade and Wage Formation

The following provides an overview of recent work on how wage formation is affected by international product market integration. The focus is on the role that endogenous changes in the trade structure have for employment creation and thus wage formation. The basic framework[1] is a simplified Ricardian trade model that allows an endogenous determination of specialization and, therefore, of which commodities become tradeables (importables and exportables) and non-tradeables, that is, the allocation of production between domestic and foreign producers is endogenous. The analysis builds on the modelling framework in Dornbusch, Fischer and Samuelson (1977), which has proved useful for analyses of international product market interactions and also the effects of further product market integration. Recent work has extended the basic model to allow for heterogeneity in wage setting, imperfectly competitive product markets, horizontal and vertical specialization, heterogeneity in trade frictions and dynamics (see e.g. Andersen (2002), Andersen and Sørensen (2003), Andersen and Skaksen (2003), Bernhard, Eaton, Jensen and Kortum (2001), Yi (2003), Melitz (2002) and Bergin and Glick (2003). Empirical work has documented the importance of these mechanisms; see e.g. Davis and Weinstein (2002), Eaton and Kortum (2002) and Bernhard, Jensen and Schott (2003).

Note that the approach taken here differs from the one taken in so-called duopoly models of reciprocal dumping, cf. Brander (1981) and Brander and Krugman (1983). In the basic variant of this model there is two-way trade in identical commodities, and trade is driven by the motivation of capturing a share of the rent accruing due to imperfect competition in the foreign markets, and vice versa. Naylor (1998) applied this framework in a setting with unionised labour markets, and this approach has since been extensively used (see e.g. Andersen and Sørensen (2001), Lommerud. Meland and Søgard (2003) and many others). The relevance of two-way trade in identical commodities can be contested. Moreover, the literature relies extensively on linear demand functions which imply that the elasticity of demand is tied to the level of demand. (Higher employment implies a less elastic labour demand.) Moreover, in a general equilibrium setting, the linear formulation implies that there are no income effects in the demand of the commodities considered[2] [see e.g. Krugman (1985)] but the model has been considered in a version where products are differentiated [see e.g. Gürtzen (2002)]. However, the specialization in production is exogenously given, i.e. countries produce given varieties of differentiated commodities. Accordingly, this type of model leaves out the basic mechanism that arises in the Ricardian models considered in the following in which the specialization in production is endogenous.

---

1 These issues have also been addressed in so-called reciprocal dumping models, see below.

2 Moreover, the literature relies extensively on linear demand functions which imply that the elasticity of demand is tied to the level of demand (higher employment implies a less elastic labour demand). Moreover, in a general equilibrium setting the linear formulation implies that there are no income effects in the demand of the commodities considered.

### 3.1 The Elasticity Effect

Consider the following stylised situation. There are two representative (European) countries – home and foreign – trading with each other in various products, subject to trade frictions, i.e. the focus is on product differentiation. An ongoing integration process reduces frictions in goods trade. To focus on employment creation and wage formation three simplifying assumptions are made, namely, real capital is disregarded, labour is assumed not to be mobile internationally, and product markets are assumed to be competitive.[3] Labour is organized in industry-specific trade unions, setting a wage under a right to manage structure. The countries are assumed to be symmetric with respect to technology and the distribution of relative factor supplies (see below).

Consider a sector $j$ for which there are a number of producers which can potentially produce various varieties of products denoted by $i$. Consumers can acquire these commodities from either domestic or foreign producers of consumption goods. A given variety $i$ in the goods category $j$ is offered by domestic producers at a price $P_{ji}$ and by foreign producers at a price $P_{ji}^*$. However, there are frictions involved in international trade (see e.g. Dornbusch, Fischer and Samuelson (1977)), which can be thought of as various non-tariff impediments to trade. These costs can also be interpreted as information or search costs concerning foreign markets, and they can include both fixed and proportional components. However, since the qualitative results of the paper hold in either case, we choose to work with the more simple case of proportional costs.

Let $z$ denote the gross costs of acquiring one unit from a foreign supplier. For simplicity the trade friction is assumed to be the same across sectors and goods (for a generalization see e.g. Andersen and Skaksen (2003)). Hence, $z \geq 1$, since acquisition of one unit of the commodity may absorb resources to overcome trade frictions. ($z$ = 1 corresponds to frictionless international trade.) A reduction in $z$ will be used in the following to capture product market integration arising from a reduction in trade frictions.

Domestic consumers choose a domestic supplier if

$$P_{ji} \leq P_{ji}^* z, \tag{1}$$

while a foreign supplier is chosen if

$$P_{ji} > P_{ji}^* z. \tag{2}$$

It follows that the consumer price $Q_{ji} = P_{ji}$ if the final good is acquired from a domestic producer, and $Q_{ji} = P_{ji}^*$ if it is acquired from a foreign producer. As-

[3] Note that the same mechanism determining the boundary between exports, imports and non-tradeables is present if firms are in a monopolistically competitive (Bertrand) position; see Andersen (2002) and Andersen and Sørensen (2003).

suming that firms in sector $j$ produce goods of type $i$ subject to a linear production technology

$$y_{ji} = A_{ji} l_{ji}, \tag{3}$$

where $A_{ji}$ is an exogenous productivity parameter. The productivity parameter allows for trade based on differences in comparative advantages (see below).

The production structure captures the fact that various producers in a certain sector convert similar kinds of inputs into different final consumption goods. There is perfect competition and, hence, the price is

$$P_{ji} = A_{ji}^{-1} \; W_j, \tag{4}$$

where $W_j$ is the wage rate in the domestic country in sector $j$, cf. the assumption of industry-specific unions. Using this price formula[4], it is possible to determine which final goods are produced domestically, and which are either imported or exported. To this end, consider first the condition ensuring that domestic consumers choose a domestic supplier of good variety $ji$ (i.e. (1) holds), which can be written as

$$A_{ji}^{-1} W_j \;\le\; z\left(A_{ji}^{*}\right)^{-1} W_j^{*}, \tag{5}$$

or

$$W_j \le W_{ji}^{I} \equiv z \frac{A_{ji}}{A_{ji}^{*}} W_j^{*}, \tag{6}$$

where $W_{ji}^{I}$ is the critical import wage in subsector $i$, that is, the wage has to be below $W_{ji}^{I}$ to prevent the commodity $ji$ from being imported. Similarly, foreign consumers choose domestic suppliers if

$$W_j \le W_{ji}^{E} \equiv z^{-1} \frac{A_{ji}}{A_{ji}^{*}} W_j^{*}, \tag{7}$$

where $W_{ji}^{E}$ is the critical export wage, that is, the level the wage has to be below for commodity $i$ to be an exportable. Note that $W_{ji}^{E} \le W_{ji}^{I}$.

[4] This also implies that $Q_j = \left[W_j^{1-\theta} \int_{i \in E_j \cup NT_j} A_{ji}^{1-\theta} di + \left(W_j^{*}\right)^{1-\theta} \int_{i \in I_j} z^{1-\theta} \left(A_{ji}^{*}\right)^{\theta-1} di\right]^{\frac{1}{1-\theta}}$

Product varieties i are ordered within sector $j$ such that $a_{ji} = \frac{A_{ji}}{A^*_{ji}}$ is increasing in $i$. We can now plot the critical import and export wage (given as the RHS of (6) and (7) respectively) as in Figure 6 and they are both increasing functions of i, which captures the relative efficiency or comparative advantage of the subsector.

**Fig. 6.** Wages and Direction of Trade

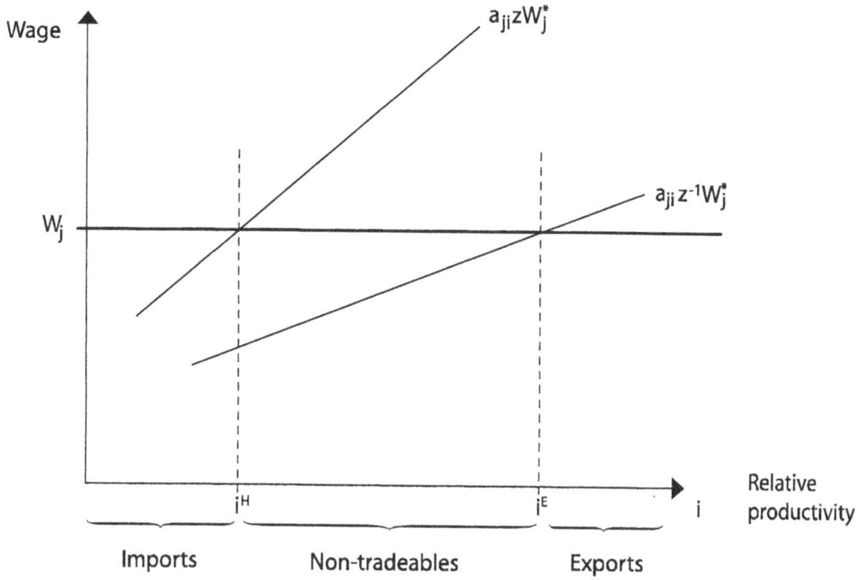


For a given wage in the sector $W_j$ it straightforwardly follows that there is a critical value of $i$ – in the following denoted $i^H$ – with the property that all goods $i \geq i^H$ are produced at home. That is, at the given wage rate these subsectors are not threatened by import. However, for all subsectors $i < i^H$ foreign firms can offer their products to the home market at a lower price than home producers can, i.e. these commodities are imported. Similarly, there is a critical value of $i$ – in the following denoted $i^E$ – with the property that for all $i \geq i^E$ domestic firms are also exporting. Note[5] that $i^E \geq i^H$, that is some of the sectors supplying the home market are also exporting, but not vice versa.

Whether a given commodity is exported, imported or non-traded is determined endogenously, depending on relative wages between the home and foreign country, comparative advantages and trade frictions. Trade is here intra-industrial trade, since there is trade within industry $j$ with some product types being exported ($i \geq i^E$) and other types being imported ($i < i^H$). It is an implication that trade is related to specialization in production, since export goods are only produced in the home country

[5] Since $z_{ji} \geq 1$, it follows that $i \in E_j \Rightarrow i \in H_j$, while $i \in H_j \Rightarrow i \in E_j$ does not apply.

and vice versa for import goods. The non-traded sector represents varieties being produced in both countries. Lower trade frictions lead to more trade (see below), a shrinking non-tradeable sector, and more specialization. Observe that there is never two-way trade of identical commodities, but there is both export and import of commodities of a given category ($j$).

**Fig. 7.** Effects of Wage Increase

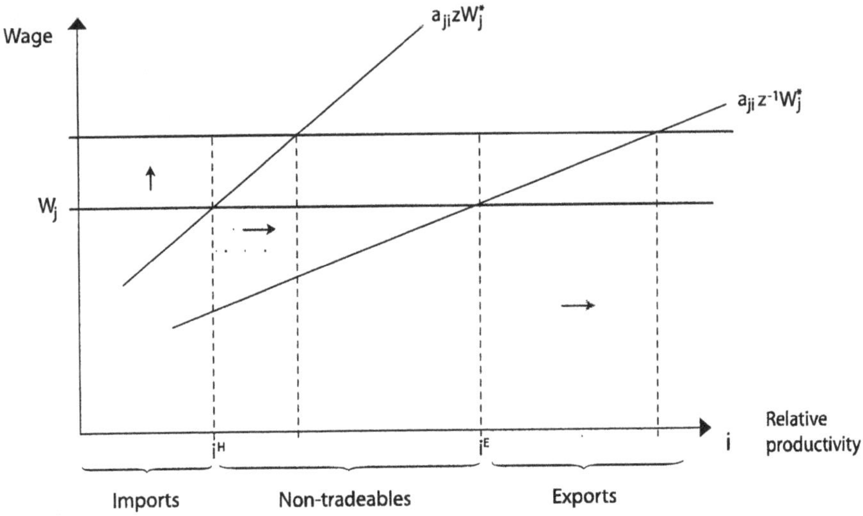


**Fig. 8.** Effects of Lower Trade Friction

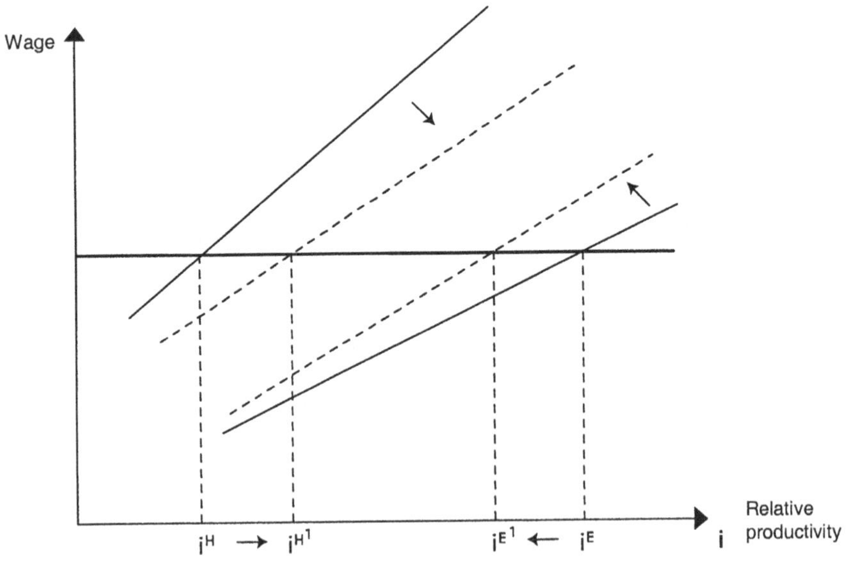

Suppose that the domestic wage increases, relative to the foreign wage; as shown in Figure 7, we have that more goods will be imported ($i^H$ increases) and fewer will be exported ($i^E$ increases). A wage increase will thus not only imply a movement up the demand curve for labour but also induce a structural shift in labour demand, due to more goods being imported and fewer exported. Note that there is indirect competition between workers in the two countries over jobs – when production shifts between the two countries it amounts to a shift in employment opportunities (job mobility). Hence, an increase in domestic wages would imply more import and less export, i.e. less domestic production and employment.

Finally, consider a reduction in the trade frictions ($z$) reflecting a process of international integration. This is illustrated in Figure 8, and it is seen to imply a decrease in the critical import wage and an increase in the critical export wage. The reason is that when the trade friction absorbs fewer resources it becomes easier for foreign firms to penetrate the domestic market and vice versa. If follows that lower trade frictions for a given wage induce an increase in both imports and exports and a reduction in the relative size of the non-tradeables sector.

### 3.1.1 Labour Demand

The demand for labour in sector $j$ can now be determined. Employment is generated from firms serving the home market ( $H = \left\{ i \middle| i \geq i^H \right\}$) as well as from firms serving the export market ( $E = \left\{ i \middle| i \geq i^E \right\}$ )

Assume for the sake of argument that the underlying demand functions for the final products have constant elasticities, i.e. the demand for a given variety $i$ in sector $j$ is given as

$$c_{ji} = \left( \frac{Q_{ji}}{Q_j} \right)^{-\theta} c_j, \qquad \theta > 1 \tag{8}$$

where total demand going to sector j is determined as

$$c_j = \left[ \frac{Q_j}{Q} \right]^{-\theta} c, \qquad \theta > 1 \tag{9}$$

in which $c$ is aggregate consumption, and $Q$ the aggregate consumer price index.

Using the demand and production functions (i.e. (9), (8) and (3)), the total labour demand in sector $j$ can be written

$$L_j = \phi^H \left( \frac{W_j}{W_j^*}, z \right) \left( \frac{W_j}{Q} \right)^{-\theta} c + \phi^E \left( \frac{W_j}{W_j^*}, z \right) \left( \frac{W_j}{Q^*} \right)^{-\theta} c^*, \tag{10}$$

where

$$\frac{\partial \phi^H}{\partial\left(\frac{W_j}{W_j^*}\right)} < 0; \quad \frac{\partial \phi^H}{\partial z} > 0; \quad \frac{\partial \phi^E}{\partial\left(\frac{W_j}{W_j^*}\right)} < 0; \quad \frac{\partial \phi^E}{\partial z} < 0; \tag{11}$$

The first part on the RHS of (10) gives the labour demand generated by supplying goods to the domestic market, and the second part is the labour demand generated by supplying to the foreign market. Note that $\phi^H$ is positively related to the share of production going to the home market, and $\phi^E$ to the share of production going to the foreign market.

One important fact concerning the demand elasticity for labour is that its numerical value is never smaller than the underlying elasticity of consumer demand, i.e. (see Andersen and Skaksen (2003))

$$\varepsilon_{L_j,W_j} < -\theta. \tag{12}$$

The intuition is that there are two dimensions of substitution, namely, between different commodities (implied by consumer preferences and here captured by $\theta$) and between domestic and foreign suppliers (implied by the possibility for trade), i.e. employment is more elastic as is the underlying final demand.[6] When demands are relocated between domestic and foreign firms, it corresponds to production (employment) being relocated across national borders even though factor mobility is absent. Note that factor mobility has here been assumed to be absent to focus on the point that changes in product markets have implications for labour markets. The immediate implication is that the labour demand elasticity is higher in an open economy than in a closed economy owing to job mobility. Moreover, the lower the trade friction ($z$) the larger (numerically) is the labour demand elasticity in most cases[7] [see Andersen and Skaksen (2003)], i.e.

$$\frac{\partial \varepsilon_{L_j,W_j}}{\partial z} > 0. \tag{13}$$

This implies that product market integration tends to reduce the effective bargaining power of unions.

---

6 In models with an exogenous production structure (specialized product models) the two tend to be equal.

7 In so-called reciprocal dumping models it is customary to work with a linear demand function. This implies that the labour demand elasticity numerically is falling in the employment level. Since more integration (with two-way trade) implies higher activity, it follows that the elasticity becomes numerically smaller; see e.g. Naylor (1998).

### 3.1.2 Wage Formation

To outline some basic mechanisms, consider the following simple wage-setting problem. Industry-specific unions determine wages with a concern for both real wages and employment, and take into account the fact that firms determine employment. This is the well-known monopoly union variant of the right-to-manage model. It is well known that it captures the qualitative implications of more rich bargaining models quite well and it is therefore a convenient simplification. Assume that workers supplying labour used for production in sector j are organized in a trade union, setting the wage under a right-to-manage structure and taking all aggregate variables as given, that is, wage formation is sectorial or industry-specific. Specifically, assume that the union objective defined over wages and employment can be written as

$$Max\ U_j = \frac{W_j}{Q}\frac{L_j}{M} - d\left(\frac{L_j}{M}\right)^{\gamma}, \tag{14}$$

where $M$ is the number of trade union members. Given this objective function, the following wage setting function follows when unions determine the wage under the constraint that employment is determined by (10)

$$\frac{W_j}{Q} = \frac{\varepsilon_{L_j,W_j}}{1+\varepsilon_{L_j,W_j}} d\gamma\left(\frac{L_j}{M}\right)^{\gamma-1}. \tag{15}$$

Equation (15) gives the wage curve as increasing in the level of employment ($\gamma - 1 > 0$). Note that the higher the mark-up parameter $\frac{\varepsilon_{L_j,W_j}}{1+\varepsilon_{L_j,W_j}}$, determined in the usual way via the elasticity of labour demand $\varepsilon_{L_j,W_j}$, the higher the wage demands at a given employment level. The wage curve (15) includes the crucial mechanism linking product markets and labour markets, namely, the elasticity $\varepsilon_{L_j,W_j}$ and, therefore, the trade-off between wages and employment faced by workers as is well known from the literature on wage bargaining. The more steep this trade-off, the higher the mark-up factor and, therefore, the effective market power of the union.

From equation (15) one key implication of product market integration for wage formation readily follows. For reasons outlined above, international product market integration is likely to increase the elasticity of labour demand, cf. (13), and the more elastic labour demand is the lower the wage demands are at any employment level. Accordingly, product market integration tends to induce wage moderation. Through this route product market integration may thus reduce wage "mark-ups", and this creates the potential for a higher steady state level of employment. This elasticity effect is a very basic channel through which product market integration affects labour markets (see e.g. Burda (1999) and Andersen et al. (2000)). Finally, observe that the above result gives an important difference to models of reciprocal dumping in which further product market integration (in the case of two-way trade) may lead to a higher wage; see e.g. Naylor(1998).

In a general equilibrium version of the above model Andersen and Skaksen (2003) show that equilibrium real wages and employment unambiguously increase following a reduction in trade frictions. That is, even though there is a reduction in the market power of unions determined by the mark-up factor, it is the case that workers become better off in terms of both employment and wages. The reason is the welfare gains following from reductions of trade frictions, more trade and specialization. This points out the importance of considering the general equilibrium effects before making any welfare conclusions.

Two extensions of the above simple model are worth mentioning. First, wage bargaining was modelled in a very stylised way in the form of the right-to-manage version of the monopoly union model. In a more general bargaining setting there are some potential important additional effects. The threat points in wage bargaining may also change in the process of product market integration. In principle, this can go to the benefit of either workers or firms. In the short run, the threat point of workers may be strengthened, since an abruption of production may be more problematic in a more competitive and integrated product market (e.g. through the importance of reliable deliveries etc.). Similarly, basing production on imported intermediaries (ordered in advance) may increase the threat point of workers (Kramarz (2003)). On the other hand, the possibility of relocating production via FDI or outsourcing improves the threat point of firms. The latter effect is likely to be larger than the former. The possibility of relocation production through FDIs can be interpreted as either an improvement in the exit option or threat point of firms or as an increase in the wage elasticity of labour demand (in the medium to long run) and this may lower wage mark-ups along the lines explained above (see Driffill and Ploeg (1995)). Looking in more detail at the possibilities of relocating production or part of it via FDIs or outsourcing, it is useful to make a distinction between horizontal and vertical investments (see Markusen et al. 1996). By horizontal investments it is understood that production is split between similar plants located in different countries (labour markets), whereas vertical investments are characterized by production being split up into separate stages, which are placed in different countries (labour markets). For horizontal investments (see Bughin and Vannini (1995), Zhao (1995, 1998) and Naylor and Santoni (1997)) the general finding is that it leads to wage moderation via essentially the elasticity effect discussed above. However, for vertical investments this need not be the case for the segment of the labour market attached to the production remaining in the home country. The reason is that domestic labour costs come to weigh less in overall costs and therefore it is possible that labour demand becomes less elastic and therefore wages increase for this group of workers; see Skaksen and Sørensen (2001). Another reason is that acquisition of intermediary inputs (imports) is a commitment on the part of firms, and this weakens the bargaining power of managers (Kramarz (2003)).

The preceding analysis considered industry-specific unions. However, international integration may be a separate cause of institutional changes in the labour market. Product market integration may affect the institutional structure through various routes. First, it is a straightforward implication that the effective degree of centralization in the labour market falls if product market integration leads to an increase in the number of firms competing in product markets, since this implies that the number of unions supplying labour to produce a certain type of commodities increases. This decrease in the effective degree of centralization has an ambiguous effect on labour markets, essentially because it depends on how the initial situation is relative to an eventual hump-shaped relation between, say, wages and the degree of centralization (Danthine and Hunt (1994) and Driffill and Ploeg (1993)). Second, product market integration may be a reason for changing institutional arrangements in the labour market. Focusing on rent extraction, Santoni (2002) shows that a reduction in product market rents (via improved possibilities for reciprocal dumping) following integration implies a reduction in the incentive for both unions and firms to have centralized wage bargaining. Along the same lines Gaston (2002) argues that the improvement in the outside opportunity of firms created by easier room for FDIs, outsourcing etc. can explain a shift towards more decentralized bargaining.

It is an implication of most of the arguments made above that, to the extent workers lose some bargaining power due to product market integration, some power can be regained by entering into trans-national cooperative arrangements for wage setting. This shows that there is a stronger incentive for unions to cooperate when the product market becomes more integrated, but it does not address the question as to how this should be implemented (a non-trivial problem, given the substantial differences in labour market institutions across EU countries). Eventually, tighter international integration of the product market and its consequences for labour markets may be the process which will add momentum to the manifesto "workers in all countries, unite".

## 3.2 Wage Spill-Over and Wage Norms

An important issue is how wage formation across countries becomes more interdependent due to tighter product market integration. Obviously, wage formation in the home country depends on wage formation in the foreign country, since the latter is of importance for the competitive margin, cf. above. This is also seen by writing the wage function (15) as the following implicit function

$$W_j = H\left(W_j^*, Q, Q^*\right), \tag{16}$$

where the H-function is homogeneous of degree one in $W_j^*$, $Q$ and $Q^*$, and where

$$1 > \frac{\partial W_j}{\partial W_j^*} > 0\,. \tag{17}$$

that is, an increase in foreign wages leads to an upward pressure on domestic wages. The intuition is straightforward: the higher the foreign wage, the higher domestic wages can be without jeopardizing competitiveness and, thus, employment.

Tighter product market integration will tend to strengthen this wage interdependence (see Andersen (2003)), that is,

$$\frac{\partial^2 W_j}{\partial z \, \partial W_j^*} < 0 . \tag{18}$$

This suggests that more integrated markets imply that more weight in wage formation is shifted towards competitors' wages, and less weight is attached to domestic market conditions. The reason is that when markets are more integrated there are more severe consequences of having, for example, wage developments out of line with those of competitors. In technical terms, the more product markets are integrated, the stronger the strategic complementarity[8] in wage setting is among labour markets. This implies that foreign wage formation becomes a stronger anchor for domestic wage formation.

The importance of the "European" element in wage formation, that is, the increased focus on competitiveness following intensified integration is visible in all EU labour markets. In various countries a "European norm" has played an either explicit or implicit role in wage formation. An interesting example is the Belgian "law on competitiveness" from 1996, which explicitly linked wage increases to wage increases for its main competitors (Germany, the Netherlands and France). This prompted the so-called "Doorn initiative", which involves unions in Germany, France, Belgium, the Netherlands and Luxembourg. The "Doorn initiative" is not an attempt at establishing trans-national wage bargaining, but rather an initiative which through exchange of information and peer pressure aims at avoiding a process of "competitive" wage cuts, or competition between different national collective bargaining systems. The initiative launched a "wage coordination formula", which defines the room for nominal wage increases as the sum of inflation and productivity growth.[9] [See also the EU Commission (2003)]. The intention is to have a norm "protecting" the labour share, and ensure a level playing field to avoid undercutting. There is, however, some ambiguity as to how to interpret the norm in respect to which measure to use for inflation and productivity. In recent years the norm has also been interpreted in a more flexible way to take into account qualitative aspects like work environment, flexible working hours, training etc. While the current status of these initiatives is open to discussion, they are interesting in the sense that they reflect a recognition of increased interdependencies in wage formation. While trans-

8 Strategic complementarity is defined as a positive relation between decision variables, cf. Cooper and John (1995). The case of a negative relationship between decision variables is denoted strategic substitutability.

9 Wage norms or formulas like this have a long history, and were, for example, a core element of the so-called Scandinavian inflation model.

national wage bargaining at present is an unlikely response, the initiatives are a way of trying to minimize the possible externalities involved in wage setting.

Empirical evidence on the strength of wage interdependencies is presented in Andersen et al. (2000), based on wage developments in the manufacturing sector for EU countries. It is found that wage setting in a number of European countries has come to follow foreign wage setting more closely. Interestingly, wage developments tend to be more similar across countries that also have tight trade links.

Beyond the structural implications of this "foreign element" for wage formation, it also has macroeconomic consequences, since it tends to imply that wage setting becomes less sensitive to domestic market conditions. Accordingly, there is a risk that stronger "European Wage Norms" would contribute to more similar wage developments but also more volatility in employment across European countries (Andersen (2003)).

## 3.3 Pressure for Wage Differentiation

The preceding analysis has taken it for granted that uniform wage settlements can be implemented. That is, it has been assumed that the union stipulates the same wage for all workers (with similar attributes) within the sector. This is in essence the limiting case of full solidaristic wage formation, since it implies that wages do not depend on firm characteristics. However, product market integration may be a reason why it becomes more difficult to maintain such wage arrangements and therefore also why it is necessary to allow for more decentralization in wage determination.

The reason is that product market integration has two immediate effects on labour markets – one is the threat of imports, that is, foreign firms capturing the domestic market, and the other is the possibility of entering the foreign market via exports, which will give new opportunities and will be good news for wages and employment. Hence, there are positive and negative effects from product market integration. Are there any compelling reasons why the gains and losses should be unequally distributed in the labour market, implying that the costs of maintaining solidaristic wage settlements increase?

To consider more closely how product market integration may put solidaristic wage solution under pressure, return to Figure 6. For any given level of productivity in a particular sector or for a given group of workers there is a critical wage – the critical import wage – above which the wage cannot be set if domestic production shall remain profitable. Similarly, there is a wage – the critical export wage – below which domestic production would also be competitive at the export market. Clearly, the critical export wage is lower than the critical import wage. This captures the standard argument that wage moderation is needed for export to be feasible. Moreover, the larger the trade frictions in product markets, the larger the difference between the two. With low trade frictions and tightly integrated product markets the difference between being in a position threatened by import and being in a position of having an export possibility is very small. On the other hand, with large frictions and little integration the margin is wider.

Figure 6 shows how the critical export and import wage depends on relative productivity (comparative advantage) – and therefore the threats and opportunities are not equally shared across all workers in a given labour market or sector. There will be a tension in the sense that when trade frictions are reduced a larger group would have an incentive to demand a higher wage, since that would still be consistent with high employment (those facing the export opportunity) while others would benefit from wage moderation to counter the import threat (those facing the import threat). This is illustrated in Figure 9. Maintaining an egalitarian wage structure – here in the extreme form of the same wage for all – would imply that there are more exports but also imports than if wages where allowed to adjust to the situation of the particular firm (subsector) (captured by the thick line allowing wages to adjust to firm-specific conditions). To put it differently, maintaining the solidaristic wage outcome would imply that the distribution of employment becomes more unequal when product markets are integrated (see Andersen and Sørensen (2003)) since wages are not adjusted to the firm-specific situation. Hence, product market integration worsens the trade-off between wage and employment equality or, to put it differently, the costs in terms of employment of maintaining egalitarian wage structures increase.

**Fig. 9.** Pressure for Wage Differentiation

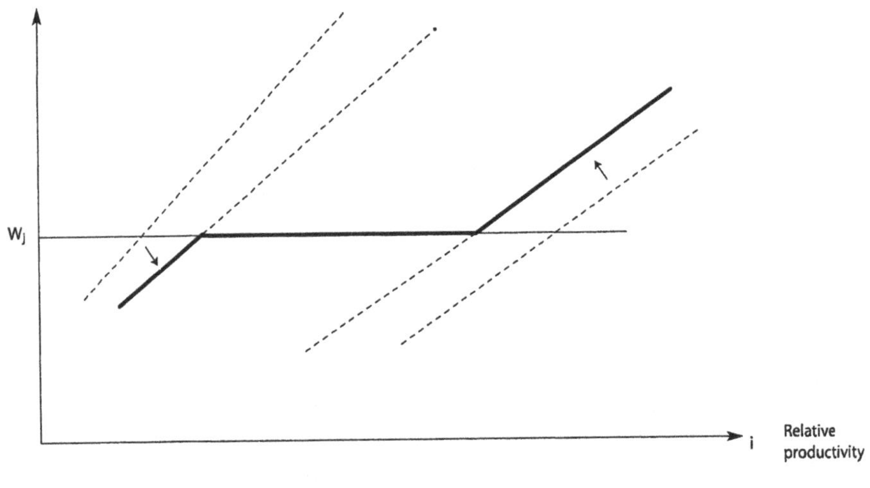


Clearly, the case considered here is very stylised, yet it captures a basic mechanism released by intra-industrial trade – there will be both import threats and export opportunities, but they would not be equally distributed even with a given sector.[10] Here the costs of maintaining an egalitarian wage structure was assessed solely from the perspective of workers to show that even among union members there may be less support to egalitarian outcomes. Clearly, in a more general setting the incentive of employers would tend to go in the same direction.

[10] Andersen and Sørensen (2003a,b) explores in more detail how this depends on market power in product markets, as well as the general equilibrium effects.

The findings above have important implications, since they affect the possibilities of achieving social objectives via lower wage limits set by either an explicit minimum wage or indirectly via unemployment benefits or social security arrangements. Term this the reservation wage. For some groups with low productivity (in general, low comparative advantage) it would be impossible to find employment at the reservation wage. The reason is that the potential jobs for this group are lost through imports, that is, domestic production is not profitable at the reservation wage. Lower trade frictions will make this a more binding constraint (affecting more sub-sectors) since the import threat becomes stronger. This implies that unemployment problems for low productivity groups will increase, and that the financial burden of maintaining social objectives through wage floors increases. This raises an obvious policy dilemma. The need for a wage floor to achieve social objectives (maintain a certain living standard) increases (see also below), because a larger proportion of the labour force is facing the import threat more fiercely, and in the absence of intervention wage dispersion would increase. Since more will be affected by this, the financial burden increases at the same time as it becomes increasingly difficult (mobility argument) or costly (the distortion argument) to finance this via taxation.

Another implication is that it points to an important difference between the short-run and long-run strategy to achieve social objectives in the labour market. The short-run implication is that it will be more costly to maintain social standards as a consequence of international integration. The long-run perspective is that since it becomes increasingly costly to maintain a qualification structure, which does not match social ambitions with respect to the wage structure. In the long run it therefore becomes important through labour market and education policy to affect the qualification structure so as to match the political objectives with respect to the distribution of pay and employment.

## 4 Risk and Insurance

The preceding discussion took the perspective that a compressed wage structure reflects egalitarian preferences. However, as pointed out by Agell and Lommerud (1992) and Agell (2002) egalitarian wage outcome or solidaristic wage settlements may also be considered as a mechanism to provide (implicit) insurance. This is so if there is some ex ante uncertainty about your future position in the labour market. This could be in respect to your skills or the specific firm in which you may end up being employed (presuming that there is some ex-post irreversibility). With uncertainty over wage and employment prospects risk-averse agents may have an ex ante incentive to enter risk-sharing agreements. Since this is associated with various incentive problems (can the risk sharing be maintained ex-post? cf. above) it is possible to think of wage setting through unions as a commitment device. Accordingly, if the union sets a more compressed wage structure than would prevail in a competitive labour market, it follows that it is effectively providing some insurance. Observe that any ex ante risk sharing arrangement would ex-post look like redistribution – from the "lucky" to the "unlucky".

Globalization may affect the incentives underlying risk sharing in two ways. As noted above, further product market integration may have the effect of making employment more sensitive to the wage rate (the demand elasticity increases), and also the underlying competitive wage structure would display more inequality. The effects of both of these changes on the insurance motive for wage compression can be inferred from Agell (2002).

Agell (2002) presents a model in which there is an underlying wage inequality related to skill levels (ex ante unknown). Agents are risk averse, and therefore union wage setting would involve some wage compression. However, since wage compression may have harmful effects for employment, it follows that full insurance or complete wage equalization is not optimal, but the wage structure is compressed relative to the competitive case. A more elastic labour demand would increase the employment costs of wage compression, and tends to imply that the union decides for a less egalitarian wage structure. However, more inequality in the underlying competitive wage structure is equivalent to more ex ante risk over your position in the labour market and this tends to increase the demand for insurance and therefore tends to imply a more compressed wage structure. In sum, product market integration will have ambiguous effects on the "insurance motive" for wage compression.

It is crucial for the above type of reasoning that there is no ex-post possibility of breaking the implicit insurance contract. It is a classic problem that there will be an ex-post incentive to deviate, since those figuring out that they are in the potential "high wage group" may see an incentive in breaking the arrangement, cf. Figure 9. Using standard reasoning from game theory the ex-ante efficient arrangement can be maintained as long as the "temptation" arising from breaking the arrangement does not exceed the "punishment" (e.g. through various forms of "harassment"). With the increased dispersion in options implied by further integration it is likely that the balance of these forces would change in the direction of making it more difficult to sustain egalitarian wage settlements, especially across very heterogeneous groups. The change in some countries away from very centralized towards more sectorial-based wage settlements, cf. section 1, can be interpreted as reflecting such changes.

If it becomes more difficult to maintain very centralized or economy-wide negotiations and therefore risk-sharing arrangements, it is important to note that the alternative is not necessarily individualized solutions. In between, there are so-called occupational or negotiated insurance schemes at the sectorial level. While not attaining the same degree of risk sharing as more universal arrangements, they allow room for solidaristic solutions. In a process of international integration, which may imply both less centralized wage settlements as well as a more binding financial constraint for the public sector, such occupational schemes may be attractive. The reason is that it would be difficult to raise the tax burden to finance extended social insurance arrangements and, moreover, with less centralization the distortionary consequences of such arrangements may increase (Andersen (2002)). Negotiated sectorial arrangements do not release these distortions to the same extent, since they are negotiated at the same level as wages. Hence, although entailing less risk sharing they have the attractive property of having small distortionary consequences (compared with universal or centralized outcomes) (see e.g. Ståhlberg (2003), Andersen (2003)).

## 5 Concluding Remarks

International integration is a process unfolding gradually and eventually affecting economic structures. A key fact concerning the ongoing process is that it is not only a quantitative increase in trade but also involves important qualitative changes. Accordingly, inferring the implications of international integration from past experience with wage formation in small and open economies may be potentially misleading. This is so, since the boundaries for which activities can be affected by international trade are changing rapidly, and they are not dictated by natural resources or the need of proximity to demanders. Accordingly, "mobility" of economic activity (and thus employment) across regions and countries is significantly affected, and this is of importance for labour markets even if labour mobility between countries remains quantitatively unimportant.

The present paper has reviewed some of the labour market implications of this process in recent work on the role of various forms of intra-industrial trade for labour markets. The main points relate to how further product market integration affects the scope for appropriating rents, increases wage interdependencies across trade partners, and has both opportunities and threats, which are unlikely to be distributed equally among all groups in the labour market. These changes are likely to affect wage formation and also, eventually, labour market institutions. The implications are, however, not simple. On the one hand, these changes would tend to affect not only bargaining power but also the need for wage formation to be more dependent on the specific qualifications of workers and the conditions in firms/sectors. On the other hand, these changes also tend to reinforce the international element in wage formation in the sense of making foreign wage development more important for wage setting. All of this also tends to go in the direction of less centralization of wage formation.

However, institutions also play a crucial role as providers of (implicit) insurance. Since wage inequality may rise and there may be more risk, the demand for such risk-sharing arrangements does not dwindle in the integration process. Since it becomes both more difficult and costly to achieve this via centralized wage setting or universal welfare arrangements via the public sector, it follows that there will be a challenge about how to meet the demand for insurance at some intermediary level. Examples[11] are already available that show that these are achieved at an intermediary level, reflecting the change in the trade-off that the benefit of such arrangements is not decreasing while it is more difficult to achieve in a centralized way.

[11] One example is the development of bargaining labour market pensions schemes in Denmark during the 1990s.

## References


Agell, J. (2002): On the Determinants of Labour Market Institutions: Rent-sharing vs. Social Insurance, *German Economic Review, 3*, 107–135.

Agell, J. and Lommerud, K.E. (1992): Union egalitarianism as income insurance. *Economica, 59*, 1992, 295–310.

Andersen, T.M. (2002): Product Market Integration, Unemployment and Wage Dispersion, IZA Working Paper 276. Labour Economics (to appear)

Andersen, T.M. (2003): Welfare Policies, Labor Taxation and International Integration, International Tax and Public Finance, 10, 43–62.

Andersen, T.M., Haldrup, N. and Sørensen, J.R. (2000): Labour Market Implications of EU Product Market Integration, *Economic Policy, 30*, 107–133.

Andersen, T.M. and Skaksen, J.R. (2003): Product Market Integration, Comparative Advantages and Labour Market Performance, IZA Working Paper 698.

Andersen, T.M. and Sørensen, A. (2003): Product market integration, rents and wage formation, CEPR Working paper 3995.

Andersen, T.M. and Sørensen, J.R. (2000): Product Market Integration and Wage Formation, *Journal of Economic Integration, 15*, 281–293.

Barth, E., Moene, K. and Wallerstein, M. (2003): Likhet under press – udfordringer for den skandinaviske fordelingsmodellen, Makt- og demokrati-udredningen 1998–2003.

Bergin, P.R. and Glick, R. (2003): Endogenous Nontradeability and Macroeconomic Implications, NBER Working Paper 9739.

Bernhard, A.B. and Bradford Jensen, J. (1999a): Exceptional exporter performance: cause, effect or both? *Journal of International Economics, 47*, 1–25.

Bernhard, A.B. and Bradford Jensen, J. (1999b): Exporting and Productivity, NBER Working Paper 7135.

Bernhard, A.B., Eaton, J., Bradford Jensen, J. and Kortum, S. (2001): Plants and productivity in international trade, NBER Working Paper 7688.

Bernhard, A.B., Bradford Jensen, J. and Schott, P.K. (2003): Falling Trade Costs, Heterogeneous Firms, and Industry Dynamics, NBER Working Paper 9639.

Blanchard, O. and Fischer, S. (1989): Lectures on Macroeconomics, MIT Press.

Boeri, T., Brugiavini, A. and Calmfors, L. (eds.) (2001): The Role of Unions in the Twenty-First Century, *Oxford University Press.*

Booth, A., Burda, M., Calmfors, L., Checchi, D., Naylor, R. and Visser, J. (2001): The Future of Collective Bargaining in Europe, in T. Boeri, A. Brugiavini, and L. Calmfors, eds., The Role of Unions in the Twenty-First Century, *Oxford University Press, 2001.*

Brander, J.A. (1981): Intra-Industry trade in identical commodities, *Journal of International Economics, 11*, 1–14.

Brander, J.A. and Krugman, P.R. (1983): A Reciprocal Dumping Model of International Trade, *Journal of International Economics, 15*, 313–323.

Bruce, N. and Purvis, D.D. (1985): The Specification of Goods and Factor Markets in Open Economy Macroeconomic Models, ch. 16 in R.W. Jones and P.B. Kenen (eds.), *Handbook of International Economics*, vol. 2, North-Holland.

Bughin, J. and Vanini, S. (1995): Strategic direct investment under unionized oligopoly, International Journal of Industrial Organisation, 13, 127–145.

Burda, M. (1999): European labour markets and the Euro: How much flexibility do we really need? Discussion paper.

Cooper, R. and John, A. (1988): Coordinating Coordination Failures in Keynesian Models, *Quarterly Journal of Economics, 103*, 441–463.

Coppel, J. and Durand, M. (1999): Trends in Market Openness, OECD Working Paper 221.

Danthine, J.-P. and Hunt, J. (1994): Wage Bargaining Structure, Employment and Economic Integration, *Economic Journal, 104*, 528–541.

Davis, D.R. and Weinstein, D.E. (2002): An Account of Global Factor Trade, *American Economic Review 92*, 1423–1453.

Dornbusch, R., Fischer, S. and Samuelson, P.A. (1977): Comparative Advantage, Trade and Payments in a Ricardian Model with a Continuum of Goods, *American Economic Review, 67*, 823–839.

Dowrick, S.J. (1989): Union oligopoly bargaining, *Economic Journal, 99*, 1123–1142.

Driffill, J. and van der Ploeg, R. (1993): Monopoly Unions and Liberalisations of International Trade, *Economic Journal, 103*, 379–385.

Driffill, J. and van der Ploeg, R. (1995): Trade liberalization with imperfect competition in goods and labor markets, *Scandinavian Journal of Economics, 97*, 223–243.

Eaton, J. and Kortum, S. (2002): Technology, geography and trade, *Econometrica, 70*, 1741–1779.

EU commission, European Economy, 2003.

Feenstra, R.C. and Hanson, G.H. (2001): Global Production Sharing and Rising Inequality: A Survey of Trade and Wages, NBER Working Paper 8372.

Flanagan, R.J. (1999): Macroeconomic Performance and Collective Bargaining: An International Perspective, *Journal of Economic Literature*, XXXVII, 1150–1175.

Grossman, G.M. and Helpman, E. (1995): Technology and Trade, in G. Grossman and K. Rogoff (eds.), *Handbook of International Economics*, vol. III, Elsevier Science B.V.

Gürtzen, N. (2002): Trade liberalization and union wages in a differentiated Bertrand duopoly, *Open Economies Review, 13*, 133–151.

Hummels, D., Rapoport, R. and Yi, K.-M. (1998): Vertical Specialization and the Changing Nature of Trade, Federal Reserve Bank of New York, *Economic Policy Review*, 4/2, 79–99.

Jean, S. and Nicoletti, G. (2001): Product Market Regulation and Wage Premia in Europe and North America: An Empirical Investigation, OECD Working Paper 218.

Jones, R.W. and Neary, J.P. (1991): The positive theory of international trade, Ch 1 in R.W. Jones and P.B. Kenen (eds), Handbook of International Economics, Vol. I, North-Holland.

Kramarz, F. (2003): Wages and International Trade, CEPR Discussion Paper 3936.

Lockwood, B. (2000): Commodity Taxation and Tax Coordination under Destination and Origin Principle, CEPR DP 2556.

Lommerud, K.E., Meland, F. and Sørgard, L. (2003): Unionised oligopoly, trade liberalisation and location choice, *Economic Journal, 113*, 782–800.

Madsen, J.S., Andersen, S.K. and Due, J. (2001): Fra centraliseret decentralisering til multiniveau regulering – Danske arbejdsmarkedsrelationer mellem kontinuitet og forandring. Fafo Working paper 032.

Markusen, J.R., Venables, A.J., Konan, D.E. and H:Zhang, H.K. (1996): A unified treatment of horizontal direct investments, vertical direct investment and the pattern of trade in goods and services. NBER Working Paper 5696.

Melitz, M.J. (2002): The Impact of Trade on Intra-Industrial Reallocations and Aggregate Industry Productivity, NBER Working Paper 8881.

Middelfart-Knarvik, K.H., Overman, H., Redding, S. and Venables, A. (2000): The Location of European Industry, Economic Papers 142, European Commission, Directorate-General for Economic and Financial Affairs.

Naylor, R. (1998): International trade and economic integration when labour markets are generally unionized, *European Economic Review, 42*, 1251–1267.

Naylor, R. and Santoni, M. (1997): Wage bargaining and foreign direct investment.

Nicoletti, G., Bassanini, A., Ernst, E., Jean, S., Santiago, P. and Swaim, P. (2001): Product and Labour Market Interactions in the OECD, OECD Working Paper 312.

OECD (1997): Economic Outlook.

OECD (1999): Open Markets Matters.

OECD (2001): Employment Outlook.

Rodrik, D. (1997): Has Globalization Gone too Far? Institute for International Economic Studies, Washington.

Santoni, M. (2002): Product Market Integration and Endogenous Market Structure, Unpublished Working Paper.

Skaksen, M. and Sørensen, J.R. (2001): Should trade unions appreciate foreign direct investment, *Journal of International Economics, 55*, 379–390.

Slaughter, M.J. and Swagel, P. (1997): The Effects of Globalization on Wages in Advanced Economies, IMF Working Paper, 97–43.

Ståhlberg, A.-C. (2003): Occupational Welfare, in Andersen, T.M. and Molander, P. (eds.), Alternatives in Welfare Policies – Coping with Internationalization and Demographic Change, Cambridge University Press.

Summers, L., Gruber, J. and Vegara, R. (1993): Taxation and the structure of labor markets, *Quarterly Journal of Economics, 94*, 385–411.

Yi, K.-M. (2003): Can Vertical Specialization Explain the Growth of World Trade?, *Journal of Political Economy, 111*, 52–102.

Zhao, L. (1995): Cross-hauling direct foreign investment and unionized oligopoly, *European Economic Review, 39*, 1237–1253.

Zhao, L. (1998); The impact of foreign direct investment on wages and employment, Oxford Economic Papers, 50, 284–301.

# Comment on Torben M. Andersen's Paper

Pekka Ilmakunnas

Department of Economics, Helsinki School of Economics
Helsinki, Finland

Torben Andersen's paper provides a nice summary of recent research by himself and others on the issues of globalisation and bargaining. The paper presents a pedagogically useful model that can be described with a few curves. It is easy for readers to experiment with different kinds of changes in the economy and to see their effects in the figure.

Andersen highlights the increasing importance of trade, especially intra-industry trade, caused by the reduction of trade frictions. Another aspect of globalisation is increasing foreign direct investment (FDI), which is discussed less in the paper. My comments deal with this issue and on what implications it may have on bargaining. Additionally, I will discuss discontinuities in labour demand caused by plant closings. These may be related to multinationals relocating production to plants in other countries, or by the kind of shifts between exporting and importing that Torben Andersen describes in his model.

One aspect of FDI is that foreign-owned firms have been observed to have higher productivity than domestic firms (see e.g. Bellak, 2004)[1]. This is usually interpreted to follow from firm-specific assets, like knowledge capital, that can be flexibly used within the firm in its different units. The multinationals can also enjoy economies of scale and scope. However, higher productivity is more related to multinationality rather than foreign ownership, since domestically owned multinational firms also tend to have higher productivity than purely domestic firms. This productivity impact is additional to the higher productivity in exporting firms that Andersen points out.

As discussed by Andersen, labour demand is more elastic in open economies. Besides the kind of shifts between exporting and importing that are included in the model, there is an additional effect when capital is mobile capital and there are potentially "footloose" multinationals. Jobs are transferred within multinationals to plants in low-wage countries. This phenomenon ("the China syndrome") has re-

[1] In Finland, Ilmakunnas and Maliranta (2003) report that foreign-owned plants (those that have at least 50% foreign ownership) have some 12–14 per cent higher total factor productivity than domestically owned plants. This effect consists of two factors. The group of plants that at some stage become foreign-owned, either when they are established or when they are acquired by a foreign company, have 2 to 4 per cent higher productivity than plants that are never in foreign ownership. When these plants actually are foreign-owned, they get an additional 10 per cent productivity gain.

ceived lots of attention in the Finnish media. It is noteworthy that it is not only foreign-owned multinationals, but also Finnish-owned multinationals that are engaged in shifting their production.

The combination of these two facts creates a trade-off for the unions. Higher productivity that follows for international integration facilitates higher wage demands, but more elastic demand dampens the incentives for wage rises. To complicate matters, this trade-off is often a dynamic one. Higher productivity and higher labour demand elasticity may have different timing in many of the high-tech industries. At the beginning of the industry life cycle, specialized production requires high-skilled labour. Consequently, home-country production (or more generally, production in industrial countries) has an advantage. In this case, high productivity may lead to high wages without adverse employment effects, since production is growing, there is not yet much competition, and location is tied to the availability of a skilled work force. Later in the life cycle, production becomes more standardized and competition increases. Now production in low-cost countries has an advantage. As a result, there is increasing mobility of capital and production, which has adverse employment effects through plant closings and downsizing. Consequently, the bargaining position of the unions deteriorates. The problem of the union is then the timing and magnitude of demands for wage increases. Early wage moderation may slow down later relocation, but if it is known that relocation is inevitable, it may be optimal to demand high wages in the beginning.

Another issue is the evaluation of relevant labour demand elasticity. In theory, monopoly unions set wages, given labour demand, or unions and firms bargain on wages and then firms determine labour demand. In any case, the labour demand elasticity plays an important role here. If capital mobility to foreign countries is not continuous, but lumpy, labour demand changes are abrupt. Typically, parts of plants are not relocated, but rather whole plants or production lines, which creates kinks or jumps in labour demand. There is, however, not much empirical evidence on how elastic job destruction through plant closings is to wage changes. At the aggregate level, plant-level discontinuities may be smoothed, so in a theoretical model aimed at describing aggregate behaviour the discontinuities may not matter. Another way of dealing with the relocations is to think, as in Andersen's discussion, that relocation is the firm's threat point in case wage agreement is not reached.

The discontinuities in labour demand through plant closings in multinationals also have effects on wages in the long run. Evidence from the worker displacement literature shows that after plant closing re-employment often happens at a lower wage and there may be long spells of unemployment (see, for example, Kuhn, 2002). The lower wages can follow from switches of industry or occupation, or the new job may be at a lower rank than the previous one. From the labour union perspective, this creates additional problems. The new jobs may be in different industries with a different union, or part of the displaced workers may drop out of the labour force or become long-term unemployed. The issue is then how much these problems weigh in the bargaining process in the early part of the industry life cycle.

## References

Ilmakunnas, P. and Maliranta, M. (2003): "Foreign medicine: A treatment effect analysis of the productivity effects of foreign ownership", mimeo.

Kuhn, P. (ed.) (2002): Losing Work, Moving On: International Perspectives on Worker Displacement, W.E. Upjohn Institute for Employment Research, Kalamazoo.

Bellak, C. (2004): "How Domestic and Foreign Firms Differ and How Does it Matter?" *Journal of Economic Surveys*, forthcoming.

# Wage Formation under Low Inflation

Steinar Holden[1]

Department of Economics, University of Oslo, Norway

## Abstract

This paper reviews the literature on the effects of low steady-state inflation on wage formation, focusing on four different effects. First, under low inflation, downward nominal wage rigidity (DNWR) may prevent real wage cuts that would have happened had inflation been higher. Second, wages (and prices) are given in nominal contracts, and inflation affects both how often wages are adjusted, and to what extent wages are set in a forward-looking manner. Third, incomplete labour contracts may provide workers with scope for inflicting costs on the firm without violating the contract, thus forcing the firm to accept a rise in nominal wages. Fourth, if effort depends on wages relative to a reference level, and workers and firms underweight inflation when updating the reference level, positive but moderate inflation may reduce wage pressure. The paper ends by a brief survey of empirical evidence, and a discussion of whether labour markets may adapt to a low inflation environment.

## 1 Introduction

Economists and practitioners now agree that monetary policy should aim at low inflation. Yet a number of economists and observers have argued that if monetary policy aims at inflation that is too low, this may involve considerable costs for society (Tobin, 1972, Holden, 1994, Akerlof, Dickens and Perry, 1996, 2000, the Economist, 2003). A key concern is that under low or zero inflation, downward rigidity of nominal wages may induce higher wage pressure, involving higher equilibrium unemployment. Other economists have countered this view, arguing that any downward nominal wage rigidity that may exist is the result of an inflationary environment, and that society will adapt to a zero inflation policy without

---

[1] I wish to thank Mike Elsby, Karl Ove Moene, Tapio Palokangas, an anonymous referee and participants at the conference "Collective bargaining and wage formation", Helsinki, for useful comments on a previous draft.

large and persistent effects on output and unemployment (Ball and Mankiw, 1994, Gordon, 1996).

In this paper I shall review what the economic literature has to say on the effects of low steady-state inflation on wage formation.[2] Crudely, one can distinguish four arguments for why inflation may affect wage setting. First, under low inflation, downward nominal wage rigidity (DNWR) may prevent real wage cuts that would have happened had inflation been higher. Second, wages (and priccs) are given in nominal contracts, and inflation affects both how often wages are adjusted, and to what extent wages are set in a forward-looking manner. Third, incomplete labour contracts may provide workers with scope for inflicting costs on the firm without violating the contract, thus forcing the firm to accept a rise in nominal wages. Unless there is sufficient inflation to provide "room" for this "minimum" wage growth, wage pressure will rise, thus increasing unemployment. Fourth, if effort depends on wages relative to a reference level, and workers and firms underweight inflation when updating the reference level, positive but moderate inflation may reduce wage pressure.

Among many economists, these mechanisms will be met with considerable scepticism, based on the argument that rational agents care only about real variables, so that any effect of nominal variables must be due to money illusion that will disappear over time. However, as will become apparent below, many of the mechanisms are developed in models with rational agents, who only care about real variables. Thus, they are not subject to this critique. Other effects do hinge on money illusion, but these effects are accompanied by considerable supporting evidence.

A basic underlying assumption throughout the literature that I review is that there is some sort of nominal rigidity in wages. This assumption can be justified in various ways. First, it is a fact of life that, in most industrialised economies, most workers have their wage set in some type of contract, either a collective agreement or an individual labour contract. Payment is typically specified in nominal terms, although annual, partial indexation to the consumer price index is sometimes used, in particular in periods of high inflation. Such contracts are not adjusted continuously; see survey in Taylor (1999), and Calmfors et al. (2001) for documenting the extensive coverage of collective agreements in most Western European countries.

There may be several reasons for the prevalence of rigid wage contracts. One aspect is that contracts may prove useful so as to prevent continuous haggling over the wage level. Contracts might also be useful to share risk or to protect against opportunistic behaviour. Nominal contracts might be practical, as continuous or frequent adjustment to some price index might involve additional cumbersome calculations and updating. Indexation may also entail a risk (as perceived of the wage setters) that the index exhibits surprising and unwarranted changes. Gottfries (1992) provides a possible justification for why wage contracts are set in nominal terms, as seen from the point of view of the firm and the insiders (the current workforce).

---

[2] Clearly, an unanticipated reduction in inflation induces higher real wages, and thus also affects output. Such temporary effects are neglected here.

Note that what matters for the issues discussed here is not the rate of inflation *per se*, but to what extent there is room for nominal wage growth. Clearly, if there is high productivity growth, or low growth in import prices, there will be more room for nominal wage growth even at low cpi inflation. This distinction is important in empirical work and in policy discussion, but will be neglected in the following.

The paper does not aim to explore what the optimal rate of inflation is. As is well known, inflation involves a number of costs and benefits that are not directly related to wage setting (interaction with tax systems, effects on money holdings, seignorage, uncertainty and the effects of zero bound to nominal interest rates, etc.). These costs and benefits are neglected in the present paper.

The remainder of the paper is organised as follows. In section 2, I discuss the effects of downward nominal wage rigidity. The effect of inflation on staggered nominal wage contracts is surveyed in section 3. Section 4 covers the effect of incomplete labour contracts and section 5 deals with multi-level bargaining. In section 6, I discuss near-rational wage setters. Some of the empirical evidence is surveyed in section 7. Section 8 discusses to what extent society might adapt to a low inflation environment. Section 9 concludes.

## 2 The Effect of Downward Nominal Wage Rigidity (DNWR)

The seminal contribution on DNWR is Tobin (1972). Tobin argued that low (zero) inflation involves higher unemployment because nominal wages are rigid downwards. Sector-specific demand shocks imply that demand varies between different parts of the economy. In the parts of economy where there is excess demand, wages increase, while in parts of the economy with excess supply, DNWR implies that wages do not go down (or they go down less). Thus, widespread excess supply – lower aggregate employment – is necessary to keep inflation very low.

Several different justifications for DNWR have been suggested in the literature

- co-ordination failure and the concern for relative wages.
- fairness; nominal wage cuts are viewed as unfair
- legal restrictions: wages are given in contracts that can only be changed by mutual consent

Co-ordination failure was a key argument of Keynes (1936). He argued that workers are concerned about relative wages, and thus oppose nominal wage cuts as this leads to lower relative wages. Workers are less opposed to the same reduction in real wages if it takes place via higher prices, as this does not affect relative wages. Bhaskar (1990) provides additional microfoundations for this idea, based on the assumption that workers' disutility of being paid less than others is greater than the utility gain of being paid more.

The fairness argument – that employers avoid cutting nominal wages because employees and employers think that nominal wage cuts are unfair – is the common hypothesis underlying much empirical work. Many economists are sceptical towards this idea, as it involves money illusion, and thus runs counter to the standard rationality arguments. However, there is now considerable survey evidence by Bewley (1999) and Shafir, Diamond and Tversky (1997), among others, documenting that money illusion does exist. Fehr and Tyran (2001) report experimental evidence that money illusion may have important effects. Akerlof, Dickens and Perry (1996) explore the consequences of DNWR within a simulation model, formalising the ideas of Tobin (1972).

As to the legal restrictions argument, MacLeod and Malcomson (1993) point out that under European legal rules, wage contracts for individual workers can only be changed by mutual consent. (This is in contrast to US law, where workers are assumed to consent to a wage cut if they show up at work, see Malcomson, 1997.) Holden (1994) makes the same observation for collective agreements.[3] MacLeod and Malcomson (1993) and Holden (1999) show that this feature – fixed nominal wage contracts that can only be changed by mutual consent – may be crucial to prevent hold-up inefficiency, and thus induce efficient levels of invest-

**Fig. 1.** The Standard Model. Equilibrium Employment is Given by the Intersection of the Wage and Price Curves

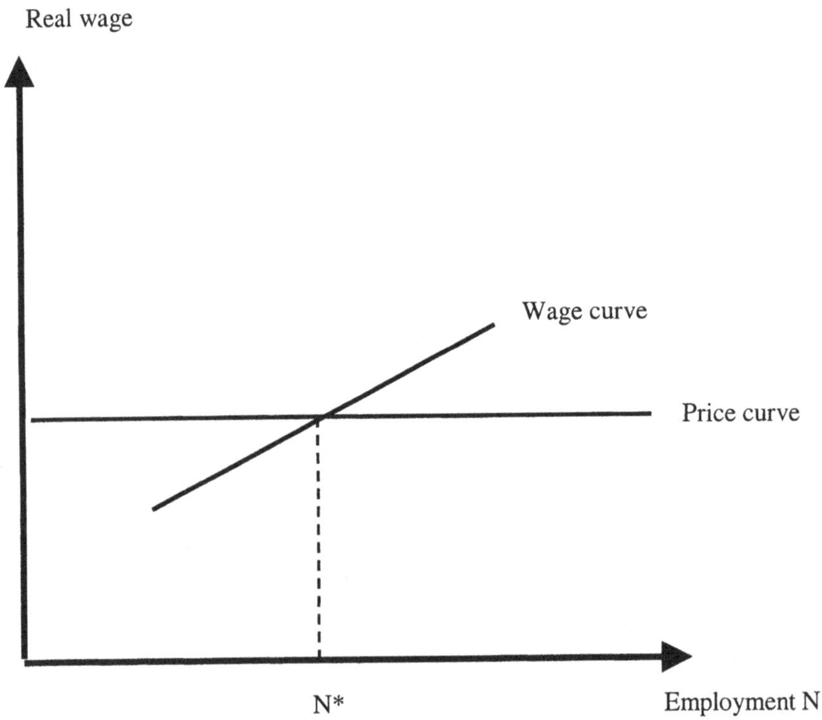


[3] The legal position of collective agreements varies between countries, and between various types of agreements within countries, but this falls outside the scope of this paper.

ment. Larsen (undated) shows how fixed wage contracts are consistent with an efficiently operating economy in a dynamic general equilibrium model.

Akerlof et al. (1996) and Holden (1994, 2004) use the same macroeconomic framework to analyse the implications of DNWR (see Andersen, 2001, for a textbook-like version of Akerlof et al.'s model, and Palley, 1994, for a related argument). Let me therefore use some space to describe this. Consider a standard monopolistic competition economy, with a large number of symmetric firms, each producing a different good. Production takes place under constant returns to scale, with labour as the only input. Firms face downward-sloping demand curves (with uniform elasticity), and set prices so as to maximise profits. As is well known, this implies that prices are set as a constant mark-up over wages, implying that the real wage is a constant, independent of the aggregate employment rate. (See the horizontal price curve in Figure 1.)

Wages are set at firm level, in a bargain between workers and firms. The outcome of the bargaining is affected by the aggregate employment rate, as a higher employment rate improves the bargaining position of the workers. Thus the wage curve, representing the outcome of the wage setting, is upward-sloping in the employment-real-wage space, see Figure 1.

Without any nominal wage rigidity, Figure 1 illustrates the standard result that the equilibrium rate of employment (and also the equilibrium rate of unemployment) is given by the intersection of the wage and price curve, and thus is independent of the rate of inflation. The model is then essentially that of Layard, Nickell and Jackman (1991) (see page 19), or Blanchard (2003, page 132), where the same figure is depicted. In this model, any change that weakens the bargaining position of the workers (e.g. a reduction of unemployment benefits) moves the wage curve downwards, raising equilibrium employment.

In Akerlof et al. (1996), a simulation model is explored where firm-specific shocks induce changes in what they refer to as the notional real wage, i.e. the real wage that would prevail without any nominal wage rigidity. If a negative shock takes place so that the notional real wage involves a nominal wage cut, Akerlof et al. assume that DNWR (due to fairness reasons) prevents the cut, implying that real wages are higher than they would otherwise have been. Under low or negative inflation, this will happen in a large part of the economy, so that wage pressure increases, the wage curve moves up in Figure 1, and the equilibrium rate of employment is reduced.

In Holden (1994, 2004), DNWR is justified by the legal feature mentioned above. Consistent with institutional regularities in many countries, it is assumed that when collective agreements are up for renewal (usually annually), they will be prolonged in nominal terms unless both parties agree to a change. Holden shows that the party that must initiate the change has a strategic disadvantage in the bargaining process. Under positive inflation, workers want a nominal wage rise, so that they have a strategic disadvantage. Thus, wage pressure is reduced, the wage curve moves downwards, and equilibrium employment increases. Under negative inflation, or under low inflation in firms experiencing a negative shock so that wages should be cut, it is the firm who wants to reduce wages, and thus have the strategic disadvantage. In this case, wage pressure is increased, the wage curve moves up, and equilibrium employment is decreased (see Figure 2). The upshot is a Phillips curve which is vertical for high inflation and negative inflation, but high

**Fig. 2.** Inflation Weakens the Bargaining Position of the Workers, Lowering the Wage Curve and Increasing Equilibrium Employment

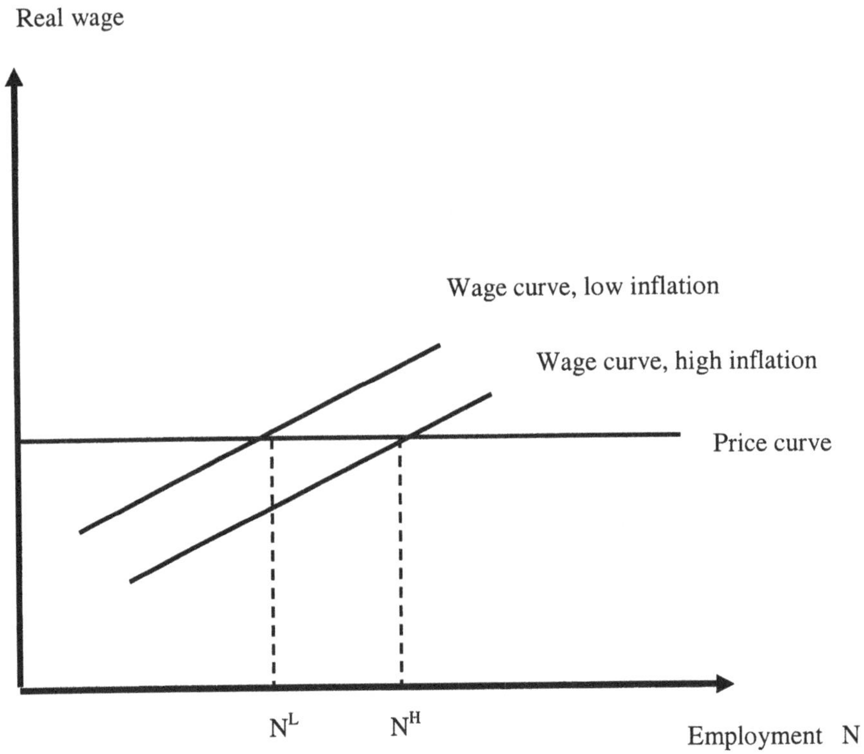


inflation involves lower unemployment than negative inflation, cf. Figure 3. (The smoothing reflects firm-specific shocks.)

Why is the party who wants to initiate the change at a strategic disadvantage? Holden analyses this in a non-cooperative bargaining model of the Rubinstein (1982) type. Both parties may disrupt production (strike or lock-out) as a means of enforcing a renegotiation of the wage contract. If a strike or lockout takes place, the outcome will be a real wage which depends on the bargaining position of the parties, including the effect of the aggregate employment rate. However, initiating a strike or lockout also involves costs to both parties, in the form of lost output during the work stoppage, and possibly also due to adverse effects on reputation, increased uncertainty etc.

To fix ideas, consider the following simple numerical illustration. (See Holden, 1994, 2004, for a rigorous treatment.) Assume for simplicity a stationary economic environment, where wage negotiations undertaken during a work stoppage (strike or lock-out) lead to a real wage of 100. Consider first an inflation scenario, where inflation has eroded the real value of the nominal wage specified in the contract. Thus, we assume that the real value of the existing contract wage is 90. Now the contract is up for possible renegotiation. If a strike takes place, there will be an agreement on a new wage of 100. Furthermore, a strike (or lock-out) will involve costs corresponding to a per time unit loss of 5 over the contract period, for both workers and firms. Thus, if the workers initiate a strike, they will obtain a payoff of 100 – 5 = 95. Clearly, strike threats are credible, as this will give the workers a higher payoff than they will obtain from prolonging the existing contract. However, if the firm offers a new contract of 95 + ε, where ε is a small positive number, strike threats will no longer be credible. Workers will obtain a higher payoff from accepting the firm's offer of 95 + ε than from initiating a strike. Thus, the workers will accept the offer, and no strike will take place.

**Fig. 3.** The Long Run Phillips-curve

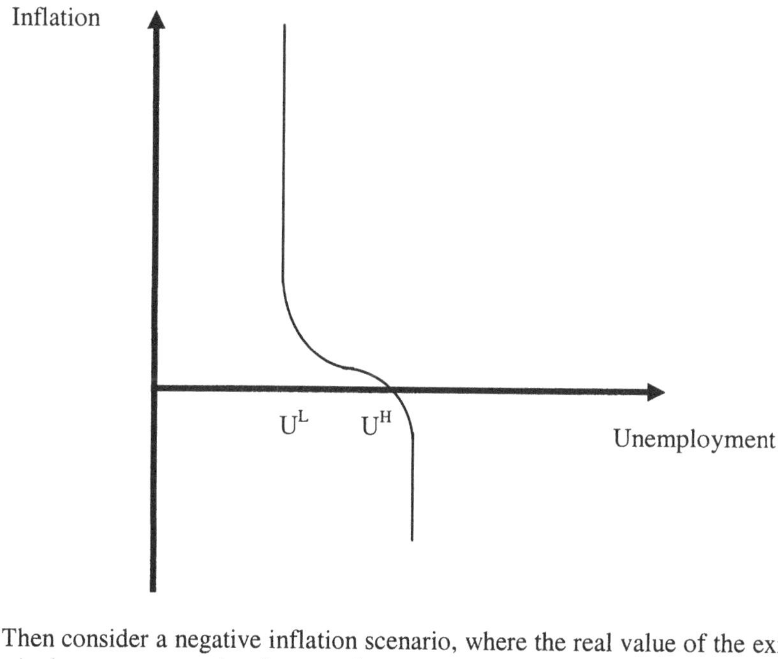


Then consider a negative inflation scenario, where the real value of the existing nominal contract wage has increased to, say, 110. In this case, it is the firm who wants to reduce wages. A lockout is credible, as it provides the firm with a payoff corresponding to a wage of 105 (wage 100 + costs 5 = 105), which is better than the existing wage of 110. But if the workers offer a wage of 105 – ε, a lockout is no longer credible, as it yields a lower payoff to the firm than the workers' new wage offer. Thus, the firm will accept the offer of 105 – ε, and no lockout will take place.

The example above shows that even if the real situation is the same in the two scenarios – absent an initial wage, the new contract should give a real wage of 100 – the existence of the initial nominal contract wage affects the bargaining outcome. High inflation erodes the real value of the nominal wage given in the contract, putting workers at a strategic disadvantage. Negative inflation, or low inflation and a firm-specific negative shock, puts firms at a strategic disadvantage.

Consider the effect of indexation in this example. Under low but positive inflation, partial indexation to the general price level will raise the nominal wage that is specified in the contract. Thus, it will raise the nominal wage at which DNWR prevails, implying that DNWR may be binding when relative wages change under higher rates of inflation than what would be the case if there were no indexation. On the other hand, under negative inflation, symmetric, partial, indexation that entails a reduction in nominal wages will work in the opposite way, reducing the nominal wage specified in the contract. However, under negative inflation, DNWR seems likely to be binding in parts of the labour market anyway.

Holden (2004) extends the analysis in the 1994 paper by also allowing for an unorganised sector. Here, DNWR hinges on the strength of the employment protection legislation, which provides workers with a means of refusing a wage cut proposed by the employer. Thus, this analysis suggests that DNWR is prevalent in countries with a high coverage of collective agreements/high union density (as unions have a stronger position to refuse nominal wage cuts than individual workers have) and in countries with strong employment protection legislation.

### Some Counter-arguments

The macroeconomic effects of DNWR implied by the models above are not undisputed cf. Hogan (1997) and Yates (1998). Most importantly, Hogan (1997) argues that if wage setting is forward-looking, firms will take the possible future effect of DNWR into consideration. Elsby (2004) takes the argument further within a fully specified forward-looking model of wage setting under DNWR arising from fairness considerations. Elsby argues that the risk of future DNWR may lead to attenuation of wage increases, i.e. that firms raise wages less than they would have done if wages were fully flexible. The attenuation of wage increases will be stronger under low inflation. The idea here is that, under high inflation, firms facing a positive demand or technology shock will raise wages considerably, as they know that the high real wage can be reversed in the future by just letting nominal wages be constant. Under low inflation and DNWR, firms facing a positive shock will be more reluctant to raise wages a lot, as raising wages increase the risk that DNWR will push up wages in the future. (Bewley, in his discussion of Akerlof et al., 2000, reports conversations with managers who express exactly this concern.) Elsby then shows that previous studies, by neglecting this effect, have overstated the costs of DNWR.

Note, however, that this argument is not fatal for the effect of inflation on the workers' bargaining position. The feature that rational agents take into consideration the possibility that DNWR may affect wages in the future, will diminish the negative effect of inflation on the union's bargaining position, but it will not remove it (Holden, 1997).

A second counter-argument by Hogan (1997) against the effect of DNWR on employment is that higher real wages need not lead to lower employment if firms hoard labour, or if higher real wages make an unemployed person more likely to accept a job. It is, however, not clear that this point is valid. If wage pressure is increased, wage and price setting are not consistent, and something has to change so as to make wage and price setting consistent. If firms hoard labour, so that unemployment does not increase, the real wage implied by the wage setting would remain higher than the real wage implied by the price setting. Thus, it seems that excessive wage pressure would prevail until firms started to shed labour, raising unemployment.

A more general argument against the idea that nominal wages affect output is based on evidence that real wages seem to be acyclical or slightly pro-cyclical. The argument runs as follows: If nominal wages are rigid, and the labour demand curve is downward sloping, demand shocks will involve movement along the labour demand curve and thus involve counter-cyclical real wages. But evidence suggests that real wages are acyclical or slightly pro-cyclical. This has been raised as a key objection to macroeconomic models with nominal wage rigidity. However, as Spencer (1998) pointed out, if there are both demand shocks and technology shocks, the latter will induce procyclical behaviour of real wages. The overall cyclicality of real wages will depend on both types of shocks. Spencer shows that US postwar data indicates that a positive demand disturbance is associated with a temporary decline in real wages, consistent with a model with nominal wage rigidity.

An interesting approach to the effect of inflation on wage setting is the Grease and Sand argument of Groshen and Schweitzer (2000). They note the well-known effect that, under downward nominal wage rigidity, inflation may facilitate changes in wage distribution across occupations (Grease). On the other hand, they also argue that inflation involves greater expectational errors that may cause unintended changes in the wage distribution across firms (Sand). These effects are analysed in a unified framework, making it possible to evaluate benefits and costs of inflation in the labour market.

## 3 The Effect of Inflation on Staggered Nominal Wage Contracts

In the literature on staggered wage and price setting, it is usually implicitly or explicitly assumed that one can abstract from trend inflation without any problems. However, as shown by Ball, Mankiw and Romer (1988), this is not so. Under high inflation, wage adjustment will be more frequent, and this will cause the short-run Phillips curve to be steeper, reducing the persistence of shocks. In related models, Helpman and Leiderman (1990) and Kolsrud and Nymoen (1998) argue that inflation reconciles the conflicting claims of workers and firms, and thus may affect the equilibrium output. More recently, Ascari (2000) has shown that inflation increases the forward-lookingness of wage setters, again reducing the persistence of shocks to the economy.

Allowing for steady-state inflation in standard staggered-contracts models has several and opposing effects on long-run output and employment. Ascari (2003) shows that under time-contingent price setting, trend inflation implies that otherwise symmetric firms will set different prices in steady state. Due to the usual non-linearities in the utility and production functions, this leads to an aggregate output loss. Ascari concludes that "a very mild level of trend inflation implies huge and unrealistic changes in the steady-state output level." In contrast, Karanassou, Sala and Snower (2003a,b) argue that the reduction in inflation over the last decades plays an important role in explaining increased unemployment. Karanassou et al. refer to their idea as "frictional growth", and the key point is as follows. Under staggered, time-contingent nominal contracts, nominal variables are a weighted average of their past and expected future variables. Owing to time discounting, wage setters will put less weight on the last part of the contract period, implying that inflation causes wages and prices to lag behind money growth. Consequently, the higher the rate of inflation, the more wages and prices lag behind money, thus increasing the real money stock, which again increases output and employment. Furthermore, Karanassou et al. argue that the weighting is amplified owing to uncertainty and multiple nominal rigidities, i.e. both rigid wages and rigid prices.

## 4 Incomplete Labour Contracts and Nominal Wage Growth

Almost all the literature on DNWR deals with the idea that nominal wages are constant in situations where flexible wages would fall. However, there is a small body of literature that argues that there are mechanisms inducing a certain nominal wage growth, implying that unless inflation is sufficiently high to allow for this nominal wage growth, other mechanisms (read unemployment) must be at work to prevent the nominal wage growth.

A key possible cause of nominal wage growth is incomplete labour contracts. As argued by Moene (1988), workers can impose costs on a firm even when working under the existing contract, e.g. by strictly adhering to the working rules (work-to-rule). Such behaviour is well known from real-world wage negotiations in many industrialised economies. On the other hand, the firm may reduce flexible types of remuneration as bonus payments etc. Yet if workers can impose larger costs on the firms than vice versa, which appears to be a plausible assumption in most cases, nominal wages increase during work-to-rule (Holden, 1997). Intuitively, firms are willing to raise the nominal wages so as to avoid a costly period of work-to-rule; see Holden (1989) for supporting empirical evidence. Nickell and Quintini (2003) find evidence for the UK that there are employees "who would have had negative nominal wage changes without the distortion who, in fact, have significantly positive, rather than zero, nominal wage changes", i.e. as predicted by the idea that work-to-rule may induce nominal wage growth, inducing higher real wages, even in a situation where real wages would have gone down had inflation been higher.

## 5 Multi-Level Bargaining and the Co-ordination of Wage Setting

Most of the literature on DNWR presumes that wage setting is unco-ordinated. Allowing for centralised or co-ordinated wage setting implies additional effects. Most importantly, several Nordic researchers have argued that multi-level wage setting systems, as in the Nordic countries, where wages are negotiated both centrally (at national and/or industry level) and locally, may cause a minimum rate of growth in nominal wages. In the literature, two versions of this feature have been discussed.

Rødseth (1985), Holden (1988), Rødseth and Holden (1990), and Calmfors (1993) argue that wage setters at the central level both generally want wage restraint, and, to a large extent, are able to predict wage growth at the local level. However, some wage growth at the local level is unavoidable, in part due to the possibility of work-to-rule under the peace clause that prevails at the local negotiations, given that the central agreements are in force. Under low inflation, wage restraint may require a nominal wage cut at the central level, and in this situation DNWR at the central level may induce higher real wages and lower employment. Holden (1998) provides empirical evidence for the existence of a floor to nominal wage growth of 2–3 percent at the central level in the manufacturing sectors of the four major Nordic countries for the period 1961–1985/92.

The other version of the inflationary bias of multi-level wage setting, advocated by, among others, Hibbs and Locking (1996) and Iversen (1999), emphasises that central wage setting has historically involved compression of relative wages. This causes a need for wage growth at the local level to restore relative wages, wholly or partially, to their market values. Under low inflation, the combination of wage growth at both levels will induce excessive real wage growth and lower unemployment.

Note that one can also argue for the opposite conclusion, that wage setting systems with a co-ordinated or centralised element are better suited to adapt to changes in the rate of inflation.[4] The idea here is that the centralised wage settlements often end up in a general increase which is a little below the sum of inflation and average productivity growth. Thus, if inflation is reduced, a coordinated, multi-level system may, in principle, easily adapt by reducing the general increase, without being bothered by coordination problems that may exist in less centralised wage-setting systems. One may argue that countries with extensive incomes policies and social pacts, like the Netherlands and Norway, have adapted better to the low inflation era than countries with less co-ordinated wage setting as France and Spain.

[4] I am grateful to an anonymous referee for providing this argument.

## 6 Near-Rational Wage and Price Setters

For decades, most economists have frowned upon explanations based on non-rational agents. While such behaviour is often viewed as plausible, many economists have argued that it is *ad hoc*. Furthermore, one has wanted to avoid a situation where different researchers invoke different behavioural assumptions as key foundations in their own theories. However, research by cognitive psychologists and experimental economists has provided strong support for behavioural assumptions that differ systematically from the standard economic main assumption (see Kahneman and Tversky, 1979, and the surveys in Rabin, 1998, and Fehr and Schmidt, 2002).

Building on this research, Akerlof, Dickens and Perry (2000) argue that wage and price setters treat inflation differently from what most economists assume. First, when inflation is low, many people ignore it. Second, workers view nominal wage increases as a sign that they are appreciated, without reflecting about nominal wage increases as being an element of a general rise in wage and price levels.

More specifically, Akerlof et al. consider a model where workers' effort depends on their wage relative to a reference level. Near-rational firms do not take low inflation into account when updating their reference level; thus, wages are increased by less than they should. Correspondingly, rational firms who know that their workers are near-rational will also underweight inflation when updating the reference level. Thus, wage pressure is reduced, and equilibrium employment increased, for positive but moderate inflation.

When inflation is high, however, underweighting of inflation will involve much larger costs. Thus, near-rational wage and price setters will take inflation fully into account when it is high. Hence, the reduction in wage pressure induced by low inflation only prevails for moderate, positive levels of inflation, and not for high rates of inflation.

## 7 Empirical Evidence

The last few years, a rapidly increasing literature has emerged testing for the existence and implications of DNWR. Due to the size and speed of increase of this literature, only a brief selective survey will be provided. Different types of evidence have been put forward. Akerlof et al (1996), Bewley (1999), Agell and Lundborg (2003) and Agell and Bennmarker (2003) report results from interviews and surveys where employers and employees are asked about (among other thing) DNWR. These studies report that nominal wage cuts are rare in the US and Sweden.

Other studies investigate DNWR in large micro-data sets based on wage surveys, administrative files, personnel files, or data for union contracts. While these studies generally find nominal wage cuts to be more frequent than one finds in interviews, the studies with few exceptions nevertheless find evidence that DNWR exists. Typically, the studies find (i) a spike in the distribution of nominal wage changes at zero and (ii) that the rate of inflation affects the distribution of nominal wage changes, both features as would be implied by the existence of DNWR. The studies include Fehr and Goette (2000) for Switzerland, Beissinger and Knoppik (2000) and Knoppik and Beissinger (2001) for Germany, Christofides and Leung (2003) for Canada, Ekberg (2002) for Sweden, Devicienti (2004) for Italy, Kimura and Ueda (1997) for Japan, Nickell and Quintini (2003) for the UK, and Altonji and Devereux (1999) and Lebow et al. (2003) for the US. (The latter three papers also discuss previous empirical findings for the UK and the US.)

The study by Lebow et al is noteworthy because it also includes data on total compensation. Lebow et al find that even if total compensation is somewhat more flexible than wage and salaries alone, there is a significant amount of rigidity for compensation. Furthermore, firms do not seem to circumvent wage rigidity by changing other types of compensation.

Few studies attempt to discriminate between the fairness- and the contract-theories of DNWR, as the key implications are shared by both hypotheses. One possible way to circumvent this problem is to compare differences between countries. Based on the cross-country differences of ten EU countries, Dessy (2002) finds evidence that DNWR is more prevalent in countries with intermediate levels of bargaining than in countries with centralized or decentralized wage setting, while high bargaining coverage seems to reduce DNWR. Holden and Wulfsberg (2004) use industry panel data from Eurostat, covering 12 countries over the period 1973–99, and find evidence that strict employment protection legislation and high union density increase DNWR, while the effect of bargaining coverage is positive but insignificant. These latter results support the contract theory of Holden (2004). On the other hand, the fact that downward nominal rigidity is also found in countries with weak legal protection of workers' nominal wages, as in the US and Switzerland, suggests that fairness considerations are also of importance.

Another way to discriminate between theories is to derive testable implications that differ. Elsby (2004) suggests a test based on the idea that the effect of inflation on DNWR differs between the fairness and the contract justifications. As explained in section 2 above, the risk of future DNWR will lead forward-looking firms to attenuate wage increases. Elsby argues that if DNWR is caused by fairness concerns, the attenuation will be weaker under low inflation (as DNWR is less likely to be binding in the future), but inflation will not affect attenuation caused by contract effects. Elsby finds evidence for the UK that attenuation of wage increases is stronger under low inflation, supporting the fairness hypothesis. Holden (2002) also suggests a test for discriminating between these two theories, but this test has not yet been implemented.

While most studies use recent data, there is also evidence for the existence of DNWR in earlier time periods. Among others, Hines (2000) shows that nominal wages were rigid in the downturns in the US in 1893, 1929 and 1981. Fregert (2000) provides evidence of downward nominal wage rigidity in Sweden during the Great Depression.

### Evidence of a Long-run Inflation-unemployment Trade-off

According to the standard view, there is no long-run trade-off between inflation and unemployment. Yet there are now a number of studies that report evidence in support of such a trade-off. Some illustrative examples are these: Bullard and Keating (1995) studying the long-run relationship between inflation and output in 58 countries over the period 1960-90. They find a positive and significant long-run response of the level of real output to a permanent inflation shock for the four European countries with the lowest rates of inflation. Karanassou et al. (2003a) find a long-run Phillips curve trade-off for a panel of EU countries for the period 1977–1998. Akerlof et al. (1996) and Karanassou et al. (2003b) find a long-run Phillips curve trade-off in the US. Ahmed and Rogers (2000) also find that the long-run effects of inflation on output in the US are positive. Lundborg and Sacklén (2001) finds evidence of a long-run Phillips curve trade-off in Sweden for the period 1963–2000, indicating that a reduction in inflation from 2 ½ per cent to zero is associated with an increase in unemployment of more than two percentage points. Correspondingly, Fortin and Dumont (2000) find evidence on Canadian aggregate data suggesting that an increase in inflation from 1 ½ percent to 2 ½ percent would reduce unemployment by 1 ½ percentage points.

These findings are consistent with other studies reporting persistent negative output effects of too strict monetary policy. Ball (1999) presents evidence supporting the view that a too strict monetary policy in the 1980s and 1990s in some European countries has led to a long-lasting increase in unemployment. Bernanke and Carey (1996) document that countries that stuck longer to the Gold standard in the 1930s, involving years with falling prices, experienced higher real wages and lower output than the countries that left the Gold standard.

So far it would, nevertheless, be fair to say that the evidence of a long-run inflation – unemployment trade-off is disputed. Among other things, several of the studies are based on rather restrictive assumptions; see, for example, the discussion of Akerlof et al. (1996) by Gordon (1996) and Mankiw (1996), as well as Canmba-Mendez, Carcia and Palenzuela (2003).

## 8 Will Society Adapt?

Many economist are sceptical towards the idea that low inflation will entail important and persistent effects on output and employment, based on the argument that any downward rigidity that may exist is the result of an inflationary environment, and that society will adapt to a zero inflation policy without a large and persistent impact on output and employment (see, for example, Gordon, 1996, Hogan, 1997, Yates, 1998). Such changes may affect the institutional setting, e.g. the type of labour contracts, or people's view of what is fair behaviour.

It seems reasonable to expect that the costs associated with higher unemployment under very low inflation will induce changes in the way labour markets operate. One would expect pay systems to become more flexible, for example by a more extensive use of bonus systems, although the evidence in Lebow et al (2003) referred to above may indicate that this will have limited effect.

Holden (2001) explores a model where firms choose between fixed wage contracts (where the employer cannot lay off the worker, and the wage can only be changed by mutual consent), or contracts where employment is at will, so that either party may terminate employment. It is shown that a fixed wage contract provides better incentives for investment and training, while employment at will facilitates efficient mobility. High inflation makes fixed wage contracts more attractive as seen from the firm, because it erodes the real value of a fixed contract wage over time, so that badly matched workers are more likely to quit for other jobs. Thus, disinflation has opposing effects on labour market rigidity: fixed wage contracts become more rigid in real terms, but fewer firms will choose fixed wage contracts.

An alternative interpretation of Holden's (2001) model is that fixed wage contracts correspond to jobs in countries with strong employment protection legislation, where labour market laws and regulations constitute important barriers to firms' possibility of unilaterally cutting nominal wages. Employment at will resembles jobs in countries with weak employment legislation, like the UK and the US, or it can be thought of as temporary jobs. Under this interpretation, a reduction in the rate of inflation will exacerbate the real wage rigidity imposed by employment protection legislation. On the other hand, firms are likely to try to opt out of the rigidity by choosing more temporary labour contracts, consistent with evidence of increased use of temporary labour contracts in Sweden in the low-inflation period in the 1990s (Agell and Lundborg, 2003). In addition, the political pressure towards a weakening of the employment protection legislation is likely to increase.

Regarding the effect of fairness, Gordon (1996) argues that in a low-inflation economy, nominal wage cuts will become more common, and there will be less reason to view them as unfair. Against this view one can argue that the fairness and legal explanations for DNWR may be complementary, and that they may strengthen each other in the sense that the existence of both makes either more persistent: The fact that many labour market participants find nominal wage cuts unfair may also contribute to the continued existence of the legal protection of nominal wages. The legal protection of nominal wages makes wage cuts rare even in a low-inflation environment, thus preventing Gordon's (1996) argument that the fairness considerations will be undermined by wage cuts being "too common".

Empirical evidence also indicates that one should not be too optimistic that labour markets and wage-setting institutions will adapt rapidly to low inflation. The extensive downward nominal wage rigidity in Sweden and Switzerland documented by Agell and Lundborg (2003) and Fehr and Goette (2000), even after years of close to zero inflation and high unemployment, also shows that rigidities may be highly persistent. Fehr and Goette also find that the wage "sweep-up" caused by nominal rigidity is strongly correlated with unemployment, suggesting that downward rigidity of nominal wages does contribute to higher unemployment.

## 9 Concluding Remarks

Let me briefly summarise the main conclusions, as seen from a policy-oriented perspective. Both the theoretical arguments and the empirical evidence indicate that wage pressure is increased under low inflation. To keep wage growth down, and to ensure consistency between the wage and price setting, higher unemployment is probably required if one aims at very low inflation. Over time, labour markets and wage setting institutions will probably adapt partially to low inflation, by increased use of flexible remuneration and temporary wage contracts. However, it is difficult to predict how far-reaching these changes will be.

In macro and monetary economics, wage and price rigidities are often the key source of inefficiencies. However, as observed above, wage and price rigidities may also play useful roles, as sharing risk or protecting against opportunistic behaviour. In particular, the legal rule that contract renegotiations require mutual consent plays an important role in ensuring efficient investments. Thus, if lower inflation leads to wages being more flexible, this would involve costs as well as benefits. Furthermore, without restrictions on the employer's right to unilaterally cut nominal wages, employment protection legislation is unlikely to be effective. Thus, proposals for changes in labour laws are likely to be met with strong resistance from unions and insiders. Evidence also suggests that the notion that nominal wage cuts are unfair is persistent. Thus it seems likely that adaptation will not be complete, so that, even in the very long run, a very low inflation target will imply permanently higher unemployment.

From a policy point of view, a key question is clearly at which rate of inflation wage pressure increases to the extent that it involves non-negligible costs. Lundborg and Sacklén (2001) find evidence for Sweden that a reduction in long-run inflation from 2 ½ to zero per cent would be associated with an increase in unemployment of more than two percentage points. In contrast, Nickell and Quintini (2003) find evidence for the UK that an increase in long-run inflation from 2 ½ to 5 ½ per cent would cause equilibrium unemployment to fall by only 0.13 percentage points. However, there is obviously a lot of uncertainty involved with these estimates, and there is also likely be considerable variation across countries with different labour market institutions. One should also remember that if low inflation is associated with high productivity growth, lower price margins or low import price growth, there will be more room for nominal wage growth, and thus fewer problems with increased wage pressure.

## References


Agell, J. and Bennmarker, H. (2002): Wage policy and endogenous wage rigidity: A representative view from the inside. CESifo WP 751.

Agell, J. and Lundborg, P. (2003): Survey evidence on wage rigidity and unemployment. *Scandinavian Journal of Economics 105*, 15–30.

Ahmed, S. and Rogers, JH. (2000): Inflation and the great ratios. Long-term evidence from the U.S. *Journal of Monetary Economics 45*, 3–35.

Akerlof, G.A., Dickens, W.T. and Perry, W.L. (1996): The macroeconomics of low inflation. *Brookings Papers on Economic Activity 1*, 1–75.

Akerlof, G.A., Dickens, W.T. and Perry, W.L. (2000): Near rational wage and price setting and the long run Phillips curve. *Brookings Papers on Economic Activity 1*, 1–60.

Altonji, J.G. and Devereux, P.J. (1999): The extent and consequences of downward nominal wage rigidity. NBER Working Paper 7236.

Andersen, T.M. (2001): Can inflation be too low? Mimeo, Department of Economics, University of Århus.

Ascari, G. (2000): Optimising agents, staggered wages and persistence in the real effects of money shocks. *Economic Journal 110*, 664–686.

Ascari, G. (2003): Staggered prices and trend inflation: some nuisances. Bank of Finland Discussion Paper 27 – 2003.

Ball, L. (1999): Aggregate demand and long-run unemployment. *Brookings Papers on Economic Activity*, September 1999.

Ball, L. and Mankiw, N.G. (1994): Asymmetric price adjustment and economic fluctuations. *Economic Journal*, 247–261.

Beissinger, T. and Knoppik, C. (2000): Downward nominal rigidity in West-German earnings 1975-1995. University of Regensburg Discussion Paper No 344.

Bernanke, B.S. and Carey, K. (1996): Nominal wage stickiness and aggregate supply in the Great Depression. *Quarterly Journal of Economics*, 853–883.

Bewley, T.F. (1999): *Why Do Wages Not Fall During a Recession?* Harvard University Press.

Bhaskar, V. (1990): "Wage relatives and the natural range of unemployment." *Economic Journal 100*, 60–66.

Blanchard, O.J. (2003): *Macroeconomics*. Third International Edition. Prentice Hall

Bullard, J. and Keating, J.W. (1995): The long-run relationship between inflation and output in postwar economies. *Journal of Monetary Economics 36*, 477–496.

Calmfors, L. (1993): Centralisation of wage bargaining and macroeconomic performance – a survey. Seminar Paper 536, IIES, Stockholm University.

Calmfors, L., Booth, A., Burda, M., Checchi, D., Naylor, R. and Visser, J. (2001): The future of collective bargaining in Europe. In T. Boeri, A Brugiavini and L. Calmfors (eds). *The Role of Unions in the Twenty-First Century* Oxford: Oxford University Press.

Camba-Mendez, G., Garcia, J.A. and Palenzuela, D.A. (2003): Relevant economic issues concerning the optimal rate of inflation. *Background Studies for the ECB's Evaluation of its Monetary Policy Strategy*, ECB.

Christofides, L.N. and Leung, M.T. (2003): Nominal wage rigidity in contract data: A parametric approach. *Economica 70*, 619–638.

Dessy, O. (2002): Nominal wage rigidity and institutions: Micro-evidence form the Europanel. Mimeo, University of Milan.

Devicienti, F. (2004): Downward nominal wage rigidity in Italy: Evidence and consequences. LABORatorio R. Revelli Working Paper No 20.

the Economist (2003): The joy of inflation. Leader, May 15$^{th}$, 2003.

Ekberg, J. (2002): Nominal wage rigidity on the Swedish labor market. Mimeo, Stockholm School of Economics.

Elsby, M. (2004): Evaluating the economic significance of downward nominal wage rigidity. Mimeo, LSE.

Fehr, E. and Goette, L. (2000): Robustness and real consequences of nominal wage rigidity. Forthcoming in *Journal of Monetary Economics*

Fehr, E. and Tyran, J.R. (2001): Does money illusion matter? *American Economic Review* 91, 1239–1262.

Fehr, E. and Schmidt, K.M. (2002): "Theories of Fairness and Reciprocity- Evidence and Economic Applications." in: M. Dewatripont, L. Hansen and St. Turnovsky (Eds.), Advances in Economics and Econometrics - 8th World Congress, Econometric Society Monographs, Cambridge, Cambridge University Press 2002

Fortin, P. and Dumont, K. (2000): The shape of the long-run Phillips curve: Evidence from Canadian macrodata, 1956–97. Mimeo, Canadian Institute for Advanced Research.

Fregert, K. (2000): The Great Depression in Sweden as a coordination failure. *European Review of Economic History 4*, 341–360.

Gordon, R.J. (1996): Comment on Akerlof, Dickens and Perry, The macroeconomics of low inflation, *Brookings Papers on Economic Activity 1*, 61–66.

Gottfries, N. (1992): Insiders, outsiders, and nominal wage contracts. *Journal of Political Economy 100*, 252–270.

Groshen, E.L. and Schweitzer, M.E. (2000): The effects of inflation on wage adjustments in firm-level data: Grease or sand? Mimeo, The Federal Reserve Bank of New York.

Helpman, E. and Leiderman, L. (1990): Real wages, monetary accommodation and inflation. *European Economic Review 34*, 897–911.

Hibbs, D. and Locking, H. (1996): Wage compression, wage drift, and wage inflation in Sweden. *Labour Economics 3*, 109–141.

Hines, C. (2000): Nominal wage rigidity and industry characteristics in the downturns of 1893, 1929, and 1981. *American Economic Review 90*, 1432–1446.

Hogan, S. (1997): What does downward nominal wage rigidity imply for monetary policy? Bank of Canada Working Paper 97–13. Canadian-Public-Policy. December 1998; 24(4): 513–25.

Holden, S. (1989): Wage drift and bargaining. Evidence from Norway. *Economica 56*, 419–432.

Holden, S. (1994): Wage bargaining and nominal rigidities, *European Economic Review 38*, 1994, 1021–1039.

Holden, S. (1997): Wage bargaining, holdout, and inflation. *Oxford Economic Papers 49*, 235–255.

Holden, S. (1998): Wage drift and the relevance of centralised wage setting. *Scandinavian Journal of Economics 100*, 711–731.

Holden, S. (1999): Renegotiation and the efficiency of investment. *Rand Journal of Economics 30*, 106–119.

Holden, S. (2001): Does price stability exacerbate labour market rigidities in the EMU? *Empirica 28*, 403–418.

Holden, S. (2002): Downward nominal wage rigidity - contracts or fairness considerations. Mimeo, available at http://folk.uio.no/sholden/#wp.

Holden, S. (2004): The costs of price stability. Downward nominal wage rigidity in Europe. Forthcoming in Economica.

Holden, S. and Wulfsberg, F. (2004) Downward nominal wage rigidity in Europe. Mimeo, available at http://folk.uio.no/sholden/#wp

Iversen, T. (1999): Contested Economic Institutions. The Politics of Macroeconomics and Wage Bargaining in Advanced Democracies. Cambridge: Cambridge University Press.

Kahneman, D. and Tversky, A. (1979): Prospect theory. An analysis of decision under risk. *Econometrica 47 (2)*, 263–292.

Karanassou, M., Sala, H. and Snower, D.J. (2003a): The European Phillips curve: Does the NAIRU exist? Mimeo, University of London.

Karanassou, M., Sala, H. and Snower, D.J. (2003b): A reappraisal of the inflation-unemployment tradeoff. Mimeo, University of London.

Keynes, J.M. (1936): The General Theory of Employment, Interest and Money. MacMillan.

Kimura, T. and Ueda, K. (1997): Downward nominal wage rigidity in Japan: Is price stability costly? Working Paper, Bank of Japan.

Knoppik, C. and Beissinger, T. (2001): How rigid are nominal wages? Evidence and implications for Germany. *Scandinavian Journal of Economics 105*, 619–641.

Kolsrud, D. and Nymoen, R. (1998): "The Open Economy Wage-Price Spiral, *Journal of Economic Studies,* 25 (1998), issue 6, 450–467.

Larsen, J.D.J. (undated). The macroeconomic implications of turnover costs and wage contracts. Mimeo, Bank of England.

Layard, R., Nickell, S. and Jackman, R. (1991): *Unemployment: Macroeconomic Performance and the Labour Market.* Oxford University Press.

Lebow, D.E., Saks, R.E. and Wilson, B.A. (2003): Downward nominal wage rigidity. Evidence from the employment cost index. *Advances in Macroeconomics vol. 3, Issue 1, article 2.*

Lundborg, P. and Sacklén, H. (2001): Is there a long-run unemployment-inflation trade-off in Sweden?. FIEF working paper 173, Stockholm.

MacLeod, W.B. and Malcomson, J.M. (1993): Investment, holdup, and the form of market contracts. *American Economic Review 37*, 343–354.

Malcomson, J.M. (1997): Contracts, hold-up, and labor markets. *Journal of Economic Literature 35 (4)*, 1916–1957.

Mankiw, G. (1996): Comment on Akerlof, Dickens and Perry, The macroeconomics of low inflation, *Brookings Papers on Economic Activity 1*, 61–66.

Moene, K.O. (1988): Union threats and wage determination. *Economic Journal 98*, 471–483.

Nickell, S.J. and Quintini, G. (2003): Nominal wage rigidity and the rate of inflation. Mimeo. *The Economic Journal 113*, 762–781.

Palley, T.I. (1994): Escalators and elevators: A Phillips-curve for Keynesians. *Scandinavian Journal of Economics 96*, 111–116.

Rubinstein, A. (1982): Perfect equilibrium in a bargaining model. *Econometrica 50*, 97–109.

Rødseth, A. (1985): Centralized unions and macroeconomic policy: A note. Memorandum 10, Department of Economics, University of Oslo.

Rødseth, A. and Holden, S. (1990): Wage formation in Norway. In L. Calmfors (ed). Wage formation and macroeconomic policy in the Nordic countries. Stockholm: SNS.

Rabin, M. (1998): Psychology and economics. *Journal of Economic Literature XXXVI*, 11–46.

Shafir, E., Diamond, P. and Tversky, A. (1997): Money illusion. *Quarterly Journal of Economics CXII*, 341–374.

Spencer, D.E. (1998): The relative stickiness of wages and prices. *Economic Inquiry* 36, 120–137.

Tobin, J. (1972): Inflation and unemployment. *American Economic Review 62*, 1–18.

Taylor, J. (1999): "Staggered wage and price setting in macroeconomics." Chapter 15 in J. B. Taylor and M. Woodford (eds). *Handbook of Macroeconomics.* North-Holland.

Yates, A. (1998): Downward nominal wage rigidity and monetary policy. Mimeo, Bank of England.

# Comment on Steinar Holden's Paper

Tapio Palokangas

University of Helsinki, Department of Economics
Finland

I found Steinar Holden's presentation very interesting. Here are my impressions of the presentation and suggestions of new ideas on the basis of my own experience.

Steinar Holden wrote, "Rational agents care only about real variables, and any effect of nominal variables must be due to money illusion that will disappear over time". I think this is a good start, because it stresses the role of microfoundations in macroeconomics. How can we then explain the salient features of modern wage settlements? Here are some suggestions.

The first thing we have to ask is why, in general, wage contracts are in nominal terms. According to contract theory, a rational contract is a function of all variables that are relevant to it. Price inflation is relevant to wage settlements, so a rational wage contract should include price indexing. Steinar Holden justifies the exclusion of indexation, because it is costly. Why are financial derivatives then used, although they are even more complicated than a price index? In many countries, indexation has been made illegal or very difficult, but then we would need a theory of why indexation is banned.

My suggested solution to this problem is the following. First, indexation leads to a stalemate, where all prices are indexed to other prices. Consequently, the overall inflation in the economy is faster and everyone loses. Hence, in the political equilibrium, where the union, the firm and the government are players, this negative externality is eliminated. We have to model this political equilibrium.

Second, in the presentation, nominal wage stickiness is based on the property that the previous contract holds over negotiations after the contract periods have expired. Steinar Holden justifies this as follows. Nominal wage contracts can be changed only by mutual consent, because otherwise there would be hold-up inefficiency in investment: firms do not invest, because they are afraid of wage increases after investment; and unions increase their wages, because they believe that, in any case, firms do not invest. According to the theory of repeated games, however, the best way of eliminating hold-up inefficiency is the formation of reputation. Employers and union leaders also know in practice that when you cheat once, your opponent remembers it for a long time.

My suggested solution to this second problem is the following. If wage contracts can be rejected after they have expired, then the likelihood of a dispute is greater and both parties will lose. Hence, there is again externality and the need of a political process to correct it. We have to model this process.

Third, Steinar Holden explains the existence of wage drifts by the assumption that wage setters at the central and local level have different preferences. This assumption, however, is not very robust, because the central and local unions have more or less the same members. My suggestion is that at the central and local levels risks, rather than preferences, are different. Therefore, according to contract theory, it is optimal to set wages in two stages, the base wage in accordance with "central" risk, and a drift in accordance with "local" risk, which, according to the law of large number, is expected to be higher than "central" risk.

Finally, Steinar Holden suggests that, owing to wage stickiness, there can be a floor to wage inflation. I would rather claim that there is asymmetry in wage adjustment on the following grounds:

- Because workers are more risk averters than firms, the average member of a union is willing to even out wages over time and unwilling to let his/her wage adjust to shocks. Consequently, a shock also has employment effects.
- Because of liquidity constraints, there is asymmetry: a downward shock decreases welfare more than the amount by which an equal upward shock increases welfare. The lower the wage inflation rate, the greater the number of households that are liquidity constrained and the lower the equilibrium level of employment.

# The Finnish Bargaining System: Actors' Perceptions

Jukka Pekkarinen and Kari E.O. Alho[1]

The Labour Institute for Economic Research, Helsinki, Finland
ETLA, The Research Institute of the Finnish Economy, Helsinki, Finland

## Abstract

The paper presents results from a survey addressing views on the wage bargaining system among Finnish employees and employers. The survey is unique in the sense that the same questionnaire was sent to a representative sample of both employee representatives and employers in the private sector in Finland, as well as, in a slightly modified form, to the leadership of the federations and confederations of employers and employees. While the survey reveals a fairly high degree of overall satisfaction with the present form of collective bargaining in Finland, it also clearly indicates that there are issues where the views of the two sides of the labour market push in different directions. The divergent views concern, in particular, the trade-off between wage flexibility and income safety. While the employers would like to see greater freedom in wage setting, the employees, particularly workers, emphasise the role of the safety net provided by the minimum tariff wages stipulated by the collective agreements for each job and skill level. In the employers' views, such contractual wage floors inhibit the creation of low-wage jobs, while the employees resist such a view. While employers clearly opt for a more decentralised form of wage bargaining than is currently the case in Finland, it appears from the survey that both employers and employees firmly resist a thoroughly atomistic system of bargaining where the decision on the peace clause would also be transferred to the firm level. In this sense, a collective bargaining system is firmly embedded in the Finnish labour market.

[1] This is part of the research project "Rules of the game in the labour market: Industrial relations, the bargaining system and income policies in the 2000s", financed by the Finnish Work Environment Fund, and carried out jointly by ETLA (The Research Institute if the Finnish Economy) and the Labour Institute for Economic Research. The authors thank Anni Heikkilä and Kenneth Snellman for comments and suggestions, and Sinikka Littu for drafting the figures.

# 1 Introduction

Wage bargaining institutions differ a lot from one industrial country to another. They extend from a highly decentralised system, say, in the United States and some other countries, to highly centralised, nation-wide negotiation systems recognisable in some small European economies. Existing bargaining systems are also continuously subject to change, responding to various sorts of changes in the economic and social environment. Yet they do not display any clear tendency to institutional convergence, notwithstanding the fact that many countries are subject to similar changes in the environment factors relevant for wage bargaining.

Existing bargaining systems thus seem to be capable of performing the same types of tasks and adjusting to similar changes in the environment through widely divergent institutional arrangements. On the basis of such divergence, one is tempted to argue that the perceptions, goals and policies of organisations and individuals who are involved in actual bargaining matter a great deal for the institutional configuration of a bargaining system and for the way in which it is evolving over time.

Nevertheless, studies investigating the bargaining agents' perceptions of the pay system's strengths and weaknesses and its development potential are not frequent (cf. Agell and Lundborg, 1995 and 1999, Campbell and Kamlani, 1997). In this paper we report some main results of a survey addressed to participants at the local, branch and national level in wage bargaining in Finland. What is, to our knowledge, unique in our survey is that we have simultaneously directed an identical questionnaire to the representatives of both the employer and the three personnel groups (workers, salaried employees, and professional employees) in the same firms in manufacturing and services in the private sector. In addition, we have addressed the questionnaire, with only minimal changes, to the representatives of employers' federations and trade unions, and also to a selected group of leaders and labour market specialists of the central organisations of employers and employees. At this last stage, the questionnaire was also directed to the leadership of employees' and employers' unions in the public sector. It is a further characteristic of our survey that our questionnaire addresses a relatively wide range of issues related to methods, objectives and assessment of wage bargaining.

As a result, our survey provides an extensive body of information that gives us an opportunity to evaluate the attitudes of the Finnish labour market partners towards the present state of the wage bargaining system as well as the need for, and the preferred forms of, its future reform. We can compare the attitudes of the national collective bargaining associations with those of the trade union representatives and employers at the firm level. It should be stressed, however, that the survey was addressed to active participants in bargaining at different levels and not to the rank and file members of trade unions.

In what follows, we shall first present some salient features of the Finnish bargaining system. Thereafter, a short description of the design of the survey as well as an outline of the survey results will follow. This discussion largely follows the succession of the sections of the questionnaire as specified below. The paper concludes with a summary discussion of the alternatives for further development of the Finnish wage bargaining institutions to cope with the changing economic and technological environment. A fuller description of the results of the survey is to be found in a book we have recently published in Finnish (Alho et. al. 2003).

## 2 The Finnish Wage Bargaining System

The Finnish bargaining system broadly represents the Nordic breed of labour market institutions. Labour markets are effectively organised; union enrolment is hovering around 80 per cent, and has remained fairly stable over the past two decades, some recent symptoms of downturn notwithstanding. By legally imposed extension, the actual coverage of collective agreements amounts to 95 per cent of the employed labour force. A high unionisation rate is supported by a Ghent type of unemployment insurance system.[2] Employers are also well organised.

Trade union organisation in Finland represents a mixture of industrial and professional unions; industrial unions are more frequent the professional type of organisation being constrained to professional employees and some segments of salaried employees. Trade unions are organised in three national confederations, representing, without much overlapping, the member unions consisting, respectively, of workers (confederation SAK, Central Organisation of Finnish Trade Unions), salaried employees (STTK, The Finnish Confederation of Salaried Employees) and professional employees (AKAVA, Confederation for Unions of Academic Professionals in Finland). There have been two employer confederations in Finland, representing manufacturing (TT, Confederation of Finnish Industry and Employers) and service sectors (PT, Employers' Confederation of Service Industries in Finland) respectively. These two confederations have just agreed to merge in a new employer and industrial confederation called EK (Finnish Industries) to be launched in the course of 2004.

In Finland, as in some other European countries, regulation of the labour market – minimum wages, working hours, working conditions etc. – to a large extent takes place through collective agreements instead of parliamentary legislation. In recent years, labour market partners at the local level have been given more flexibility in enforcing the stipulations of the collective agreements e.g. concerning working time arrangements as well as the allocation of the local share of contractual wage increases, which has increased in recent years. The local presence of the trade unions is further strengthened by the fact that in Finland there exists no competing institution similar to work councils in many other countries, for example. Local representation of employees is concentrated in the hands of shop stewards and other trade union representatives.

[2] In a Ghent system, unemployment insurance is managed by trade unions and insurance coverage is tied to trade union membership. In Finland, this is largely the case in practice as far as the earnings-related unemployment insurance is concerned, although not by law. As a matter of fact, there exists one fast growing non-union unemployment insurance fund in Finland with the same legally mandated insurance level and the same share of public funding as in the case of trade union run insurance funds.

The Finnish wage bargaining system is commonly characterised as being fairly centralised. Yet a more accurate description might be a fairly high degree of bargaining *co-ordination*. Legally binding wage contracts are concluded at the industrial level. National confederations have frequently agreed on a recommendation for average wage increases, which have been voluntarily followed by a great majority of industry-level associations in their own wage agreements. The government has been actively involved in talks on central-level recommendations, and its tax policies, as formerly many aspects of social policies too, have been made conditional on a positive outcome of the centralised pay negotiations. Nevertheless, describing the Finnish bargaining system as co-ordinated, rather than centralised, is justified by the fact that the relations between the four bargaining levels, i.e. the centralised, industry, local and individual levels, have varied in shape, and this has provided various options for flexibility at each level. First, the history of wage bargaining in Finland since the late 1960s rather represents an interconnected cycle of centralised and (industry-wise) decentralised wage rounds, where centralised agreements have been recurrently intermitted by rounds of union-level bargaining without any central-level recommendation. Nevertheless, a kind of fairly co-ordinated pattern bargaining, with certain leading sectors opening the wage round and setting the framework for other agreements, has persisted over union-level wage rounds as well, notwithstanding evidence pointing out that union-level agreements have been, on the whole, somewhat more inflationary than the centralised wage rounds (Uusitalo in this volume and Alho, 2002).

Lack of thorough-going centralisation is indicated, second, by the fact that even in the presence of a central recommendation, a small number of unions have normally stayed outside the centrally recommended frames and sought for a pay deal on their own. Nevertheless, the wage increases reached by such outsiders have normally not deviated from the centrally agreed guidelines.

In the Finnish case, the mix of the centralised and decentralised ingredients is further characterised by the fact that, third, the collectively agreed wage hikes are normally transformed in a quite straightforward way into corresponding increases in effective wages at the local level. The wage increase stipulations of the collective agreements as such are, strictly speaking, not legally binding; what they imply is rather that the employer, on the one hand, is entitled to apply this increase, and the employees, on the other hand, are bound to observe the peace clause. Yet, on mutual consent, the local partners are free to deviate from the collectively agreed wage increases; as a matter of fact, this escape route was followed, in a downward direction, in many enterprises during the crisis years in the early 1990s.

Fourth, even centralised wage rounds in the Finnish bargaining system have become less centralised in the course of the 1990s. Namely, in recent years the wage hikes entailed by centralised agreements have not been exhaustively used up by industry-level agreements, but an increasing share of the increases has been left out, to be specified in the pay talks conducted, subject to a peace clause, at the local level. One could have expected that the increased leeway for local pay talks would have led to higher wage drift; yet so far this seems not to have been the case.

The feature of a "managed decentralisation" of the bargaining system is strengthened, fifth, by the fact that the legally binding minimum, or tariff, wage, specified in collective agreements for each job, corresponds in practice to the actual wage in only a relatively few cases. At the local or individual level, the partners are free to agree on an effective wage level above the legal floor set by the collective agreement. This works for greater wage differentials, which are indeed observed if the Finnish case is compared with other Nordic countries, for example.

To summarise, in the Finnish case of managed decentralisation, the *average wage increase* is relatively effectively co-ordinated by centralised agreements or pattern bargaining, which allows for an opportunity to take into account the macroeconomic constraints of wage policy. As a result, the wage drift plays a smaller role in the Finnish bargaining system than it does, for example, in other Nordic countries. On the other hand, the *wage structure* is also shaped by decisions at the local level, reflecting the microeconomic forces acting upon the wage determination. On the whole, the wage dispersion in Finland is higher than in other Nordic countries but lower than in many other industrialised countries.

It should be noted, however, that there are divergent assessments concerning the relative influence on the wage outcome of the different features of the collective bargaining system specified above. Through centralised agreements, the trade union side has pursued its solidarity goals by insisting upon proportionally greater pay increases for low-wage industries and low-wage earners as well as for inter-industry earnings index clauses linking the actual wage developments of different sectors to one another. The impact of such a central level intervention on actual wage dispersion is open to dispute; see, however, the paper by Alho in this volume. Views also diverge on the extent to which the collectively agreed wage floors and wage increases constrain wage policies at the local level.

In fact, it is in differences in the views of the role of wage dispersion that the divergence in the standpoints of the labour market partners is at its sharpest in Finland. While employers see in greater wage dispersion a vehicle for greater labour market flexibility and higher employment, employees just as strongly resist it as a threat to the position of the weakest segment of the labour force. This watershed in the assessments of opposing parties of wage bargaining is clearly reflected in the outcome of the survey to which we now turn.

## 3 Central Results of the Survey

Our sample, stratified according to plant size, was drawn from the membership registers of the two employees' associations TT (Confederation of Finnish Industry and Employers, mainly representing employers in manufacturing) and PT (Employers' Confederation of Service Industries). The questionnaire was sent to 8296 respondents in 2074 firms, respectively. The overall reply rate was 23 per cent. In particular, the big manufacturing employers responded actively, with a reply rate of around 50 per cent, while in the service sector the reply rate was much more uniform across the firm size groups. As was to be expected, the reply rate was much higher, 51 per cent, among associations, i.e. the respondents in unions, industrial federations and national confederations.

In our questionnaire, we also asked for background information on the characteristics of the plant or firm, and 12 variables of such kind that were used in cross-tabulating the response data. In addition, the questions concerning the frequency of profit-sharing and its mode of implementation were analysed separately. As such, the direct reply distributions and their cross-tabulations with the background variables provide a huge amount of data, only the main results and findings of which will be reported below.

The questionnaire was divided into five different sections, which asked, respectively, for the respondent's views on (1) the functioning of the present system; (2) directions in which it should be developed further; (3) the interplay between wages, taxes and social security contributions; (4) the implications of membership in the EMU for wage adjustment in possible recessions; as well as (5) future challenges facing the bargaining system. We shall next summarise the survey results section by section.[3]

## 3.1 Performance of the Present System

The survey results will be presented as histograms, which show the shares of different response alternatives (usually on the scale 1 – 5), with the corresponding average scores, of the replies given by the five different employer-respondent and nine employee-respondent groups respectively (see the enclosed figures, number of responses (n) in each group in parentheses on each row). The replies from the 14 different sub-groups of respondents are classified in the figures so that the rows representing employers, workers, salaried employees and professional staff, respectively, are bundled together. Responses to a general question addressing the overall degree of satisfaction with the Finnish wage bargaining system convey a fairly positive assessment of the traditional collective bargaining framework in the country (Figure 1). While the degree of satisfaction is quite high across the board, conformity is strongest among workers and salaried employees, both at the local and at the association level. On the other hand, there exists some more dissatisfaction among the employers, particularly among the representatives of the employers' associations. Professional employees represent a middle position among employers' and employees' standpoints, the respective unions representing an attitude closer to that of the employers'. This general pattern of responses appears quite consistently throughout the survey.

In closer detail, the employee responses unravel some dispersion across industries. The degree of satisfaction is highest in the metal industries and other manufacturing industries; it is noteworthy that employees in the food and communications industries seem to be fairly happy with the present-day system – notwithstanding the fact that these industries have most frequently stayed outside centralised agreements in Finland.

[3] We shall largely omit discussion of Section 5 (challenges facing the bargaining system), as these issues can briefly be dealt with while we are discussing issues related to Section 1 (assessment of the present system).

**Fig. 1.** In General, I am Satisfied with the Functioning of the Present Bargaining System (n=number of answers)

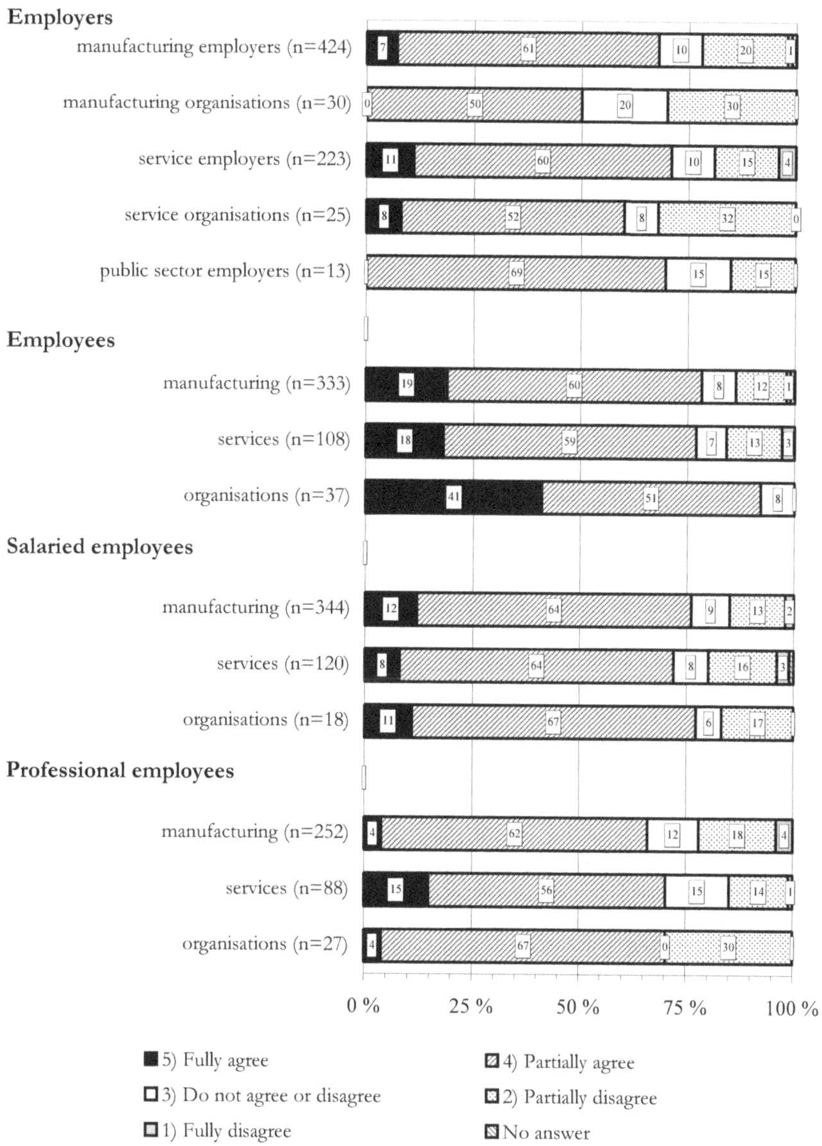

**Fig. 2.** Existing Bargaining System Allows for Sufficient Flexibility in Wages (n=number of answers)

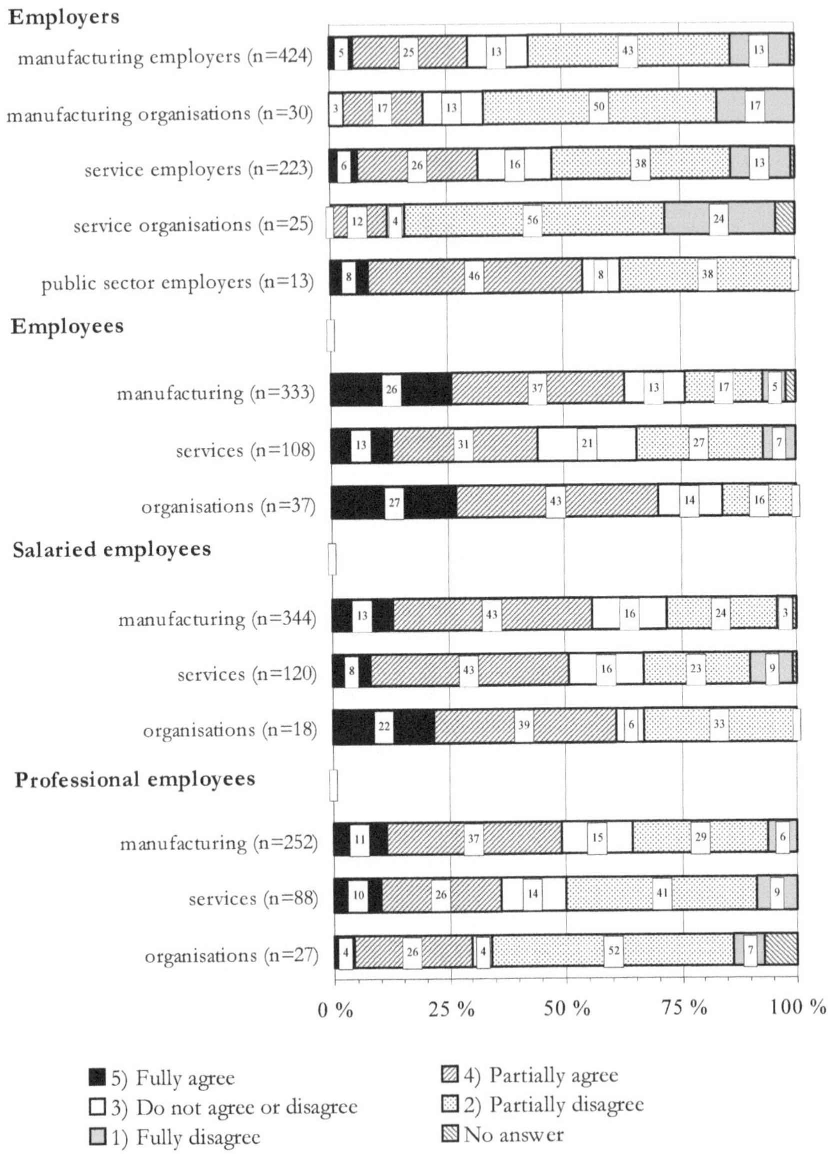

As far as the factors working for the overall positive assessment of the existing bargaining framework are concerned, the capacity of the collective bargaining to sustain peaceful industrial relations, to limit strike frequency and to provide legitimacy to the agreed pay increases strikes an overall high score, as does its capacity to enhance the stability and predictability of wage developments and to convey information about the macroeconomic factors determining the room for sustainable wage increases.

Underneath the overall satisfaction with the present system, there lies, however, a clear disagreement, which concerns assessments of the actually available room and the desired extent of *wage flexibility* in the bargaining system (Figure 2). A large majority of employers disagrees with the proposition that the present bargaining system provides sufficient room for flexibility strongly or at least partly, while, in contrast, almost as large a majority of workers and salaried employees fully or partly agrees with this proposition. The professional employees again represent a middle position between the contrasting views of employers and employees. It is also worth observing that the responses by the representatives of both the employers' and the professional employees' unions are more dissatisfied with the flexibility of the Finnish bargaining system, see Figure 3, while the degree of dissatisfaction is, in this respect, somewhat milder at the local level among the representatives of the employers and of the professional staff. On the other hand, the leaderships of the unions representing workers and salaried employees take the most positive stance towards the present system's flexibility. In other words, the divergence in the views of the bargaining partners concerning the flexibility potential of the bargaining system is at its strongest at the national level, i.e. among the leaders of the respective labour market organisations. There is more convergence in the views of the local partners, perhaps due to the fact that they have more experience with the actual flexibility potential allowed for by the bargaining system, provided, for example, by re-evaluation of jobs, bargaining on the local component of contractual wage increases and other components of the so-called wage drift.

Cross-classifications, in turn, reveal that at the local level the divergence in the views of employers and employees on flexibility is strongest in manufacturing. Moreover, increase in the size of the firm seems to increase employers' dissatisfaction with the available room for flexibility.[4]

This same pattern in the divergence of responses also consistently appears from other questions of a similar type that address the room for flexible wage adjustment allowed for by the present bargaining system. Thus, for example, employers agree, again at the association level more strongly than at the local level, with the statement that the system imposes too tight constraints on individual firms' wage policy (see Figure 3). In the same vein, employers disagree with the statement that the present bargaining system provides enough option to adjust wages to changes in profitability, this claim again receiving support from the employee side. Incidentally, agreement with this statement is characteristic of workers and salaried

[4] Similarly, the order probit estimations by Heikkilä and Piekkola in this volume reveal that the size of the firm increases the desired share of the local component of wage increases.

**Fig. 3.** Existing Bargaining System is Too Binding Concerning Firm's Wage Policy (n=number of answers)

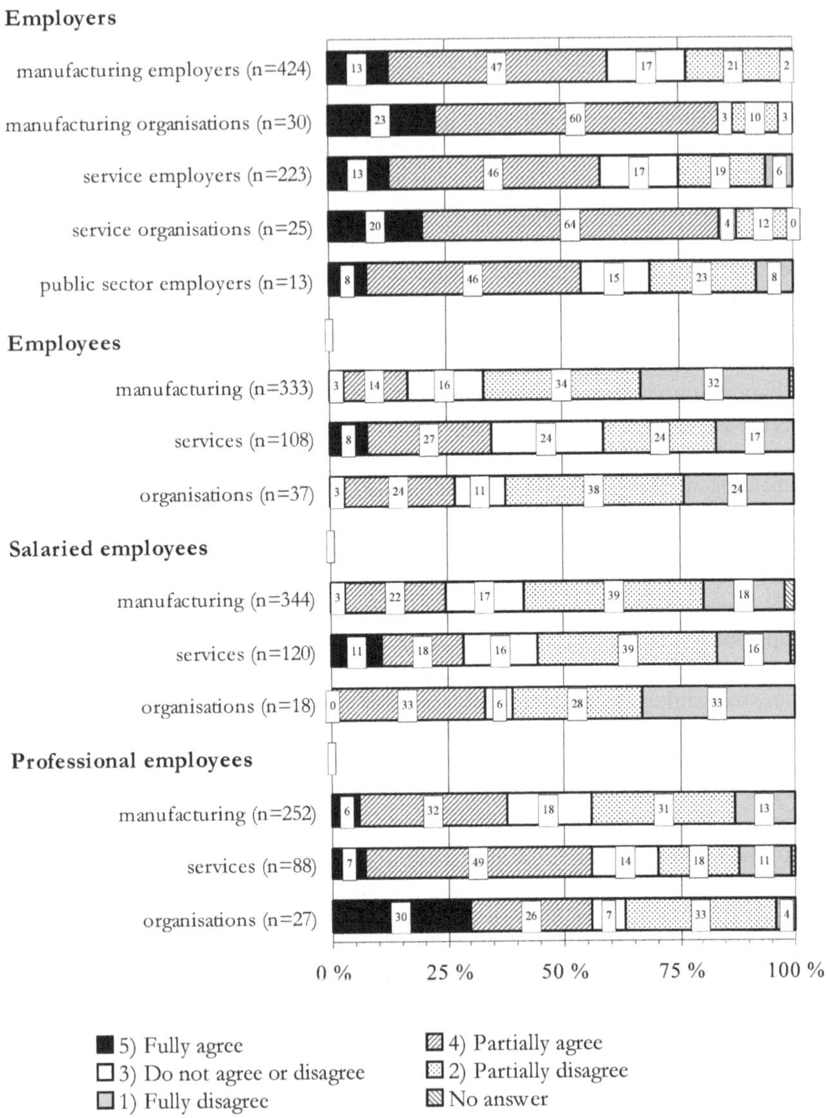

**Fig. 4.** Contractual Wage Floors Are Important Because They Provide a Minimum Income Guarantee (n=number of answers)

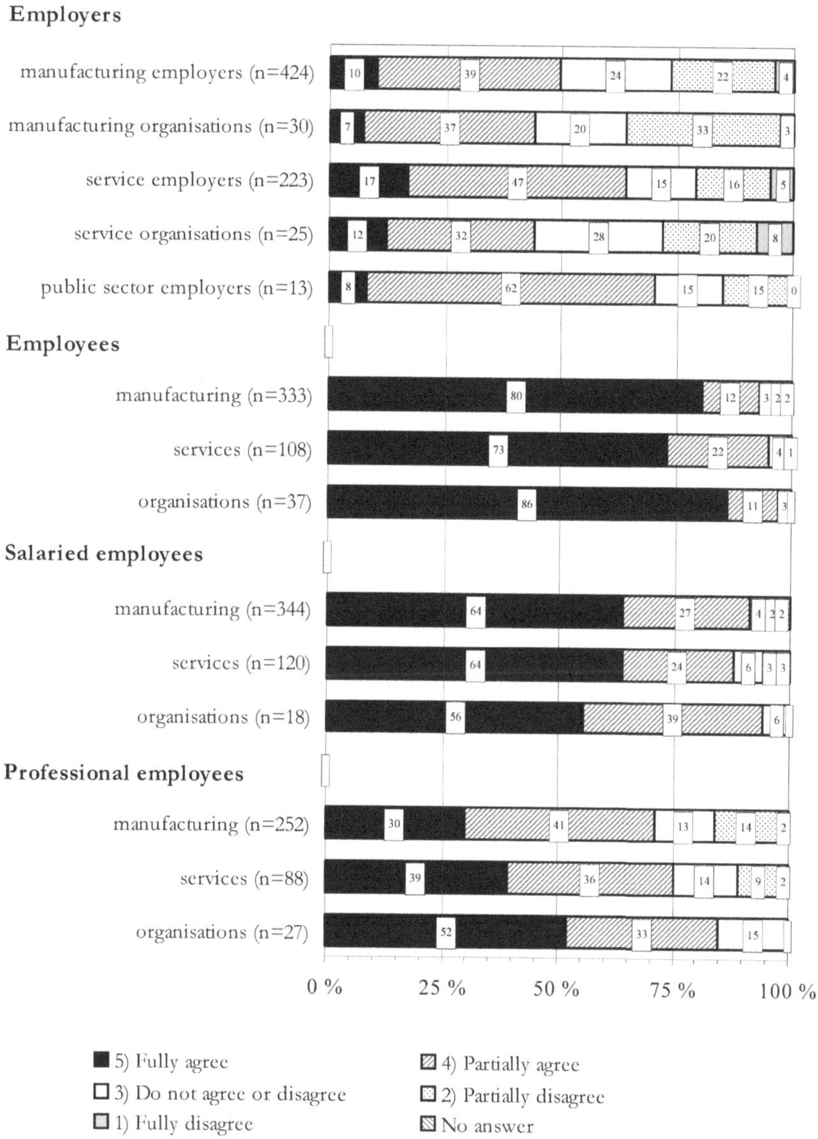

employees as well as, even more strongly, of the corresponding associations. The professional staff again represents a middle position between employers and lower-status employees.

As a counterpart to the respondents' divergent standpoints towards flexibility, partners' views also differ concerning the role of the minimum tariff wages, i.e. the wage floors task specifically stipulated in the collective agreements. In employees' views, rather unanimously all the way from workers to professional staff, such wage tariffs provide a safety net that guarantees a subsistence income (Figure 4). Even employers partly agree with this view, although to a clearly lesser extent than employees. On the other hand, employers dissociate themselves from the workers and salaried employees, by agreeing with the proposition that extra increases in tariff wages also push actual wages upwards, regardless of the fact that only a small share of employees may, in fact, have been hired at wages corresponding to the contractual minimum (Figure 5). By the same token, employers support the view, denied by employees, that one weakness of the present bargaining system is that the minimum contractual wages inhibit the creation of low-wage jobs.

A critical watershed thus seems to be formed between the employers' and employees' (particularly workers' and salaried employees') views, on the one hand, of the degree of flexibility that the present collective bargaining system leaves for employers to adjust wages to local conditions and, on the other hand, of the role of the tariff wages as a necessary safety net for employees. The contrast in the views of the role of tariff wages indicates that while the employers consider tariff wages as a constraint on their freedom of action, employees, particularly at the lower end of the wage spectrum, consider them as a necessary guarantee for the required minimum income. It is also interesting to note that this conflict appears most prominently in the survey responses by the respective labour market associations, while at the local level this conflict is somewhat milder and the confidence in the ability of the bargaining system to manage it is correspondingly stronger.

In a survey conducted in Sweden a few years ago, both employees and employers agreed with the statement that the need to preserve a good atmosphere in the work place prevents firms from employing unemployed people at wages corresponding to the contractual wage floors; this kind of minimum wages should thus prevent the creation of low-wage jobs (Agell and Lundborg, 1995 and 1999). Responses to a similar type of question in our survey suggest that such a fairness consideration is not particularly relevant in the Finnish labour market. Employers at the local level in particular take a view that disagrees with the statement that contractual wage floors which are below the going wage are relevant as concerns the recruitment of unemployed persons (Figure 6).

## 3.2 Views on Reform Needs in the Bargaining System

A separate section was allocated to inquire into the views of the social partners on the need for reform of the bargaining system and its future shape.

Employers and employees agree that certain basic features of the bargaining system should be upheld, but there is a disagreement on the preferred extent and direction

**Fig. 5.** Increase in Contractual Wage Floors Is Bad, Because It Pushes Actual Wages Upwards Across the Board (n=number of answers)

**Fig. 6.** Contractual Wage Floors Do Not Prevent the Creation of Low-Wage Jobs, Because Employers Would Actually Not Employ Unemployed People for These Jobs Due to the Fear of Damaging the Atmosphere in the Work Place (n=number of answers)

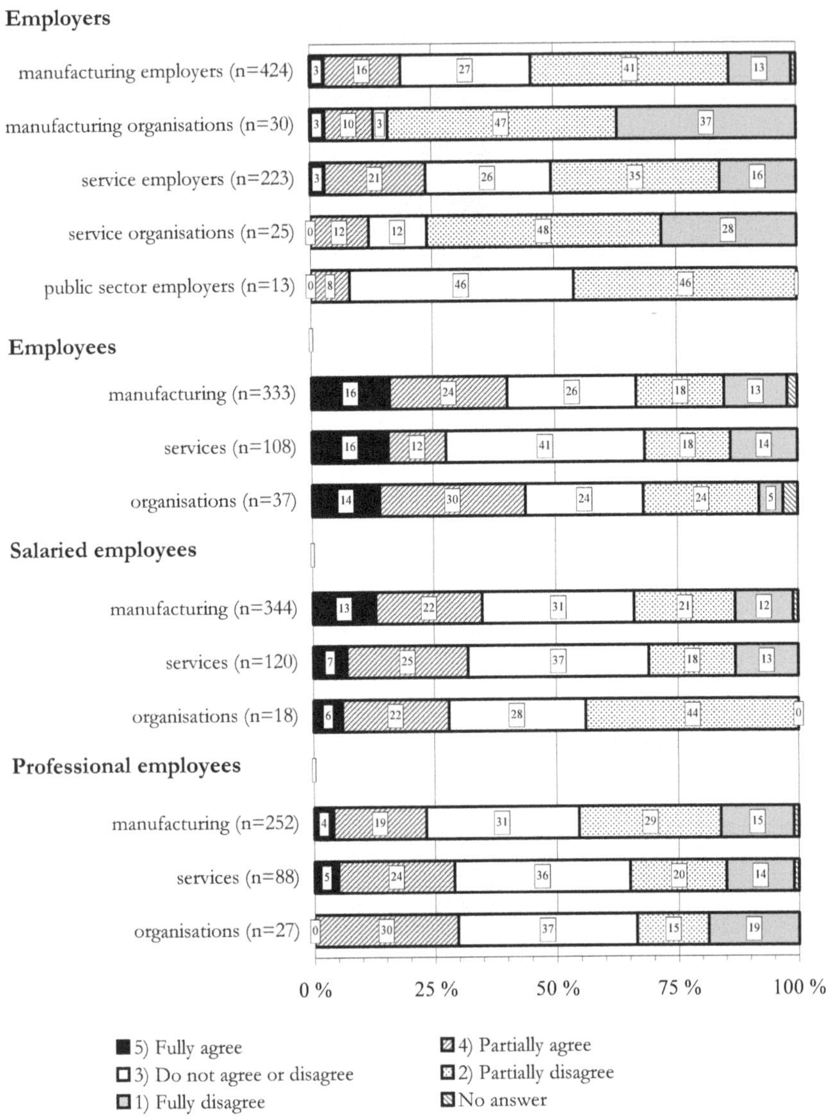

of reforms. In general, there is stronger pressure for reforms on the employers' than the employees' side. The blue-collar workers value the present system's capacity to provide minimum security, while the employers would like to proceed towards more freedom in wage setting to provide higher incentives for the employees.

Among employees, the attitudes and views of the professional employees are again closest to those of employers, while the blue-collar workers display the largest disagreement with the employers' views, and salaried employees occupy a middle position.

One question in this development set concerned the appropriate level of bargaining on the wage hikes. The respondents were asked for preferences on five possible levels: the individual level, the firm level, the industry level, nation-wide incomes policy agreements, and the European level. In their replies, both employers and employees uniformly discard the process towards a European level of wage bargaining as a future option. Collective bargaining is conceived as a national endeavour. It also appears from other parts of the survey that both sides of the labour market consider wage co-ordination at the national level as an important means of adjustment and economic policy making in the EMU age.

Among the other alternatives, the industry level appears as the most favoured if we calculate the overall average score of the alternatives (Figure 7). Centralised income policy agreements are the most favoured alternative for workers and salaried employees, but overall this is a less favoured option than industry-level bargaining. The support for the firm level agreements is high in large firms on the employers' side, but the representatives of the employees of these firms prefer collective bargaining to take place at the union level. The individual level gets only a relatively little support overall, but this receives most support in small firms and in firms where the personnel has a low average age.

One of the questions asked for the preferences (in order) of various combinations of increases in tariff wages, general wage hikes and application of the peace clause. The alternative to maintain the present system intact was favoured more by employees than by employers. Different combinations of general wage hikes, minimum guaranteed wage increases and wage floors received a somewhat mixed response in the survey. On the whole, employers seem to support a model where the minimum wage increase would be agreed upon by a bargain taking place at the industry level between the union and the respective employer federation, while on the firm level there should take place, subject to a peace clause, local bargaining on additional wage increases. It should be noted, however, that all parties were unanimous in resisting a shift towards a completely atomistic bargaining system, where both the wage settlements and decisions on the peace clause would be moved to the firm level (Figure 8). Reliance on co-ordinated bargaining in the sense that the peace clause is imposed at the industry level and local wage settlements take place under this constraint thus enjoys strong support among the social partners is Finland. Pure localisation of wage bargaining, i.e. a system where wage increases, strikes and lock-outs are decided at the firm level, is firmly resisted. This is one of the central conclusions from the survey.

The next question concerned the suitable criterion for negotiated wage increases, the so-called wage norm. Preferences on five alternative wage norms were

**Fig. 7.** Wage Increases Should Be Settled at the Industry Level (n=number of answers)

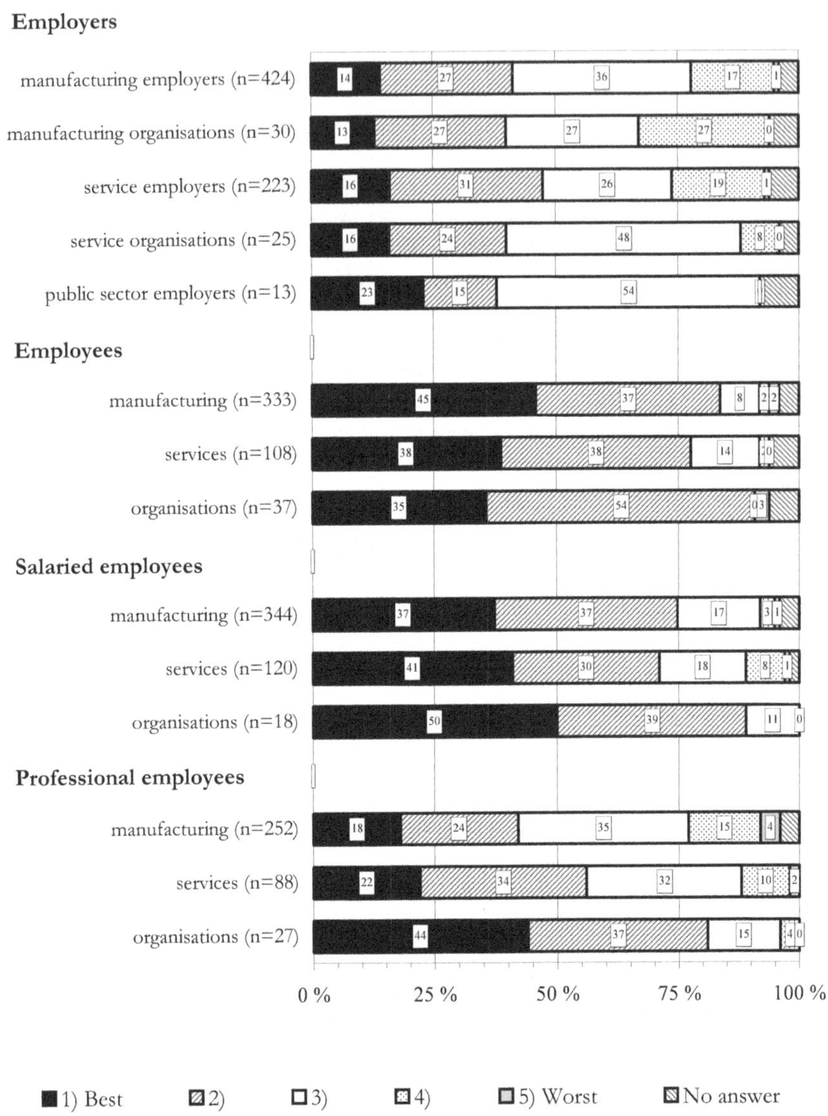

**Fig. 8.** In Future, Contractual Wage Floors and Wage Increases Should Be Suspended; Instead, Wage Settlements and Deciding on the Peace Clause Should Be Transferred to Firm Level (n=number of answers)

asked for: the profitability of the firm; the increase in labour productivity in the respective industry added by the inflation norm of the ECB (industry norm); the same formula but applied to the productivity increase in the whole of the economy (national norm); the average wage rise in the euro area (euro norm); and, finally, the wage increase linked to the level of unemployment in the domestic labour market (unemployment norm).

Of these alternatives, the euro norm receives only scanty support. The unemployment norm is rejected still more overwhelmingly; this may suggest that there prevails a kind of insider behaviour in Finnish wage bargaining. On an overall score, the most popular is the industry norm, which is favoured by the employees in particular. On the other hand, on the employee side, especially among unions and central organisations, the national norm gets the strongest support (Figure 9).

On the basis of the cross-tabulations, employers in the big and internationalised companies would clearly like to proceed towards company-level wage bargaining. However, at the same time, this tendency is most strongly opposed by the personnel in the same type of firms; the personnel prefer to keep the present forms of collective bargaining.[5] One background variable shaping the differences in the replies is also the industry concerned. This provides broad support for the existing industry-level organisation of the social partners in Finland and makes it understandable.

It should also be noted that the electronics industry, which has increased rapidly in Finland in recent years and undergone a radical structural change, does not display any significant deviation from the average responses to any of the questions concerning a move toward company-level wage settlements. On the other hand, the forest industry, the traditional key sector in Finnish manufacturing, is among the most eager to proceed towards company-level bargaining. Among service sector industries, finance displays similar attitudes. In general, the younger the age of the personnel, the more inclined the personnel is to move towards of individual bargaining EMU-level bargaining. The issue as to whether this will imply a gradual change in the pattern of wage bargaining in the future cannot be settled on the basis of one cross-cut questionnaire but remains to be seen in the future. Finally, the prevalence of more permanent job tenures in the firm seems to make the employees more favourable towards company-level bargaining.

## 3.3 Views on Reform Towards Company-level Wage Formation

An important issue in the labour market is the ongoing gradual shift towards more leeway in wage determination at the company level. In our questionnaire, many questions in the section on the reform needs addressed this issue, which will be dealt with in what follows. For instance, respondents were asked to assess as to whether both the employers and the personnel were ready for a shift in which there should be more freedom to agree on wages at the company level. In Figure 10 we see how the actors assess the employees' readiness for local bargaining to

[5] The same result also appears in the estimates of Heikkilä and Piekkola (2004b).

**Fig. 9.** Contractual Wage Increases Should Be Raised Based on the Productivity Gains in the Whole Economy Added to the Inflation Target (n=number of answers)

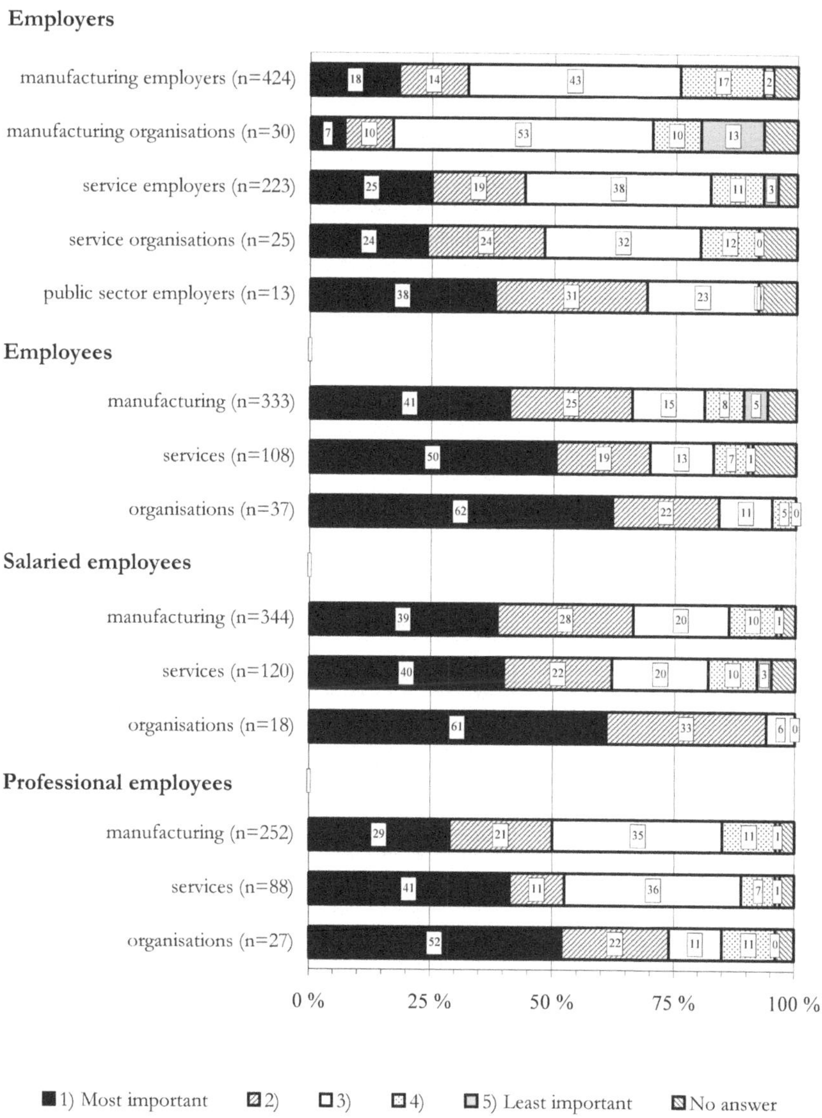

**Fig. 10.** The Personnel is Ready to Accept that the Local Partners Would Have More Freedom in Bargaining on Wages (n=number of answers)

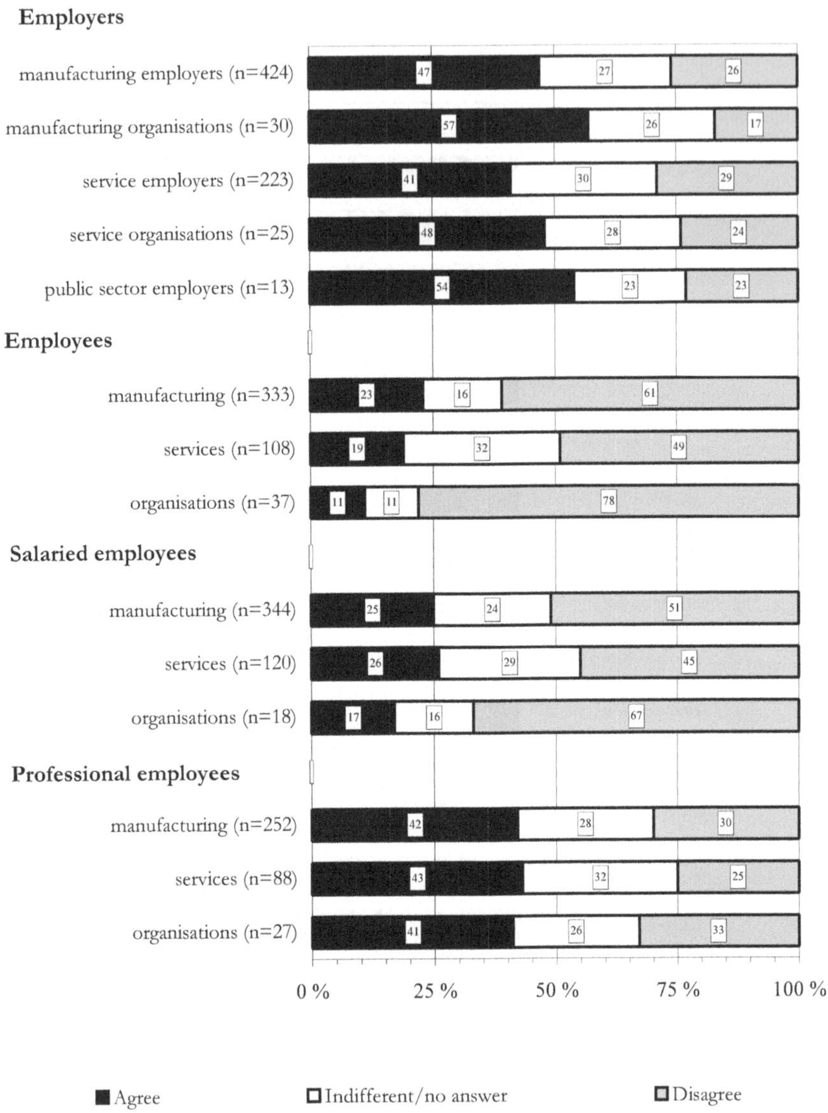

move towards company level bargaining. The employers seem to think that the personnel is ready for such a move, while the employees, especially workers, believe that the personnel is against such a shift. The professional employees occupy a middle position between employers and employees on this issue. In a similar vein, in the employers' view, company-level bargaining would benefit the firm, while employees, particularly workers, are doubtful of such a statement.

In the questionnaire, we also asked for views as to the desired share of the whole wage increase to be agreed upon at the company level, and how to agree on its allocation among the employees. Responses to these questions are analysed in detail by Heikkilä and Piekkola in their article in this volume. Let us here only briefly point out that employers and their federations favour a larger emphasis to be put on the firm-level wage bargaining. Professional employees, who already have the individual level of wage settlements, have a more positive attitude towards company-level wage bargaining. Workers and salaried employees and their unions in general support collective bargaining taking place at the local level between the employer and the shop stewards too, while the professional employees and the employers favour more individual-level negotiations. There is also a disagreement in that the employers prefer allocating the company-level wage rises so as to provide more incentives for their employees, while workers would like to channel them to low-wage workers.

The employers in manufacturing have the most favourable attitude towards firm-level wage rise so that 30 per cent of them would like to have the company-level component to be more than half of the total wage rise. Of the service sector employers, one fifth are of this opinion. The drive for company-level wage agreements is stronger in cyclically sensitive industries, in the export sector, in foreign-owned companies and in internationalised companies. But, on the other hand, among employees the support of company-level bargaining is smaller in large companies.

The probit regressions, carried out by Anni Heikkilä and Hannu Piekkola (see Alho et al. 2003, chapter 6), reveal that if the employer is dissatisfied with the present wage bargaining system, he or she also strongly favours more room for company-level wage bargaining. Profit sharing has increased rapidly in Finnish firms in recent years. The attitudes on both the employer and employee side are quite positive towards it as a local form of wage formation. In the open questions where the respondents could mention, in their view, the most important issues of development as to the wage-bargaining system, profit sharing and its ground rules were, on the other hand, mentioned most often.

## 3.4 Taxes, Social Security and Incomes Policy

The section of the survey addressing taxation and social security brought out two policy-relevant conclusions: A positive result from the point of view of economic and labour market policies is that tax cuts are generally perceived as an efficient means to sustain wage moderation and that the labour market partners accept linking tax cuts to wage moderation. An awkward outcome is, on the other hand, that the majority of the employee respondents resist attempts to promote employment through wage subsidies. i.e. by allowing for lower wages than at present and supporting the purchasing power of low-wage workers through higher social transfers instead. This issue also seems to be divisive among employers, as a half of them is positive to such an approach and the other half is of the opinion that a full-time wage earnings should be high enough so that even a low-wage worker can live on it.

The attitudes also differ as concerns the impact of social security on labour market participation. Employers quite strongly support the view that increased social security benefits have led to a lower intensity to participate in the labour market, while the employees, especially workers, oppose this claim.

### 3.5 EMU Adjustment

There are some survey studies on the views of wage flexibility with relation to unemployment (see Campbell and Kamlani, 1997 and Agell and Lundborg, 1995, 1999). We formulated a question in a similar manner as in Campbell and Kamlani (1997) to discover the attitudes concerning the preferred mode of wage adjustment in a hypothetical recession in the EMU age. The alternatives were, first, that employment could be fully maintained by labour shedding amounting to 10 per cent of the labour force, or, second, through a 10 per cent cut in every employee's wage, or, third, by a combination of these two alternatives so that the wage bill of the firm is cut by 10 per cent, or, fourth, through running down the financial reserves accumulated in the balance sheet of the firm. What is different in our survey compared to the previous ones is that we also collected views from the employee side and submitted more alternatives to the respondents. Apart from the opinion on the desired way to adjust to a recession, the respondents were also asked what way they considered to be the likely one to be carried out in reality.

A conclusion from these replies is that, realistically, the adjustment to a recession is most probably expected to take place through dismissals. On the other hand, the need to develop modes of wage adjustment, which at least to some extent could be used in a recession to cushion the impact of the negative shock on labour shedding is acknowledged by respondents in principle. As such a cushion, combining wage and employment cuts received stronger support in our survey than full reliance on wage or, respectively, employment adjustment.

## 4 Conclusions

We have here presented only a basic outline of the results of our survey, which is unique in its design in the sense that the same questions concerning views on the present shape of the Finnish bargaining system and its desired course of development were addressed to both the employer and employee sides of the labour market. The usefulness of the survey material is increased by the fact that the questionnaire includes a number of relevant background variables related to a firm's size, its industry of operation, profitability, extent of foreign ownership, reliance on profit-related pay etc. It should be kept in mind, however, that the population covered by the survey consists of the active participants in collective bargaining at different levels, i.e. management and shop stewards at the firm level as well as the leadership in industry-level labour market federations and national confederations.

Our preliminary analysis of the results reveals that, generally speaking, labour market partners in Finland are reasonably satisfied with the existing framework of collective bargaining owing to its stabilising influence on labour market relations and overall wage developments. It is also widely conceived that the wage-moderating role of co-ordinated bargaining is made more important by the fact that membership in the EMU excludes adjustment of competitiveness through changes in the nominal exchange rate.

As a counterpart to such a stability of the Finnish wage front, there exists, however, a problem of rigidity about which the employer and the employee side have sharply contrasting views. Employers, particularly the respective federations, emphasise the need to make the bargaining system more flexible by shifting the locus of bargaining towards the enterprise level. Employees, particularly local representatives of workers, together with leadership of the unions representing them, on the other hand, emphasise the role of fixed negotiated tariff wages and nationally negotiated, universally applicable wage increases as a safety net necessary for the income security among the low wage segment of the labour force. This contrast of views seems to be at its sharpest in large manufacturing forms, where the employers look forward to a rapid move towards enterprise level bargaining while the personnel just as strongly rejects this. On the other hand, among the employees, the professional salaried employees display a middle position between typical employers' and employees' standpoints in their views on the flexibility issue.

On the whole, it seems that it is the trade-off between stability on the one hand and flexibility on the other that the participants in the Finnish bargaining system will have to deal with in further development of the bargaining system.

On the basis of our survey, an intelligent development of various forms of firm-level wage bargaining, profit-related pay and other forms of local flexibility seems to offer the most promising avenue for striking a sustainable working compromise between stability and flexibility in the future bargaining system. The local leeway allowed for by the bargaining system should be targeted to modify the main course of wage developments, determined at the central or industry level, to local conditions. Both sides of the negotiation table at all levels of bargaining seem to be ready, in principle, to proceed along this route. It is in the speed of such a move towards local bargaining and the nationally agreed conditions under which it should take place that the views of the labour market partners differ.

## References

Alho, K. (2002): "Kannattaako tulopolitiikkaa jatkaa" (Is It Worth While to Continue Incomes Policies?) (in Finnish) The Research Institute of the Finnish Economy (ETLA) Discussion Paper, No. 837.

Alho, K., Heikkilä, A., Lassila, J., Pekkarinen, J., Piekkola, H. and Sund, R. (2003): *Suomalainen sopimusjärjestelmä – työmarkkinaosapuolten näkemykset* (Finnish Bargaining System: The Views of the Labour Market Partners). The Research Institute of the Finnish Economy (ETLA) Series B, No. 203, and Labour Institute for Economic Research, Studies, No. 89. Helsinki.

Agell, J. and Lunborg, P. (1995): Theories of pay and unemployment: Survey evidence of Swedish manufacturing firms. *Scandinavian Journal of Economics 97*, 295–307.

Agell, J. and Lundborg, P. (1999): Survey evidence of wage rigidity and unemployment: Sweden in the 1990s. IFAU Working Paper 1999:2.

Campbell, C.M. and Kamlani, K.S. (1997): The reasons for wage rigidity: Evidence from a survey of firms. *Quarterly Journal of Economics 112*, 759–789.

Heikkilä, A. and Piekkola, H. (2004a): Local bargaining opinions of employers and cooperation in decision making with employees. In Piekkola, H. and Snellman, K. (eds.) *Collective Bargaining and Wage Formation – Performance and Challenges*. Springer-Verlag.

Heikkilä, A. and Piekkola, H. (2004b): Decisions for local bargaining and divergence of opinions among employers and employees. Evidence from Finnish survey. The Research Institute of the Finnish Economy (ETLA) Discussion Papers No. 910.

Uusitalo, R. (2004): Do centralized bargains lead to wage moderation? Time series evidence from Finland. In Piekkola, H. and Snellman, K. (eds.) *Collective Bargaining and Wage Formation – Performance and Challenges*. Springer-Verlag.

# Productivity, Incentives and Relative Wages

Kari E.O. Alho[1]

ETLA, The Research Institute of the Finnish Economy
Helsinki, Finland

## Abstract

The relation between productivity and relative wages is in many ways crucial as to the functioning of the labour market and the wage bargaining system. This is addressed from three angles in the paper. We first present data, which show that there has been a regulation in the Finnish labour market with respect to low-wage employees and low-productivity workers and industries so that the relative wage there clearly exceeds the respective relative productivity. Then, a model is built, which analyses the effects of this kind of regulation and its alleviation in the labour market. The outcome is that such a regulation of the non-skilled sector of the labour market hurts the skilled labour in the form of a lower wage. The possibility to compensate the losers by means of the winners of a deregulation of this type of wage formation is then evaluated. Next, an extended model incorporating efficiency wages, but now with two components of labour, is presented, where the effort of an employee is endogenous and depends on the relative wage rate. This model explains the empirical fact that the relative wages tend to remain unchanged, even though there is a regulation raising the low wages. Finally, we briefly discuss the lesson given by the optimal contract theory on relative wages and their link to productivity.

[1] This is part of the research project *Rules of the game in the labour market: Industrial relations, the bargaining system and income policies in the 2000s*, financed by the Finnish Work Environment Fund, and carried out jointly by ETLA, The Research Institute of the Finnish Economy, and the Labour Institute for Economic Research. The author thanks Jaakko Kiander of the Government Institute for Economic Research, Jukka Lassila and Hannu Piekkola of ETLA and Kenneth Snellman of the Labour Institute for Economic Research for comments and helpful suggestions. The usual disclaimer applies.

# 1 Introduction

If we go five years or so backward in time, the key challenge - which was also widely and unanimously acknowledged by both the employers and trade unions - was the preparation of the economy and the labour markets for the future EMU membership of Finland. This called for adoption of a strict wage norm, consistent with the low inflation target of the single monetary policy. Finland had a past of high wage hikes and inflation, leading in times to devaluations in order to improve the competitive position of the firms in the export sector. All this had to be discarded and replaced by a new sense of discipline in wage bargaining. We may, on good grounds, argue that the constraint of this new era on macro-level wage policy has also been successfully internalised, at least so far, as the rise of the average wage rate has been less than 5 per cent p.a. for a decade already.

However, at the moment, all this macro-coherence in the labour market that has been achieved seems to belong to the past. It is severely challenged and under pressure, especially from the employers' ranks. There has been dissatisfaction with the uniform wage formation, as stipulated in the recent nationwide centralised incomes policy agreements. The norm where all the wage rises have followed the average rise in productivity in the whole economy in times of wide disparities in productivity rises in various sectors, even within manufacturing, has aroused indignation among employers. Firms, especially the big internationalised companies, are also dissatisfied with their overall freedom of manoeuvring in wage policies. This was also a clear outcome of the recent survey conducted by ETLA and the Labour Institute; see Alho et al. (2003) and Pekkarinen and Alho in this volume.

The Finnish wage-bargaining system has rested on the implicit agreement that the labour unions obey, on average, a moderate wage and incomes policy, but at the same time the biggest of them have the power to influence the pattern of wage rises over the wage scale in a decisive way. This has led to solidaristic wage formation and excessive rises in the wages at the lower end of the wage distribution and in firms and industries with lower than average productivity. It is easy to imagine that, consequently, there has also been dissatisfaction among professional employees, situated at the upper end of the wage scale. Due to the technological change (skill-biased technical change) and globalisation, i.e. intensified import competition from the low-wage countries, it is no longer so easy to continue with such policies without major setbacks in employment; see e.g. Andersen in this volume.

There are three key dimensions in the labour market negotiation system and wage formation, according to which its individual elements and the whole system and its future evolution can and should be evaluated. These are illustrated in Fig. 1. The relevant goals are macroeconomic stability, microeconomic efficiency and efficient risk-sharing. There may be a substitution with respect to an instrument so that if one goal is promoted by it, this can lead to a setback with respect to the other. But it may be that such a conflict does not exist. Take, for example, profit sharing, which has become more and more widely applied in Finnish firms. This may both enhance macro stability and increase incentives and, if applied within meaningful limits, may neither be in conflict with the minimum security. Such a measure should meet wide acceptance among all the parties, and indeed this holds in practice; see Alho et al. (2003). However, such a coincidence does not apply to many other instruments in labour market policies.

So, referring to what was stated above, if we consider the present and future focus in the wage-bargaining system, on the employers' side it is shifting from preserving macro-stability, if by this is meant inflation control, towards enhanced micro-efficiency and sufficient incentives in wage formation and better correspondence between productivity and wage rises on a sectoral level. The employers also want to get rid of bigger rises in low wages than on average. On the trade union side, however, there is still a widespread adherence towards the security created by minimum wages and so-called tariff wages, i.e. the minimum norm at which a worker can be employed in a specific task. This result was also reached in the Finnish survey mentioned above.

Based on these conflicting aspirations, a likely outcome is that there will be more tensions in the Finnish wage-bargaining system in the coming years. We have come to a watershed, and we do not yet know how the new situation will emerge and what it will be like.

**Fig. 1.** The Goals and Respective Instruments of Labour Market Policies as to Wage Formation

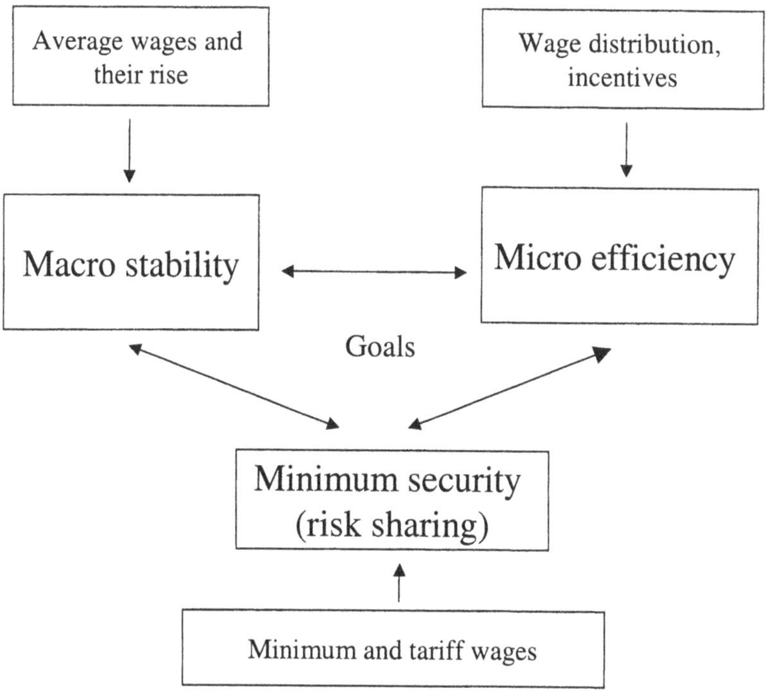


In this paper, it is the aim to first analyse one key feature, where disagreement prevails among the social partners, namely the labour market regulation in the lower

end of the productivity and the wage scale and its effects on the whole labour market. This problem, linked to the high unemployment of the low-wage employees, has received a lot of interest in economic and employment policies in the EU and in Finland, too. We are especially interested in the general equilibrium effects of this regulation on other sectors of the labour market-, not under regulation, and with respect to the relative wages. The basic outcome is that such a regulation hurts the other sector of the labour market so that its relative wage is pushed down. Next, we enlarge the focus to consider the links between incentives, productivity and relative wages. In this larger framework, we now find that the firms are willing to preserve the relative wages at their initial level, although the low wages are pushed upwards. Finally, we tackle the issue as to what this relation should be from the perspective of an efficient incentive contract between the firm and an employee.

In Section 2 we first present some data on relative wages and productivity in the Finnish and US manufacturing industries to see the similarities and differences in their relation in Finland and in a country with a flexible labour market. Section 3 proceeds to specify a simple two-sector model of the labour market and derives the outcome of labour market regulation on wage setting, the cost of this kind of regulation, and discusses possibilities to undergo a deregulation of the system by combining a compensation scheme with it. Section 4 enlarges the analysis into a more realistic model, where the productivity of a worker is endogenous in the manner suggested by the efficiency wage theory. Section 5 presents a brief look into what microeconomic theory tells us about incentives, productivity and wage formation, and what in this sense can be a problem under widespread wage bargaining. Section 6 concludes.

## 2 Productivity and Wage Distribution in Finland in Comparison to the US

Let us first have a look at data on the distribution of productivity and wage rates. We contrast the Finnish case with that in the US, which is normally conceived to have a flexible labour market. Fig. 2 depicts the situation in Finland. The corresponding relation for the US is depicted in Figure 3.

Let us first condense these findings in Table 1. From the figures and the table we see some important similarities, but also dissimilarities between Finland and the US. In the figures we have also drawn the lines of perfect correspondence between the relative labour productivity and relative wage levels. We see that in the US the correspondence between productivity and wages is much tighter than in Finland. The dispersion of wages is much smaller than that of the productivities, but the relation between these two variables is identical in Finland as compared with the US. However, the lower end of the wage and productivity scale is very much different in these two countries. In Finland the relative wage rate there exceeds the relative productivity level by 17 percentage points, three times as much as in the US.

**Fig. 2.** Relative Labour Productivity and Relative Wage in Industries in Manufacturing in Finland in 1998*

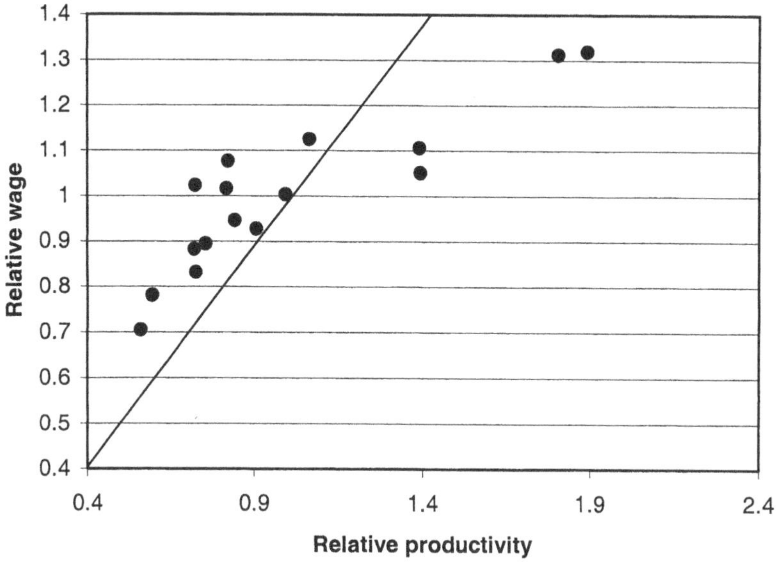


*Relative productivity (wage) = productivity (average wage) in the industry / the weighted average productivity (average wage) in total manufacturing.

**Fig. 3.** Relative Labour Productivity and Relative Wage in Industries in Manufacturing in the US in 1998*

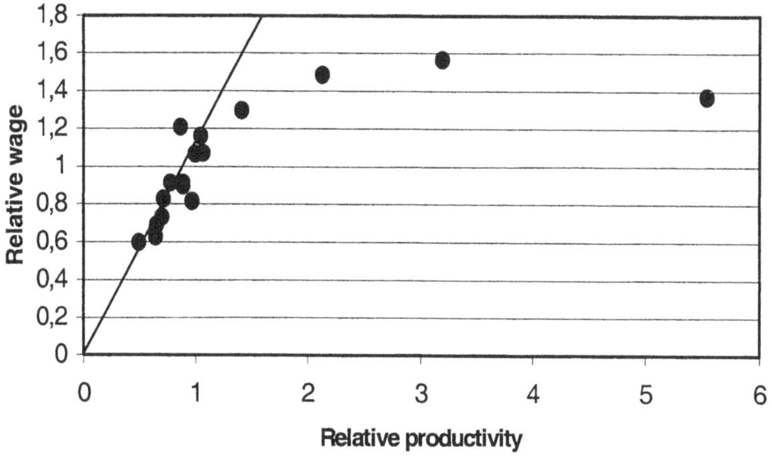


* For explanations, see Fig. 2.

So, even this simple data suggests that in Finland quite far-reaching regulation at the lower end of the wage scale has been pursued. However, it is quite striking that this has not been similarly reflected in a lower share of total employment of these industries in Finland than in the US. It may look as if the problem lies in insufficient incentives for labour to shift towards more productive firms and industries, and not so much in a lack of demand for the low productivity workers. However, other evidence shows that unemployment among the low-skilled workers in Finland is markedly high in an international comparison; see e.g. Holm and Vihriälä (2002).

**Table 1.** The Distribution of the Relative Wage and Relative Productivity in the Industries in Finnish and US Manufacturing in 1998, per cent*

| Variable | Finland | USA |
|---|---|---|
| (1) St. dev. of wage rates | 15.1 | 24.1 |
| (2) St. dev. of productivity | 44.3 | 73.3 |
| (1)/(2), % | 34.1 | 32.9 |
| 5 industries of lowest prod., average rel. wage – rel. productivity, % | 17.1 | 5.4 |
| The share of these industries in total employment, % | 28.5 | 22.4 |

* Relative productivity (wage) = productivity (average wage) in the industry / the weighted average productivity (average wage) in total manufacturing. The standard deviation is weighted with the respective employment shares of the industries, and multiplied by 100.

## 3 A Model of Labour Market Regulation and Relative Wages

In this section we formulate a simple model of labour market regulation and wage formation assuming exogenous productivity, i.e. effort. A model of endogenous productivity in the spirit of efficiency wage theory will be formulated in the next section.

Let us for simplicity distinguish only two types of labour, skilled ($L_1$) and non-skilled ($L_2$) labour, which operate in production with the fixed capital stock (K). The production function F for the volume of production Q is generally ($F_{ij}$ being the partial derivative of function F with respect to variables i and j),

$$Q = F(K, e_1L_1, e_2L_2), \quad F_i > 0, F_{ii} < 0, F_{ij} > 0, \tag{1}$$

where $e_i$ is the efficiency parameter describing internal productivity of labour component i, reflecting its accumulated human capital through education and training.

We can think of some special cases of (1), such as the CES and the Cobb-Douglas (C-D) cases

$$Q = K^{\alpha}\left[a_1(e_1L_1)^{\sigma} + a_2(e_2L_2)^{\sigma}\right]^{\frac{1-\alpha}{\sigma}}, \sigma \leq 1 \text{ and} \tag{2a}$$

$$Q = K^{\alpha}(e_1L_1)^{\beta}(e_2L_2)^{\chi},\ 0<\alpha,\beta,\chi<1, \alpha+\beta+\chi=1. \tag{2b}$$

We now assume that, through a regulation in the wage setting, referred to in the introduction, and on which evidence was given in the previous section, the wage rate in the non-skilled sector is exogenously fixed at b to be higher than the market clearing level. We simply assume that the skilled sector is one of full employment with market-determined wages. The demand for non-skilled labour is given by the marginal productivity condition,

$$e_2F_{L2} = b, \tag{3}$$

where b is now an exogenous wage. In effect, this condition determines the ratio of the skilled to non-skilled workers demanded by the firms as a function of b. Similarly, we get from the condition for the demand for the skilled labour that

$$e_2F_{L2} = W_1, \tag{4}$$

where $W_i$ is the wage rate of labour component i ($W_2 = b$). Once we assume a specific production function, we can derive a number of results on the determination of the relative wages as a function of the efficiency parameters $e_i$, i = 1,2, and of the relative supplies of factors; see Alho (2002a) on them.

One important finding is reached in the simple C-D -special case (2b) with no capital, where we get the result,

$$\frac{W_1}{W_2} = \frac{e_1}{e_2}\left(\frac{b}{e_2}\right)^{-\frac{1}{\beta}} \frac{\beta}{(1-\beta)^{1-1/\beta}} \tag{5}$$

This expression shows that *the relative wage of the skilled vis-à-vis the non-skilled depends on the respective relative efficiency $e_1/e_2$, and is compressed to be lower, the higher the wage rate set in the non-skilled sector fixed in relation to the respective efficiency is. This reaction has an elasticity in excess of unity.*

The intuition behind this negative spillover result is that the firms have to cut the demand for skilled workers as well, when the wage rate of the regulated sector and their overall costs are raised. This need for adjustment will then be reflected in the wage rate of the skilled labour. This fact may be one explanation for the compression of the wage distribution in Finland and in Europe more generally. This result holds in general under any smooth production function with the property of cooperative factors of production.[2]

[2] We also get from (5) a result showing that the regulation of the low-skilled sector may entail an incentive problem in that, even if $e_1 > e_2$, the equilibrium wage rate of the skilled labour will be lower than that of the low skilled, which the firms cannot, of course, normally put into effect in practice. We shall in this paper skip this complication.

What is the cost of this kind of regulation? The loss related to it is the reduction in output in relation to that under a flexible wage. We can first derive from (3) in the simple C-D case that the demand for low-skilled is

$$L_2 = \left( \frac{b}{e_2(1-\beta)} \right)^{-\frac{1}{\beta}} \frac{e_1}{e_2} N_1 < N_2 \,, \tag{6}$$

where $N_i$ is the size of labour force i. So we have as the loss of regulation in relative terms of output reduction

$$\begin{aligned} Loss &= \varepsilon(Q, L_2)\, d\ln\left(L_2\right) = (1-\beta)\frac{N_2 - L_2}{N_2} \\ &= (1-\beta)\left[1 - \left(\frac{b}{e_2(1-\beta)}\right)^{-\frac{1}{\beta}} \frac{e_1 N_1}{e_2 N_2}\right] \end{aligned} , \tag{7}$$

where ε(y,x) is the elasticity of variable y with respect to x, ε(y,x) = (dy/dx)(x/y).

We get the result that *the efficiency loss from labour market regulation Is the bigger, the higher is the wage rate of the non-skilled labour fixed in ratio to its efficiency, i.e. b in relation $e_2$. On the other hand, there is no loss if $b/e_2 = 1-\beta$, (being less than unity) and if the education system provides both the sectors to be in efficiency units ($e_iN_i$) of equal size.*

However, as also with other combinations of the parameters, this loss can be eliminated.[3]

The policy question is then what one should do with this regulation. There are basically two alternative paths. First, we could transform the wage setting behaviour towards being less regulated and more competitive and, secondly, we could channel wage subsidies to firms and workers, or combine elements of both these policies. Economists have usually avoided considering the first opportunity and, instead, have considered wage subsidies directed to employers of the low-wage workers, as suggested for Finland in the paper by Holm and Vihriälä (2002), which has also aroused much publicity and attention by the policy-makers. There are, however, a number of problems with such wage subsidies. There is, for example, a substantial dead-weight loss, as the already employed workers will also receive the subsidy.

It is, in principle, an important policy question as to whether a compensation scheme could be established in such a manner that nobody loses from a deregulation of the wage formation. So, let us carry out an evaluation to see whether it is possible to carry out a compensation for the low-skilled, when their relative wage

[3] Technically, the expression (7) can give as a result also a positive value, i.e. efficiency gain. This is due to the fact that the demand for non-skilled labour, if their reward b is very low, exceeds their supply. In this case there is no efficiency loss in the above sense.

falls and the wage of the skilled rises, as implied by expression (5). The situation is something like that in Figure 4. In the specific C-D case, it holds that the gain in wage income of the skilled is just enough to offset the loss of the employed non-skilled, i.e. area A = $B_1$ in Fig. 4. But the compensation cannot be extended so that there would be an extra gain (area $C_2$) directed to the newly recruited non-skilled so that their income would be raised to be same as that of employed non-skilled before the reform. This last component would be based on the fact that within transfer and tax systems we are normally bound to obey equal treatment of workers without reference to the time of their being employed.

**Fig. 4.** The Deregulation of Wage Formation and Its Compensation*

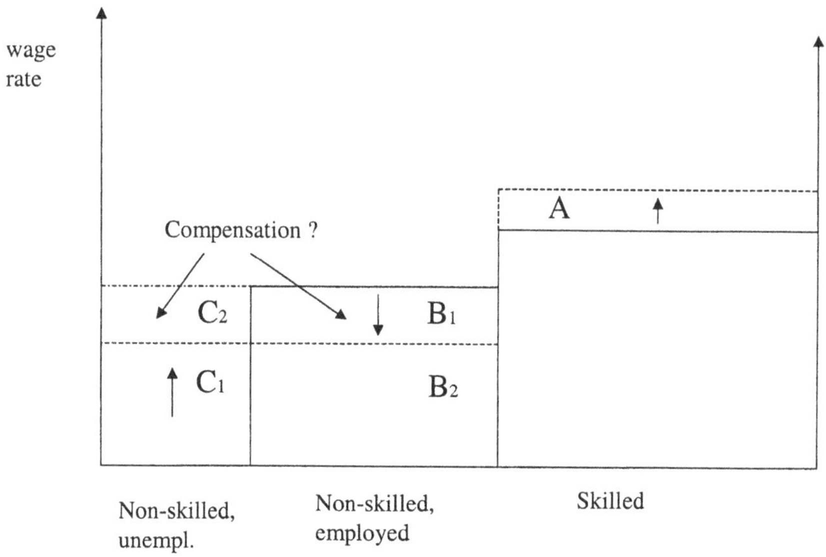


* For explanations, see the text.

CEPR (1996) reached the outcome that the gains of deregulation of the European labour markets are quite small in comparison to the consequent cost in terms of a markedly widening income distribution. However, such a static exercise may not be the most relevant reference point in a dynamic economy. Namely, as the factors of production are cooperative, the unemployment in the non-skilled sector also falls on capital, through reduced marginal productivity and is, thereby, also reflected in a reduced rate of return on the existing capital stock. Over time, this leads to less investment and lower factor rewards for labour as well. Over time, the gain from a deregulation outweighs the cost related to it. So, the above compensation problem may only exist as a temporary one.

The macroeconomic analysis of labour market deregulation should be accomplished by microeconomic risk-sharing argumentation. Wage rigidity is not only a bad feature, as there do not, in general, exist such widespread income transfers through which the workers could insure themselves against adverse shocks to flexible wages; see the analysis by Dreze and Gollier (1993) on this. But it would be meaningless to argue that all kind of wage rigidity is welfare-improving and welcome.

## 4 Incentives and Wage Formation

Let us now take a broader view of wage formation within firms and consider proper incentives, which were largely omitted above, and their role in the equilibrium in the labour market. There are two basic aspects in the relation between the firm and the worker from the firm's point of view: a) to give the worker enough incentives to produce effort and b) to extract rents from the worker; see Moen and Rosén (2003). The optimal situation, analysed by the optimal contract theory, is a balance between these two conflicting goals and will be briefly discussed in Section 5. However, we should add a third essential aspect to these: c) to organise the firm internally efficiently so that the workers cooperate with each other in an efficient way, and to form the incentive mechanism so that it is also efficient in this sense.

The above considerations in Section 3 were carried out in a simple general equilibrium type of framework. The general outcome of this exercise was that a regulation in one sector in the labour market hurts the other. However, the actual situation in the labour market may be something else, where this kind of equilibrating forces are put aside and do not determine the actual wages as was assumed for skilled labour in Section 3. A classical explanation for disequilibium in the labour market is the efficiency wage theory. It also involves the incentive mechanism of wage setting by the firms so that the efficiency parameters ($e_i$), treated as fixed above, respond to wages set by the firm and thereby become endogenous. The basic idea of the efficiency wage theory is that, through setting wages above the full employment level, the employers are able to give incentives for the workers to deliver more effort.

The effort by a worker is positively influenced by the wage offered to him by the firm. For this phenomenon, there are a number of intuitively plausible explanations; see e.g. Heijdra and van der Ploeg (2002). Of these, we take here, as the starting point, the sociological explanation that a worker's effort depends not only on his or her own wage, but also on it in relation to what his or her workmates get. If the worker gets a poor wage in relation to others, corrected by the internal efficiency, like education, the motivation of the worker to give effort will be undermined. So, let us now specify that in (1),

$$e_i = p_i \eta_i \,, \tag{8}$$

where $p$ is the effort and $\eta$ is the human capital of an employee. The first component can be influenced by the wage policy of the firm, but the second is exogenous to the labour market. According to the stated idea, let us assume that the effort given by the skilled labour ($L_1$) positively depends on its wage in relation to the human capital, and in an inverse way on the wage offered to the non-skilled workers in relation to their human capital. So, we have for skilled labour the following specification g [4]

$$p_1 = g^1\left(\frac{W_1}{\eta_1}, \frac{W_2}{\eta_2}\right), \; g_1^1 > 0, \; g_2^1 \le 0 \; . \tag{9}$$

The latter reaction depends on the fact that if the wages of non-skilled labour are raised in relation to the respective human capital, the motivation to work of the skilled workers will be lower. A similar expression holds for the non-skilled labour. This formulation will change the situation from what it was in Section 3. Now the wage rate is also a policy parameter of the firms. The firm then maximises the profit $\pi$,

$$\pi = F(K, \, p_1\eta_1 L_1, \, p_2\eta_2 L_2) \; - \; w_1 L_1 \; - \; w_2 L_2 \tag{10}$$

with respect to the labour inputs $L_1$, $L_2$ and the wage rates $W_1$ and $W_2$ when the capital stock is predetermined. Now we get the optimality conditions,

$$\begin{aligned} F_2\eta_1 p_1 &= W_1 \\ F_3\eta_2 p_2 &= W_2 \\ F_2\eta_1 L_1 (p_1)_{W_1} + F_3\eta_2 L_2 (p_2)_{W_1} &= L_1 \\ F_3\eta_2 L_2 (p_2)_{W_2} + F_2\eta_1 L_1 (p_1)_{W_2} &= L_2 \end{aligned} \tag{11}$$

Inserting the first two equations into the last two in (11), we get the basic result of a modified efficiency wage model,

$$\begin{aligned} &\varepsilon(p_1, W_1) + \frac{W_2 L_2}{W_1 L_1}\varepsilon(p_2, W_1) = 1 \quad \text{and} \\ &\varepsilon(p_2, W_2) + \frac{W_1 L_1}{W_2 L_2}\varepsilon(p_1, W_2) = 1 \, , \end{aligned} \tag{12}$$

where $\varepsilon(y,x)$ is again the elasticity of variable y with respect to variable x.

---

[4] This can be derived from a utility function U, involving group incentives, like $U_1 = W_1 p_1 - C(p_1)\frac{W_2/\eta_2}{W_1/\eta_1}$, where C is the convex cost of effort function. See Encinosa et al. (1997) on the general idea that group norms have an impact on wage formation.

In the standard efficiency wage theory with only one type of labour - or two mutually independent types of labour in our setting - we get the result from (12) that in the optimum the elasticity of effort with respect to the wage rate is unity. In our extended formulation with two components of labour, in the optimum this elasticity is, in general, higher than unity, because the second term on the left-hand side of (12) is negative. This causes the fact that the wage rate of the skilled workers is less (point $O_2$ in Fig. 5) than what would prevail (in point $O_1$), if the negative spillover from the high wages of the skilled to the effort by the low-skilled did not exist. This is due to the "envy" property of wage setting, specified above in (9), which the employers have to take into account. The same holds for the non-skilled labour. So, there are lower wages but also a lower effort when the two types of labour are rivals in wage formation.

**Fig. 5.** The Basic Determination of the Efficiency Wage with Two Components of Labour*

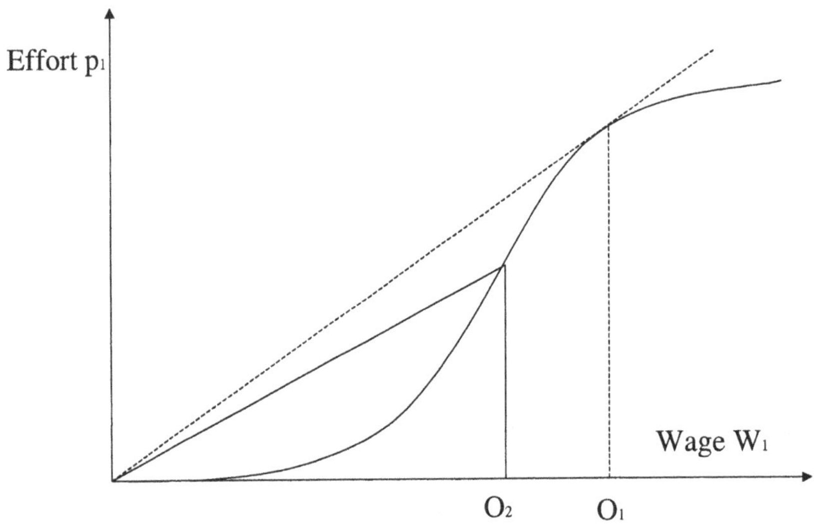


* For explanations, see the text.

Assume next again as, in Section 3, that the wage rate $W_2/\eta_2$ in the non-skilled sector is fixed to the firms from outside, through the bargaining system, to be above the firm's optimal level. In practice, this means that in the wage negotiation an agreement is reached, in which the minimum wages and the tariff wages are raised more than the negotiated wage rise for those having higher wages. What is the reaction now by the employers to this kind of a situation? This is depicted in Fig. 6. The motivation of the skilled workers will be scaled down due to this rise in wages of the low skilled as incorporated in specification (9) above. The proper reaction by the employers is now, in contrast to the outcome reached in the previous full equilibrium model, to raise the wage rate of the skilled as well. The old optimum was in point $O_2$ and the new one is in point $O_3$. So, we get the situation that there is a higher wage of the skilled combined with a lower level of effort. A wage-wage linkage emerges between the two components of labour, but now through policies of the employers. The employers are in a situation with smaller profits than in the first-best situation, determined by expression (12).

**Fig. 6.** The Change of the Skilled Wage as a Reaction to the Rise in the Tariff Wage

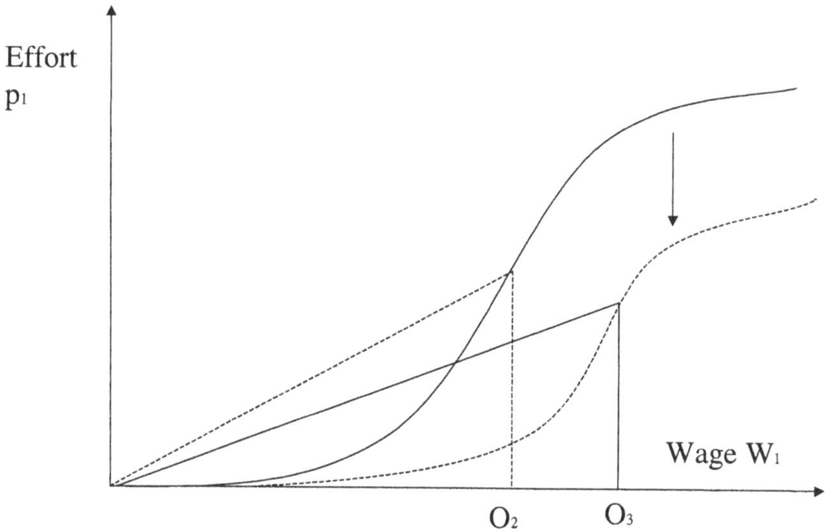


Turn again then to the policy question, discussed in Section 3, of labour market policies with respect to the lower end of the wage distribution. To sharpen the analysis, we suggest an assumption that the "envy" behaviour is typically asymmetric in the sense that there is a more vigorous reaction in wage claims with respect to the worsening of the relative position than to an improvement in it, analogously as in Encinosa et al. (1997). So, we write

$$\left|\frac{dp_i}{dW_j}\right|_{W_j \text{ rises}} > \left|\frac{dp_i}{dW_j}\right|_{W_j \text{ is lowered}}, \quad i \neq j. \tag{13}$$

In Figure 7, we have again depicted the regulated wage (RW) line corresponding to the equilibrium model of Section 3. As stated there, this is downward sloping. The efficiency wage theory implies a line (EW) that is upward sloping in the manner explained above, when the regulated wage $W_2$ is raised. However, if we have reached a point like B on this curve and again consider a deregulation of the low wages, the burden of adjustment now falls disproportionately on low-wage earners, through the asymmetric property stated in expression (13). This is depicted as the BL curve in the figure. The firms' profits are raised, and the relative incentives increased for the skilled labour in comparison to the non-skilled. This describes the situation prevailing in practice, according to which the employers strive to give more weight to the incentives in the wage formation by widening the wage distribution. We shall return to this issue once more in the next section[5].

**Fig. 7.** Adjustment in a Two-sector Efficiency Wage Model

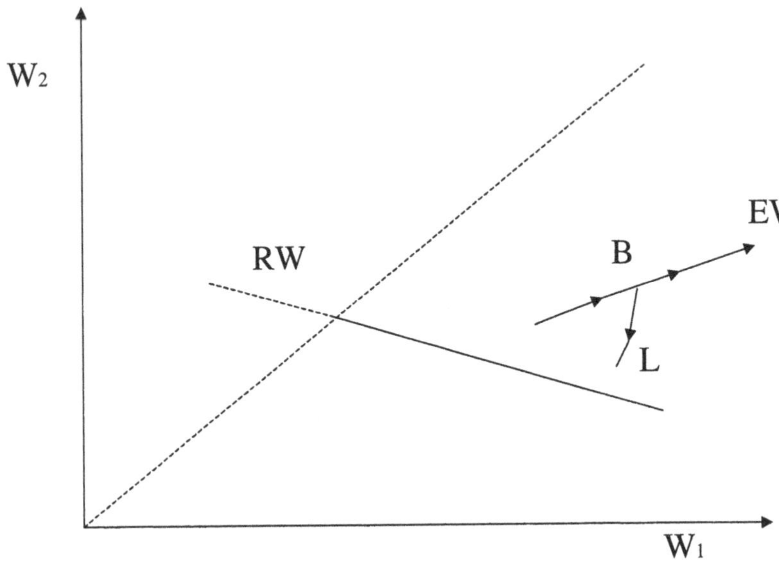


## 5 A Note on Incentives, Individual Effort and Wage Bargaining

Above, we have only considered the case of two types of labour, being homogeneous within each type of labour. This is, however, not a very realistic situation in practice. We mentioned in the introduction that the incentive mechanism is becoming all the more important in the labour market, and thereby its connection to the collective bargaining system will also emerge as an essential feature in the future, so that it deserves more attention in the research field as well. The contract theory builds various kinds of models, where individual workers are identified as separate entities; the individual effort can either be monitored or not, and the output of a worker can be identified or not.

[5] See also the analysis of wage drift in an efficiency wage framework, but with a single type of labour, by Muysken and van Leen (1996).

Theoretically, the optimal link between productivity and wage formation is analysed by the optimal contract theory; see e.g. the recent paper by Moen and Rosén (2003). In their model the effort of a worker is not observable to the firm, but output is, and it can be the basis of a wage contract. Without going into the details of their model, I just want to raise one further issue here. The model replicates the situation which prevails in the data (see Table 1) that the distribution of wages is more compressed than that of productivities. But, according to the optimal contract, typically the marginal reward from productivity rises and the whole marginal product will be given to the most productive worker; see Fig. 8.

However, in reality the wage scale is typically convex, so that smaller or equal marginal rewards are given to the more productive workers. This situation can be explained by the wage bargaining model with a fixed outside option; see e.g. Alho (2002b), and it is depicted in Figure 9.

This discrepancy between these two models raises two questions, which, to my knowledge, have not been tackled in the literature:

1) Is the model of the optimal contract theory in some way inconsistent with the empirical facts of wage formation?
2) Is the typical outcome of Figure 9, in contrast to Figure 8, an indication that there is an inefficiency in wage formation and insufficient incentives in labour markets characterised by widespread collective bargaining?

**Fig. 8.** Incentives Given by the Optimal Contract Theory *

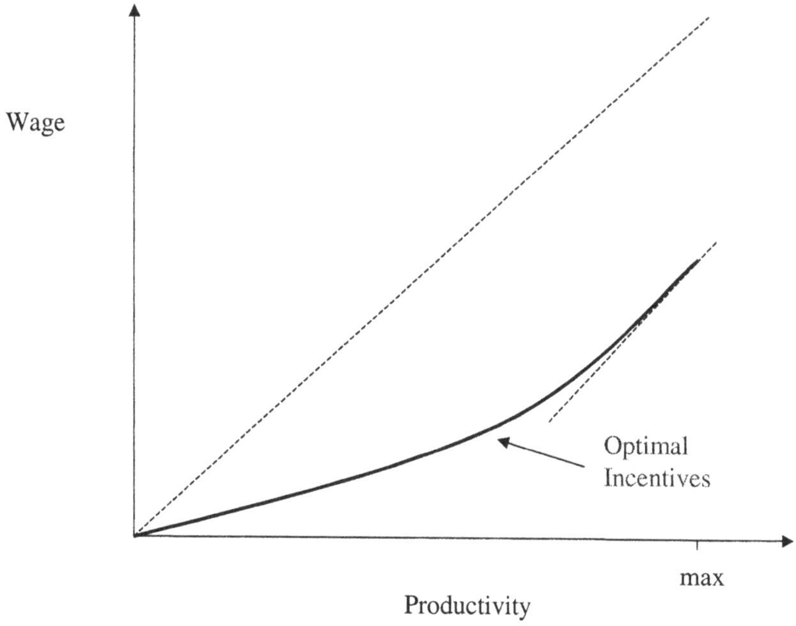


* Based on Moen and Rosén (2003).

If we answer 'yes' to Question 2, we should turn to the policy question, as to how to improve the existing wage bargaining system to produce a better incentive scheme than that in Figure 9. It seems that the solution to this problem lies in transforming the unemployment benefit scheme (the outside option) so that it should also be convex, like the incentive curve in Figure 8 (but located in a lower position, of course). We know that typically the unemployment benefit scheme is either flat, or concave with lower marginal benefits, the higher the wage rate of the individual. I leave here this interesting issue for further analysis.

A complete analysis of wage formation is needed, and it should combine the three aspects, mentioned above in the beginning of Section 4, and so the last of them on group incentives also deserves attention, which was to some extent tackled in Section 4 above.

**Fig. 9.** The Bargaining Outcome with a Fixed Outside Option

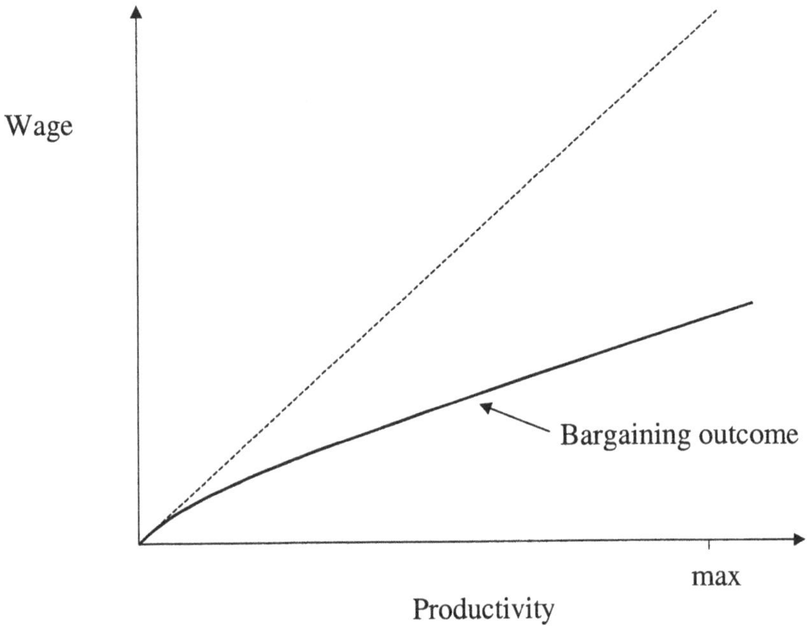


## 6 Conclusion

We have, in this paper, tried to analyse some possible issues which are important, but also likely to cause mutual conflict in the Finnish labour market wage bargaining system in the future. The analysis of the labour market bargaining system has had a pervasive aspect of the macro-economy in Finland. It is true that this remains an essential issue in the EMU age as well, but it is not sufficient, neither in policy-making nor in the studies of the labour market.

## References


Alho, K. (2002a): "Productivity, Relative Wages and Wage Bargaining" (in Finnish), paper given at the seminar of The Research Institute of the Finnish Economy (ETLA) & Labour Institute for Economic Research research project, January 2002, Helsinki.

Alho, K. (2002b): Is It Worth While to Pursue Incomes Policies?" (in Finnish), The Research Institute of the Finnish Economy (ETLA) Discussion paper, No. 837.

Alho K., Heikkilä, A., Lassila, J., Pekkarinen, J., Piekkola, H., and Sund, R. (2003): The Finnish Wage Bargaining System – Views of the Social Partners", (in Finnish), The Research Institute of the Finnish Economy (ETLA) series B, No. 203.

Andersen, T.M. (2004): International Product Market Integration and Wage Bargaining. In Piekkola, H. and Snellman, K. (eds.) *Collective Bargaining and Wage Formation – Performance and Challenges.* Springer-Verlag.

CEPR (1996): Unemployment: Choices for Europe, Monitoring European Integration, 5.

Dreze, J.H. and Gollier, C. (1993): "Risk Sharing in the Labour Market and the Second-Best Wage Rigidities", *European Economic Review*, Vol. 37, No. 8, December, 1457–1482.

Encinosa, W.E., III, Gaynor, M. and Rebitzer, J.B. (1997): "The Sociology of Groups and the Economics of Incentives: Theory and Evidence on Compensation Systems", NBER, Working paper, No. 5953.

Heijdra, B.J. and van der Ploeg, F. (2002): *Foundations of Modern Macroeconomics*, Oxford University Press.

Holm, P. and Vihriälä, V. (2002): A Subsidy to Labour of Low Productivity" (in Finnish, with English summary), Pellervo Economic Research Institute, Working Papers, No. 57.

Moen, E. and Rosén, Å. (2003): "Equilibrium Incentive Contracts", CEPR Discussion paper, No. 3790.

Muysken, J. and van Leen, T. (1996): "Efficiency Wages and Local Wage Bargaining", *Scandinavian Journal of Economics*, Vol. 98, No. 1., 119–127.

Pekkarinen, J. and Alho, K. (2004): The Finnish Bargaining System: Actors' Perceptions. In Piekkola, H. and Snellman, K. (eds.) *Collective Bargaining and Wage Formation – Performance and Challenges.* Springer-Verlag.

# Local Bargaining and Employers' Co-operation Options

Anni Heikkilä and Hannu Piekkola[1]

ETLA, The Research Institute of the Finnish Economy
Helsinki, Finland

## Abstract

Finnish employers want the locally bargained wage share to be approximately half of the total wage rise, which is significantly more than the locally bargained share in the current centralised wage agreement. However, employers' attitudes towards local bargaining vary a lot depending on firm characteristics. The aim of this paper is to explain employers' opinion of the proper locally bargained share of contract wages and also about who they think should decide on this wage share. It is shown that employers in large firms and in the financial services sector demand the largest locally bargained share of contract wages. When low competition in the product market is considered a challenge, employers may favour centralised wage setting instead of local bargaining. Employers are willing to involve employees in local bargaining decisions when the firm size is 30–299 employees or when the firm is profitable and operates in the service sector.

## 1 Introduction

The Finnish labour market has traditionally been comprehensively organised (for a description, see Vartiainen 1998, or Alho and Pekkarinen 2004, and Uusitalo 2004 in this book). Collective bargaining affects over 90% of wages and also covers the majority of non-union members. (Union membership is over 80%.) However,

[1] This is part of the research project Rules of the game in the labour market: Industrial relations, the bargaining system and income policies in the 2000s, financed by the Finnish Work Environment Fund, and carried out jointly by ETLA, The Research Institute of the Finnish Economy, and Labour Institute for Economic Research. We would like to thank Roope Uusitalo and Antti Kauhanen for very helpful comments, and seminar participants at the University of Jyväskylä for comments on an earlier draft. The usual disclaimer applies.

Piekkola and Marjanen (2003) argue that wage negotiations in Finland have changed since 1992, allowing more flexibility at both the industry level and the local level. New work relations have emerged, particularly in individual wage settlements and especially for salaried employees. For example, the use of performance-related pay (PRP) has become more common. By 2001, as much as 67 per cent of the industrial and 49 per cent of the service sector personnel working in member firms of the Confederation of Finnish Industry and Employers belonged to a PRP scheme.

The main elements of the Finnish collectively negotiated wage increases are the centrally agreed overall increase and a wage increase that is left to be bargained at either the industry or the firm level. (For a survey, see Marjanen 2002.) In addition to these, employers can pay a voluntary wage drift. In the centralised income policy agreement for the years 2003–2004, the wage share negotiated at either the firm or the industry level accounts for 31 per cent (in 2003) and 23 per cent (in 2004) of the total centrally bargained wage increase. Industrial unions and employers' federations can agree on a partial transfer of this wage share to be bargained at the firm level. Previously, local application of collective agreements has taken place rather mechanically, since employers have simply added the collectively negotiated increase to all wages (see Vartiainen 1998). However, recent globalisation and EMU membership-related changes in the business environment of Finnish companies may oblige employers to apply local wage bargaining more efficiently than before.

The research problem of this paper is to explain employers' desire for local flexibility in wage setting and, more specifically, their opinion of the proper locally bargained share of contract wages. Additionally, we examine employers' opinion of who should decide on the locally bargained wage share (the employer alone, the employer together with the employee/employees or the employees alone). The accompanying paper also considers employees' opinion of the locally bargained wage share (see Heikkilä and Piekkola 2004). Our empirical results indicate that employers exhibit a large variability in their local bargaining opinions, depending on several firm characteristics.

This paper is organised as follows. Section 2 explains the empirical data, variables and methods which are used. Section 3 provides the empirical analysis of employers' desire for local bargaining under the current system of centralised wage negotiations. Section 4 concludes.

## 2 Data and Methods

### 2.1 Data

Empirical data are from a questionnaire study 'The Performance of the Finnish Wage Bargaining System 2002–2003' carried out by The Research Institute of the Finnish Economy and The Labour Institute for Economic Research. The firm-level questionnaire study was directed at a sample of 2074 members of the Confederation of Finnish Industry and Employers and the Employers' Confederation of Service Industries. (For sample weights see Table A1 in the Appendix.) The questionnaire was sent to the representatives of the following four groups in each firm: the employer, the workers, salaried employees and professionals. The total response rate was 22.9%, which can be regarded as satisfactory. The employers' response rate was higher, 30.4%. Employers belonging to the Confederation of Finnish Industry and Employers had a higher response rate (33.8%) than employers belonging to the Employers' Confederation of Service Industries (25.3%). In their article Pekkarinen and Alho (2004) give additional information about this questionnaire study.

The first dependent variable is the respondent's answer to the question "One part of the collectively bargained wage increase is determined at the local level. In your opinion, how large should the locally bargained share of contract wage increases be?" The respondents were given five mutually exclusive response alternatives: 0, 1–24, 25–49, 50–74 or 75–100%. The second dependent variable is the employer's opinion of who should decide on the locally bargained share of contract wages. This dependent variable has four categories: a unilateral decision by the employer, determination in an individual wage settlement, determination in co-operation with employers and employees, and a unilateral decision by employees.

The independent variables of our empirical estimations are based on the background information about the firms that was inquired in the employers' questionnaire forms. The variable 'challenges of uncompetitive product market' is, however, generated from answers to question on the degree of challenge that low competition in the product market creates for labour market relations (see Appendix). We interpret challenges of low competition to be an indication of inefficiency or even monopoly power in the product market, which may cause challenges to labour market relations (e.g. employees insisting on receiving their share of the abnormal profits). Because of the relatively small number of observations, we have used a rougher classification of independent variables than in the original questionnaire. The industry variable, in particular, is classified more roughly than usual. The independent variables used are described in greater detail in the Appendix.

The following tables show detailed distributions of employer opinions concerning our two dependent variables. Table 1 shows that employers prefer around half of the wages to be locally bargained. To be precise, 33% of employers prefer 25–49% local wage share and 20% of them prefer 50–74% local wage share. The higher popularity of local bargaining among manufacturing sector employers is explained by different firm characteristics (disappears when controlled for). It is also seen that the representatives of the Confederation of Finnish Industry and Employers (TT) and the Employers' Federation of Service Industries (PT) usually prefer a higher share of local bargaining than the respective employers.

Table 2 shows employer opinions of who should decide on the locally bargained wage share. It is seen that about half of the employers prefer the locally bargained share to be decided solely by employers or in individual negotiations with employees. Representatives of the Employers' Federation of Service Industries (PT) seem to be most positive towards employers' unilateral local wage decisions, whereas service sector employers support mutual local negotiations relatively most of all.

**Table 1.** Desired Locally Bargained Share of Wage Rise, %

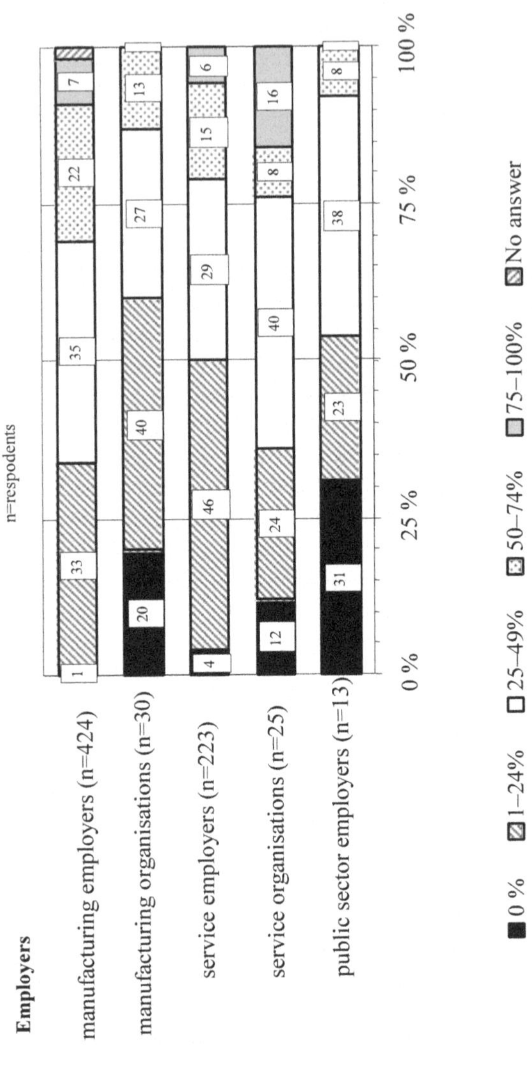

**Table 2.** Decision on Locally Bargained Wage Share

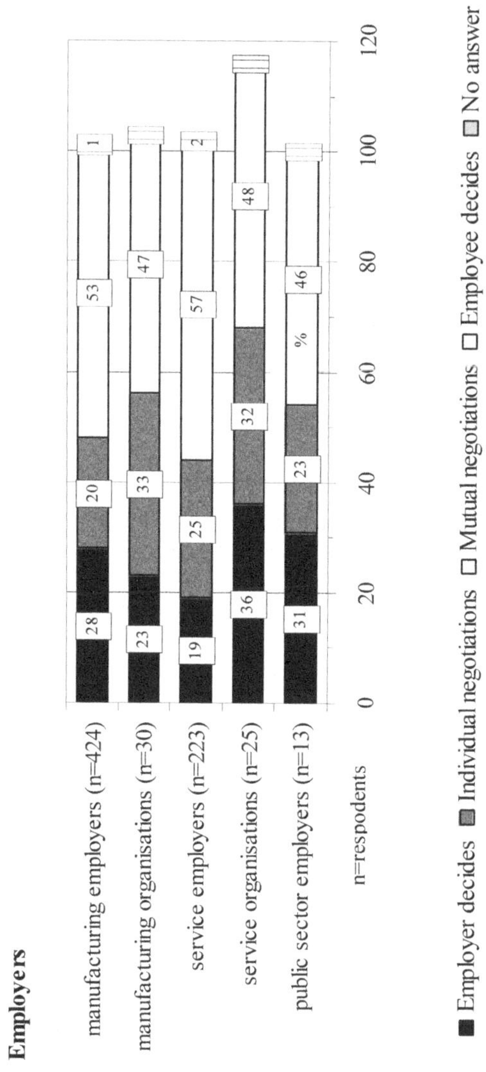

## 2.2 Methods

The first and most important dependent variable in our estimations, the answer to the question about the desired share of locally bargained wages, is multinomial with its five categories, and these categories are in order. We use the interval regression model to describe the probability of favouring a certain locally bargained share of contract wage increases (0, 1–24, 25–49, 50–74 or 75–100%) as a function of the independent variables. We chose interval regression since the quantitative outcome we are explaining is grouped into intervals and thus the cut points do not need to be estimated as when using the ordered probit model (Wooldridge 2002, 508–509). When it comes to the second dependent variable, the employer's opinion of who should decide on the locally bargained share of contract wages, we apply the ordered probit model. This qualitative dependent variable has four categories, which are inherently ordered, but the cut point parameters are unknown and have to be estimated together with the coefficients $\beta$.

Interval regression allows us to interpret the magnitude (marginal effect) of the positive or negative effects that the estimated coefficients $\hat{\beta}$ have on the dependent variable. For example, when considering the 'size of the firm' variable, coefficient 0.066 of the category of 30–99 employees will be interpreted so that when the firm size increases from 5–29 to 30–99 employees, the desired locally bargained wage share increases by 6.6%. Due to the non-linearity of the ordered probit model the estimated parameters $\hat{\beta}$ cannot be interpreted as marginal effects. Thus, when it comes to the interpretation of our ordered probit estimation results, we are only able to interpret the sign of the effects, not the magnitude.

The questionnaire data of this study was collected by the use of a weighted sampling method so that in different firm size groups the sample proportion of the population varies. The conventional way to do sample weighting for estimations would be to use inverses of sample proportions as estimation weights. In the present study, however, conventional sample weighting would overemphasise smaller firms' opinions since larger firms' employer opinions represent a significantly larger number of employees and their wage negotiation systems. Thus, we multiplied the inverses of sample proportions by the average number of personnel in each firm size group. This measure returned the importance of large firms' opinions compared with small firms' opinions and thus made the sample weights reasonable in the context of our empirical research problem.

# 3 Employers' Desire for Local Bargaining

In this section we present and analyse our estimation results concerning Finnish employers' opinions of the proper locally bargained share of contract wage increases and who should decide on local bargaining. We begin our analysis by presenting cross-tabulations of the most important explanatory variables and the desired locally bargained share of contract wages.

### 3.1 Descriptive Analysis

Cross-tabulation results in Table 3 indicate that firm size seems to be positively related to an employer's desire for local bargaining. This effect is particularly strong when we compare firm-size category of 30–99 employees with the lowest category of 5–29 employees. The positive effect might imply that large firms have more need for local leeway in their wage setting or that employers in small firms regard local wage bargaining as too complex and time-consuming.

**Table 3.** Firm Size and the Desired Locally Bargained Wage Share

| | Desired locally bargained wage share | | | | | |
|---|---|---|---|---|---|---|
| **Firm size** | **0 %** | **1–24%** | **25–49%** | **50–74%** | **75–100%** | **Average** |
| **5–29 employees** | 8.5 % | 54.9 % | 19.5 % | 15.9 % | 1.2 % | 2.46 |
| **30–99** | 2.1 % | 41.5 % | 34.5 % | 15.5 % | 6.3 % | 2.82 |
| **100–299** | 1.7 % | 34.5 % | 35.0 % | 20.3 % | 8.5 % | 2.99 |
| **300–** | 0.0 % | 29.5 % | 36.9 % | 24.9 % | 8.8 % | 3.13 |
| **Total** | 2.1 % | 37.1 % | 33.5 % | 20.2 % | 7.1 % | |

The results in Table 4 show a preliminary positive connection between firm profitability and the desired locally bargained share of contract wages. However, we have to be careful when interpreting results related to firm profitability because our cross-sectional empirical data contains information only on current profitability and not profitability over longer period.

**Table 4.** Profitability and the Desired Locally Bargained Wage Share

| | Desired locally bargained wage share | | | | | |
|---|---|---|---|---|---|---|
| **Net profit margin** | **0 %** | **1–24%** | **25–49%** | **50–74%** | **75–100%** | **Average** |
| **Less than or equal to 5%** | 3.0 % | 42.3 % | 30.2 % | 19.5 % | 5.0 % | 2.81 |
| **More than 5%** | 1.3 % | 32.2 % | 36.6 % | 20.9 % | 9.1 % | 3.04 |
| **Total** | 2.1 % | 37.1 % | 33.5 % | 20.2 % | 7.1 % | |

When the employer considers the challenges of uncompetitive product market to be moderate or high, the desired locally bargained wage share is smaller than when the uncompetitive product market is regarded only as a minor challenge (Table 5 below). However, when challenges of low competition grow from moderate to high, the size of the desired locally bargained wage share does not decrease equivalently but remains almost the same.

**Table 5.** Low Competition and the Desired Locally Bargained Wage Share

| | Desired locally bargained wage share | | | | | |
|---|---|---|---|---|---|---|
| **Uncompetitive product market** | **0 %** | **1–24%** | **25–49%** | **50–74%** | **75–100%** | **Average** |
| **Minor** | 0.0 % | 27.6 % | 31.0 % | 27.6 % | 13.8 % | 3.28 |
| **Moderate** | 1.8 % | 38.8 % | 34.7 % | 18.8 % | 5.9 % | 2.88 |
| **High** | 2.4 % | 37.5 % | 33.7 % | 19.9 % | 6.5 % | 2.91 |
| **Total** | 2.0 % | 36.9 % | 33.7 % | 20.4 % | 7.0 % | |

We assume that the industry of the respondent's firm would have a notable effect on the size of the desired locally bargained wage share. The cross-tabulation results in Table 6 indeed show us that there seems to be variation according to the industry of the employer, although the significance of this variation remains questionable until econometric estimations are carried out. Employers in financial services and other private sector services seem to demand the relatively largest scope for local wage bargaining, whereas employers in education and welfare services, as well as those in trade, seem to be satisfied with the relatively least flexible local wage setting.

**Table 6.** Industry and the Desired Locally Bargained Wage Share

| | Desired locally bargained wage share | | | | | |
|---|---|---|---|---|---|---|
| **Industry** | **0 %** | **1–24%** | **25–49%** | **50–74%** | **75–100%** | **Average** |
| **Metal** | 1.0 % | 32.7 % | 38.8 % | 19.4 % | 8.2 % | 3.01 |
| **Food, forest and other** | 0.0 % | 31.4 % | 34.9 % | 25.4 % | 8.3 % | 3.11 |
| **Electronics and IT sector** | 2.6 % | 43.6 % | 28.2 % | 20.5 % | 5.1 % | 2.82 |
| **Construction and transportation** | 3.1 % | 37.5 % | 31.3 % | 21.9 % | 6.3 % | 2.91 |
| **Trade** | 5.6 % | 46.1 % | 29.2 % | 14.6 % | 4.5 % | 2.66 |
| **Financial services** | 0.0 % | 27.6 % | 31.0 % | 24.1 % | 17.2 % | 3.31 |
| **Other private sector services** | 1.8 % | 25.5 % | 36.4 % | 27.3 % | 9.1 % | 3.16 |
| **Education and welfare services** | 4.0 % | 53.3 % | 32.0 % | 8.0 % | 2.7 % | 2.52 |
| **Total** | 2.1 % | 37.1 % | 33.5 % | 20.2 % | 7.1 % | |

According to the cross-tabulations shown in Table 7, use of profit sharing seems to be positively related to the need of large, locally bargained wage shares. According to Alho (1998), Kauhanen and Piekkola (2002) and Kruse (1996), one of the main motives to use profit sharing is that it enables flexibility in wage expenses. Thus, similar flexibility-seeking motives that explain the use of profit sharing may also be connected to the employer's desire for a large, locally bargained wage share.

**Table 7.** Use of Profit Sharing and the Desired Locally Bargained Wage Share

| | Desired locally bargained wage share | | | | | |
|---|---|---|---|---|---|---|
| **Use of profit sharing** | **0 %** | **1–24%** | **25–49%** | **50–74%** | **75–100%** | **Average** |
| **No** | 3.7 % | 46.1 % | 30.6 % | 15.1 % | 4.5 % | 2.71 |
| **Yes** | 1.1 % | 31.1 % | 35.4 % | 23.6 % | 8.8 % | 3.08 |
| **Total** | 2.1 % | 37.1 % | 33.5 % | 20.2 % | 7.1 % | |

## 3.2 Econometric Analysis

In the estimations of Tables 8 and 9 we have used the tobit interval regression technique and hence we are able to interpret the percentual (marginal) effects that independent variables have on the dependent variable, the desired locally bargained share of contract wages. In Table 10 we have used ordered probit technique and thus only the signs of the coefficients can be interpreted.

**Table 8.** Employers' Desired Locally Bargained Share of Contract Wages

| | Employers Tobit Interval Regression | |
|---|---|---|
| **Variable** | **Coefficient** | **S.E.** |
| **Firm Variables** | | |
| Firm Size 30–99 | 0.066 | (0,035)* |
| 100–299 | 0.101 | (0,035)*** |
| 300– | 0.114 | (0,034)*** |
| Export Share 40–59% | 0.070 | (0,046) |
| 60%– | 0.019 | (0,033) |
| Uncompetitive Product Market Moderate | -0.104 | (0,04)*** |
| High | -0.087 | (0,037)** |
| Net Profits per Sales/100 | 0.002 | (0,002) |
| Share of Employees Abroad 60%– | 0.045 | (0,044) |
| Foreign Owned Partly or Wholly | 0.053 | (0,029)* |
| Food, Forest and Other Industries | 0.066 | (0,035)* |
| Electronics Industry and IT Sector | -0.017 | (0,048) |
| Construction and Transportation | 0.037 | (0,048) |
| Trade | 0.062 | (0,045) |
| Financial Services | 0.270 | (0,079)*** |
| Other Private Sector Services | 0.061 | (0,045) |
| Education and Welfare Services | 0.042 | (0,048) |
| **Personnel Variables** | | |
| Profit Sharing Used | 0.007 | (0,025) |
| Share of Salaried Employees 40%– | -0.026 | (0,024) |
| Share of Professionals 40%– | 0.047 | (0,037) |
| Share of Female Employees 60%– | -0.079 | (0,029)*** |
| Average Age of Employees 40 years– | -0.024 | (0,026) |
| Share of Permanent Employments 80%– | 0.039 | (0,031) |
| Constant | 0.284 | (0,065)*** |
| No. Observations | 573 | |
| Log Likelihood | -445814 | |

Note. The dependent variable is the desired locally bargained share of contract wages (0–100%). Table reports coefficients and standard errors using robust estimates. The base for the firm-size dummy is firms with 5–29 employees. The base for industry dummies is the metal industry. * Significant at the 90% confidence level. ** Significant at the 95% confidence level. *** Significant at the 99% confidence level.

### Firm Variables

In conformity with the earlier cross-tabulation results, the estimation results in Table 8 show that employers in large firms clearly prefer a higher share of local bargaining than employers in small firms. Increase in the firm-size variable from 5–29 employees to 30–99 employees increases the desired locally bargained wage share by approximately 7%. Employers in firms employing 100–299 people demand a 10% larger locally bargained wage share than employers in the smallest firms. When it comes to the largest firms employing at least 300 people, the desired locally flexible wage share is 11% larger than in the smallest firms. Large firms are also more likely to use profit-sharing than smaller firms (see Kauhanen and Piekkola 2002). Profit-sharing may help in decreasing the large employee supervision costs of large firms that stem from incomplete information of on-the-job performance. Supervision costs and, hence, the need to allocate local wage increases in a motivating way may explain large firms' desire for locally determined wages in general. The second explanation for the positive firm-size effect can be that employers in small firms want to avoid complex and time-consuming local wage negotiations and thus they are relatively satisfied with common, centrally negotiated wage increases.

The coefficients of export share dummies in Table 8 are positive but insignificant. Thus, employers in export-intensive firms are not significantly more interested in large locally bargained wage shares than employers in domestically oriented firms.

Severe competition in the product market and the firm's poor profitability can create demand for local bargaining in order to ensure sufficient wage flexibility. The low competition variable ('challenges of uncompetitive product market') has statistically significant, negative coefficients in Table 8. The negative effect of low product market competition on wage flexibility demands is slightly larger when low competition is regarded as a moderate challenge compared with when it is regarded as a high challenge. This was already seen in cross-tabulations presented earlier. However, our results indicate that centralised wage setting appears to be preferred under uncompetitive product market circumstances.

Profitability of the firm has surprisingly little effect on the desire for local bargaining among Finnish employers. The coefficient of our profitability variable is positive but very small and statistically insignificant in Table 8. One explanation for this finding can be the low probability of any need for wage cuts when the firm is profitable. Another explanation can be that employers in profitable firms are reluctant to increase the scope of local bargaining because it may encourage employees to demand a higher share of the firm's profits. However, later estimations reported in Table 9 show that employers in profitable service sector firms support local bargaining.

In many countries, the USA probably being the best example, firm-level wage setting is substantially more flexible than in Finland. Thus, we assume that Finnish employers who have the majority of their workforce working abroad would like to adopt this flexibility also in Finland. In Table 8 the share of employees working abroad has a positive but insignificant coefficient. When it comes to the 'foreign ownership of a firm' variable, our results in Table 8 show that employers in partially or wholly foreign-owned firms demand a significantly larger locally bargained wage share than employers in domestically owned firms. To be precise, when the firm is at least partially foreign-owned, employers demand an approximately 5% larger locally bargained wage share than employers in domestically owned firms. This result may be explained by Finnish employers' desire to meet the profitability demands of foreign (institutional) investors by increasing the scope of their firms' wage flexibility.

### *Personnel Variables*

Cross-tabulations presented earlier indicated that employers' desire for local bargaining may be connected to the same flexibility-seeking motives that explain the use of profit-sharing. It should be noted, however, that profit-sharing adjusts wages automatically downwards in financial downturns, but locally bargained wage contracts always need to be approved by both the employer and the employees' representatives. In Table 8 the profit-sharing coefficient is positive but small and remains statistically insignificant. Hence, Finnish employers already using PRP schemes seem to think that they do not need large locally bargained wage shares to ensure the flexibility of their wage costs. This is perhaps not surprising, since Alho et al. (2003) report almost unanimous satisfaction with profit-sharing among Finnish employers who are currently using it.

Locally bargained wage shares allow employers to differentiate local wage increases in order to motivate specific employee groups and thus decrease shirking-related monitoring costs. Salaried employees' effort is likely to be more difficult to monitor than blue-collar workers' effort in all firms. When the proportion of salaried employees increases, the employer may thus become more interested in large locally bargained wage shares. On the other hand, when nearly the whole workforce consists of salaried employees the employer may lose interest in large locally bargained wage shares because he cannot differentiate local wage increases between specific groups any more. Our estimation results in Table 8 indicate that a high share of salaried employees has a negative, insignificant effect on the employer's demand for a locally bargained wage share. A high share of professionals has a positive effect, which also remains insignificant.

The share of female employees in a firm is the only significant personnel variable in Table 8. In firms where more than 60% of workforce is women, employers demand approximately an 8% smaller locally bargained wage share than employers employing a smaller proportion of women. One possible explanation for this result might be the differences in firm- and individual-level wage negotiating cultures in female and male employee-dominated firms. However, we have to bear in mind that the effect of female dominance is highly dependent on the industry of the firm and our roughly classified industry dummies may not control all of this effect.

When the average age of the personnel is 40+, employers seem to favour smaller locally bargained wage shares compared with employers with a workforce whose average age is less than 40 years. This result is statistically insignificant, but it is in conformance with the idea that employers with a young workforce who are willing to try new negotiation practices may see local bargaining as a real opportunity to increase the flexibility of their wage expenses.

Azfar and Danninger (2001) show that profit-sharing decreases worker mobility. In a similar way local bargaining can also create stable job relations between employee and employer, which enables the accumulation of firm-specific human capital. The more stable and established the firm's workforce, the easier it may be for the employer to implement large-scale local wage bargaining. On the other hand, the effect of workforce stability might also be opposite, because an unstable workforce may have less bargaining power, which increases employers' interest in local wage bargaining. Our estimation results in Table 8 give some support to the idea of a positive relationship between the share of permanent employments and the desire for a large locally bargained share of contract wages. However, the positive coefficient of the 'share of permanent employments more than 80%' variable remains statistically insignificant.

### *Variation by Industry*

Industry dummies are expected to have positive coefficients when industries are more volatile than the reference industry (metal) and negative coefficients in the opposite case. The forest and construction industries, as well as the financial services sector, can be regarded as cyclically volatile and are expected to have positive coefficients. In addition, current inflexibility in the wage setting of a specific industry may arouse a need for more locally flexible wages. Our industry coefficients in Table 8 mostly have expected signs, except for the negative (but insignificant) coefficient of the electronics and IT sector. Only the positive coefficients of financial services and the food, forest and other industries are statistically significant. Compared with all other coefficients in Table 8, financial services has an exceptionally large coefficient, which indicates that employers in this sector would like to have a 27% larger locally bargained wage share than employers in the metal industry. The Finnish financial services sector suffered more than most other Finnish industries from the economic downturn at the beginning of the 21st century, and cost cutting in wage expenses became everyday life for these firms. Our result also reflects the large structural change going on in the financial services sector.

Industry dummies indicate that employers in service industries seem to favour larger locally bargained wage shares than employers in the metal industry, but in some other manufacturing industries (especially the food and the forest industries) there is also a demand for local wage flexibility. The following table, Table 9, shows employer opinions by industries.

Table 9 shows some clear industry variation in local bargaining opinions. It is seen that a positive firm-size effect is most prevalent in the manufacturing sector. Demand for local bargaining is strongest among employers in middle-sized manufacturing firms (100–299 employees) and large manufacturing firms (at least 300 employees). Coefficients show that employers in these firms would like to have approximately 11% larger locally bargained wage shares than employers in small manufacturing firms (5–29 employees). On the other hand, service sector firms with profit sharing are remarkably positive towards large locally bargained wage shares. Foreign ownership and a large share of professionals also show up as important reasons to prefer local bargaining in the service sector. The negativity of 'female employees more than 60%' variable can be traced back to the manufacturing sector employer opinions.

**Table 9.** Employers' Desired Locally Bargained Share of Contract Wages in the Manufacturing and Service Sectors

| | Confederation of Finnish Industry and Employers TT Tobit Interval Regression | | Employers´ Federation of Service Industries PT Tobit Interval Regression | |
|---|---|---|---|---|
| **Variable** | **Coefficient** | **S.E.** | **Coefficient** | **S.E.** |
| **Firm Variables** | | | | |
| Firm Size 30–99 | 0.063 | (0,048) | 0.046 | (0,048) |
| 100–299 | 0.114 | (0,049)** | 0.048 | (0,05) |
| 300– | 0.107 | (0,051)** | 0.039 | (0,05) |
| Export Share 40–59% | 0.094 | (0,047)** | -0.171 | (0,14) |
| 60%– | 0.029 | (0,034) | -0.173 | (0,208) |
| Uncompetitive Product Market Moderate | -0.105 | (0,05)** | -0.120 | (0,065)* |
| High | -0.083 | (0,048)* | -0.095 | (0,06) |
| Net Profits per Sales/100 | 0.390 | (0,257) | 0.004 | (0,002)* |
| Share of Employees Abroad 60%– | 0.053 | (0,046) | -0.062 | (0,14) |
| Foreign Owned Partly or Wholly | 0.040 | (0,033) | 0.191 | (0,066)*** |
| **Personnel Variables** | | | | |
| Profit Sharing Used | -0.021 | (0,031) | 0.096 | (0,046)** |
| Share of Salaried Employees 40%– | -0.022 | (0,03) | -0.012 | (0,036) |
| Share of Professionals 40%– | 0.036 | (0,047) | 0.119 | (0,058)** |
| Share of Female Employees 60%– | -0.106 | (0,045)** | 0.007 | (0,037) |
| Average Age of Employees 40 years– | -0.029 | (0,036) | -0.050 | (0,039) |
| Share of Permanent Employments 80%– | 0.030 | (0,045) | 0.026 | (0,042) |
| Constant | 0.312 | (0,076)*** | 0.203 | (0,196) |
| No. Observations | 386 | | 187 | |
| Log Likelihood | -320492.76 | | -118799.49 | |

See note in Table 8. Estimation includes industry dummies.

## 3.3 Decision on the Locally Bargained Wage Share

Table 10 shows employer opinions concerning who should make the decision on the locally bargained wage share. Estimations in Table 10 have been carried out using the ordered probit technique. A positive coefficient indicates that the employer is willing to give more decision-making power to employees (unilateral decision-making by employees is the extreme) and a negative coefficient indicates the opposite (unilateral decision by the employer is the extreme).

**Table 10.** Employer's Opinion on Who Should Decide on Locally Bargained Share of Contract Wages

| | Employers Ordered Probit | | Confederation of Finnish Industry and Employers TT Ordered Probit | | Employers' Federation of Service Industries PT Ordered Probit | |
|---|---|---|---|---|---|---|
| **Variable** | **Coefficient** | **S.E.** | **Coefficient** | **S.E.** | **Coefficient** | **S.E.** |
| **Firm Variables** | | | | | | |
| Firm Size 30–99 | 0.487 | (0,269)* | 0.553 | (0,411) | 0.431 | (0,425) |
| 100–299 | 0.516 | (0,258)** | 0.624 | (0,404) | 0.449 | (0,365) |
| 300– | 0.238 | (0,256) | 0.323 | (0,418) | 0.007 | (0,371) |
| Export Share 40–59% | -0.115 | (0,284) | -0.079 | (0,286) | 18.535 | (0,704)*** |
| 60%– | -0.015 | (0,195) | -0.033 | (0,196) | 1.213 | (0,934) |
| Uncompetitive Product Market Moderate | 0.066 | (0,239) | 0.371 | (0,261) | -0.847 | (0,668) |
| High | -0.200 | (0,222) | 0.068 | (0,242) | -1.039 | (0,564)* |
| Net Profits per Sales/100 | 0.024 | (0,006)*** | 0.742 | (1,372) | 0.023 | (0,007)*** |
| Share of Employees Abroad 60%– | -0.127 | (0,226) | -0.194 | (0,221) | -0.157 | (0,743) |
| Foreign Owned Partly or Wholly | 0.095 | (0,15) | 0.265 | (0,165) | -0.628 | (0,334)* |
| **Personnel Variables** | | | | | | |
| Profit Sharing Used | 0.272 | (0,22) | 0.230 | (0,248) | 0.638 | (0,385)* |
| Share of Salaried Employees 40%– | -0.101 | (0,146) | -0.099 | (0,165) | 0.327 | (0,363) |
| Share of Professionals 40%– | -0.322 | (0,251) | -0.259 | (0,316) | -0.678 | (0,476) |
| Share of Female Employees 60%– | 0.080 | (0,197) | -0.046 | (0,227) | 0.358 | (0,414) |
| Average Age of Employees 40 years– | 0.160 | (0,165) | 0.081 | (0,188) | 0.330 | (0,389) |
| Share of Permanent Employments 80%– | 0.295 | (0,238) | 0.295 | (0,303) | 0.251 | (0,465) |
| No. Observations | 394 | | 297 | | 97 | |
| Log Likelihood | -511.64 | | -382.09 | | -108.18 | |
| Pseudo $R^2$ | 0.026 | | 0.033 | | 0.141 | |

See note in Table 8. Estimation includes industry dummies.

It is seen that employers in middle-sized firms (30–299 employees) are more willing to involve employees in locally bargained wage share decisions than employers in small firms (5–29 employees). Another significant determinant of willingness to empower employees is firm profitability. The significance of profitability is explained by the opinion of service sector employers, in particular. The willingness of profitable firms to negotiate should be contrasted with the insignificant effect of profitability on the magnitude of the desired locally bargained share. Employers in profitable firms have evidently less pressure for wage flexibility, so in case they want to use local bargaining it is justified by other motives. When increasing the flexibility of labour costs is not the underlying motive for local bargaining, it is evident that negotiations with employees are more easily carried out. On the other hand, employers in non-profitable firms may support local bargaining for flexibility-seeking reasons, which explains their willingness to retain the decisive power for themselves.

When a service sector firm exports 40–59% of its turnover or uses performance-related pay schemes, the employer is likely to be willing to involve employees in local wage bargaining. On the other hand, foreign ownership in the service sector shows up as a significant reason to prefer unilateral employer decisions or to allow only minor employee participation in local bargaining decisions.

# 4 Concluding Remarks

In this paper we studied Finnish employers' desire for local wage bargaining under the current predominantly centralised Finnish wage bargaining system. Employers want, on average, half of the rise in wages to be negotiated at the local level, which is significantly more than the locally bargained share in the current centralised wage agreement. However, our results show that employers differ significantly in their opinions on the proper locally bargained share of contract wage increases.

Employers in large firms clearly prefer a larger share of local bargaining than employers in smaller firms. When the firm employs at least 100 people, the employer wants approximately a 10% larger locally bargained wage share than an employer employing 5–29 people. Large firms' desire for local bargaining can be explained by an employer's attempt to decrease supervision costs or by small firms' reluctance to enforce complex and time-consuming local wage negotiations.

The profitability of the firm has surprisingly little effect on the desire for local bargaining among Finnish employers. An explanation for this finding can be the minor interest in the local labour cost flexibility in profitable firms. It is interesting that, despite the lack of interest in large locally bargained wage shares, the firm's profitability leads to employers' greater willingness to negotiate with employees, especially in the service industry. Thus, it seems that in firms with poor profitability labour cost flexibility is demanded, and employers think that relatively little of this should be agreed with employees. This opinion is not surprising, since wage-cutting negotiations are naturally more difficult than discussions on how to share profits.

Our results indicate that the severity of product market competition affects the desire for local bargaining. The low competition variable has statistically significant, negative coefficients, which means that the greater the employer perceives the challenges of low competition, the less he advocates a large locally bargained share of contract wages. We came to the conclusion that low product market competition makes employers vote for centralised wage setting instead of local bargaining.

Contrary to our expectations, employers using PRP schemes are not interested in additional locally bargained wage shares. Alho et al. (2003) report almost unanimous satisfaction with PRP schemes among Finnish employers who use them. This may explain that employers do not need additional local flexibility to their labour costs Variables for the share of salaried employees, the share of professionals and the share of permanent employments also remain insignificant.. The only significant personnel variable is the share of female employees. When the proportion of the female workforce exceeds 60%, employers desire an 8% smaller locally bargained wage share than employers employing a smaller percentage of women. This effect is highly dependent on the industry of the firm and the negativity of 'female employees more than 60%' variable can be traced back to the manufacturing sector's employer opinions.

Employers are most willing to involve employees in local bargaining decisions when the firm size is 30–299 employees. Employers in profitable service sector firms are also willing to empower employees in local wage negotiations. Foreign ownership in the service sector shows up as an important reason to prefer unilateral employer decisions or to allow only minor employee participation in local bargaining decisions. At the same time, employers in partially or wholly foreign owned firms are willing to increase the scope of local wage bargaining in their firms.

## References

Alho, K. (1998): Tulospalkkaus – EMU-ajan palkkausmuoto. *Research Institute of the Finnish Economy,* Series B 146. Taloustieto Oy, Helsinki.

Alho, K., Heikkilä, A., Lassila, J., Pekkarinen, J., Piekkola, H. and Sund, R. (2003): Suomalainen sopimusjärjestelmä – työmarkkinaosapuolten näkemykset. *Research Institute of the Finnish Economy,* Series B 203. Taloustieto Oy, Helsinki.

Azfar, O. and Danninger, S. (2001): Profit-Sharing, Employment Stability, and Wage Growth. *Industrial and Labour Relations Review,* 54, 619–630.

Centralised Income Policy Agreement for Years 2003–2004.

Heikkilä, A. and Piekkola, H. (2004): Desire for Local Bargaining and Divergence of Opinions among Employers and Employees - Evidence from Finnish Survey. *The Research Institute of the Finnish Economy, Discussion papers.* Forthcoming.

Kauhanen, A. and Piekkola, H. (2002): Profit Sharing in Finland: Earnings and Productivity Effects. *The Research Institute of the Finnish Economy, Discussion papers* no. 817.

Kruse, D. L. (1996): Why Do Firms Adopt Profit-Sharing and Employee Ownership Plans? *British Journal of Industrial Relations,* 34, 515–538.

Marjanen, R. (2002): Palkkaratkaisujen sisältö ja toteutuminen tulopolitiikan aikakaudella. *Research Institute of the Finnish Economy,* Series B 188. Taloustieto Oy, Helsinki.

Pekkarinen, J. and Alho, K. (2004): Finnish Bargaining System: Actors' Perceptions. In Piekkola, H. and Snellman, K. (eds.) *Collective Bargaining and Wage Formation – Performance and Challenges.* Springer-Verlag.

Piekkola, H. and Marjanen, R. (2003): Palkoista sopiminen ja palkkaliukuma: Tulopolitiikan uudet kulissit. *Research Institute of the Finnish Economy,* Series B 202. Taloustieto Oy, Helsinki.

Vartiainen, J. (1998): The Labour Market in Finland: Institutions and Outcomes. *Prime Minister's Office Publications* Series 1998/2.

Wooldridge, J. M. (2002): *Econometric Analysis of Cross Section and Panel Data.* MIT Press, Cambridge, MA.

## Appendix

In the estimation the independent variables are generated as follows:

*Firm size categories*: 5–29 employees, 30–99 employees, 100–299 employees, at least 300 employees.

*Export share of the firm's turnover*: 0–39%, 40–59%, 60–100%.

*Respondent's estimation of the challenge of low product market competition*: Based on questionnaire question E1_14: "How big a challenge do you consider low product market competition is for the Finnish wage bargaining system?" 1=No challenge at all,..., 5=Very big challenge. We created a new variable for the estimations: Challenges of uncompetitive product market: minor (category 1), moderate (category 2), high (categories 3, 4 and 5).

*Profitability of the firm*: Net profits per sales (net profit percentage). We divide net profits per sales by one hundred to obtain a reasonable coefficient for this independent variable.

*Share of employees working abroad*: 1–59%, 60–100%.

*Foreign ownership:* No foreign ownership, partial or whole foreign ownership.

*Industry*: Metal industry, food, forest and other industries, electronics industry and IT sector, construction and transportation, trade, financial services, other private services, education and welfare services.

*Use of profit sharing:*

1 if profit sharing is used for at least one of the following personnel groups: workers, salaried employees, professionals,

0 if profit sharing is not used for any of the groups mentioned above.

Based on the background information asked in the questionnaire form: "What kind of payroll systems are used in your firm?" Either more or less than half of the amount of profit sharing may depend on the net profit of the firm.

*Share of salaried employees:* 0–39%, 40–100%.

*Share of professionals:* 0–39%, 40–100%.

*Share of female employees*: 0–59%, 60–100%.

*Average age of employees*: less than 40 years, 40 years or more.

*Share of permanent employments*: 0–79%, 80–100%.

**Table A1.** Sample Weights and Sizes in the Questionnaire

| | **TT Employers Federation Manufacturing** | | **PT Employers Federation Service** | |
|---|---|---|---|---|
| **Firm size** | **Sample weight %** | **Obs** | **Sample weight %** | **Obs** |
| over 300 | 100 | 356 | 100 | 184 |
| 100–299 | 40 | 300 | 50 | 163 |
| 30–99 | 20 | 300 | 20 | 221 |
| less 300 | 10 | 300 | 5 | 250 |
| All | | 1256 | | 818 |

# Do Centralized Bargains Lead to Wage Moderation? Time-Series Evidence from Finland

Roope Uusitalo[1]

The Labour Institute for Economic Research
Helsinki, Finland

## Abstract

Empirical research usually generally supports the view that the countries with a more centralized bargaining system have more favourable outcomes than countries where bargaining occurs at the industry level. These studies are usually based on cross-country data. This paper examines the relationship between the degree of centralization and wage increases within a country across years with different degrees of centralization. The key finding is that both bargained and actual nominal wage increases are lower when bargaining takes place at a national level.

## 1 Motivation

Empirical research generally supports the view that the countries with more centralized bargaining systems have more favourable economic outcomes than the countries where wages are bargained at the industry level. Co-ordination of wage bargaining leads to lower wage increases and lower unemployment than industry-level bargaining, because the bargainers take into account the consequences of bargaining outcomes to the aggregate inflation and unemployment. Calmfors and Driffil (1988) argue that the relationship between centralization and unemployment is hump-shaped so that the most centralized (nationwide) and the most decentralized (firm-level) negotiations lead to lower unemployment than industry-level bargaining.

However, the existing empirical evidence is almost entirely based on cross-country comparisons. A problem in these studies is that with a limited amount of

[1] This is part of the research project "Rules of the game in the labour market: Industrial relations, the bargaining system and income policies in the 2000s", financed by the Finnish Work Environment Fund, and carried out jointly by ETLA, The Research Institute of the Finnish Economy and the Labour Institute for Economic Research. I am grateful to Steinar Holden, Pekka Sauramo and Hannu Piekkola for useful comments.

data it is difficult to disentangle the effects of bargaining systems from the other differences across countries that affect inflation and unemployment. Even when panel data on countries is available, the differences across countries typically dominate so that the results are driven by cross-country differences rather than different changes over time (e.g. Nickell and Layard 1999). Furthermore, the cross-country comparisons are sensitive to the classification of countries in the different bargaining regimes. These classifications are based on crude indexes of co-ordination and centralization. Different criteria lead to the somewhat different ranking of countries and, hence, different results. For example, Flanagan (1999) concludes in his survey that differences in country rankings produced by nuances of definition have a dramatic effect on the correlation between institutional structure and economic performance. Finally, cross-country studies often ignore the variation in the degree of centralization within countries over time. This variation may be substantial and yet indexes of centralization (e.g. OECD 1997) typically rank countries similarly from year to year.

In this paper I present evidence on the wage-moderating effects of centralized bargaining based on time-series data from Finland. Finland is an interesting example of a country where there are substantial differences in the degree of centralization across time. During the past thirty years most wage bargains have been negotiated at the national level between confederations of unions and employer organizations, often with substantial government involvement. However, national bargains have not been achieved every year; seven bargaining rounds have been conducted at the industry level. Also, in the years when a national bargain has been agreed upon, some unions have opted out from the national bargain, creating additional variation in the degree of centralization.

Focusing on the data from a single country has several benefits compared with the cross-country studies. First, it can be argued that the consecutive wage bargaining rounds within a country are more comparable than different countries. Macroeconomic conditions at the time of wage negotiations certainly affect both the likelihood of obtaining centralized agreement and the outcome of the bargaining process, but it is far from clear that the possible bias is more severe than the bias caused by omitted variables in cross-country comparisons. The second advantage is that the details of the bargaining process can be studied better within a country. The cross-country comparisons rely on crude indexes of co-ordination or centralization. Constructing such indexes requires judgment and is subject to criticism. Within a country it is possible to construct more objective measures of centralization based on data on, for example, the share of wage earners covered by the central bargain.

This paper is certainly not the first attempt to study the effects of coordination on economic outcomes by using time-series data. The analysis in this paper resembles an earlier study by Barkbu, Nymoen and Roed (2001), who use time variation in wage coordination between the bargaining rounds to identify the effect of wage coordination on unemployment in Sweden and Norway. However, this paper differs from Barkbu et al. and from most previous papers by focusing on the nominal wage increases instead of differences in unemployment or real wage growth. The natural motivation is that nominal wages are what the wage negotiations are about. Even if the bargainers really care about real wages and unemployment, the nominal wage increases are the only instrument that they have for achieving these goals. Focusing on the nominal wage increases does not imply that inflation expectations are unimportant. In their simplest form the expectations are accounted for by the inclusion of past inflation in the equation explaining wage increases.

**Fig. 1.** Union Density in Finland

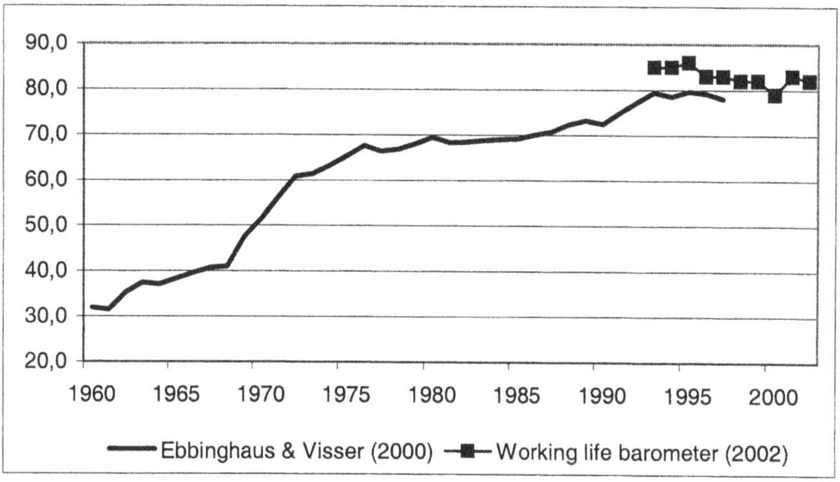


Note: Numbers from Ebbinghaus and Visser refer to net density i.e. active membership (excluding pensioners, students) as share of the gainfully employed wage and salary earners (excluding the unemployed). The working life barometer reports the share of union members based on a survey of employed wage and salary earners.

Collective agreements also cover non-union members in the sectors where at least half of the employees are employed by the employers that are members of the employer organizations. Owing to the extension of the union contracts to non-union workers, the changes in the union density are less important for the bargaining outcomes than the coverage of the union contracts. Currently the union contracts cover roughly 95 per cent of all employees.

Most bargaining rounds have started with negotiations between confederations of employer and employee unions, creating a high degree of co-ordination in the individual union contracts. The union bargains have then been negotiated, based on the wage increases agreed in the central agreement. However, there is no legal basis for the economy-wide wage negotiations. Central organizations cannot negotiate agreements that would be legally binding for the member unions or employer organizations. Even if negotiations at the central level are successful, individual unions may, and often do, opt out from the centrally negotiated agreement.

There has been considerable variation in the degree of centralization between the different bargaining rounds. During the period 1969–2002, there have been seven bargaining rounds (1973, -80, -83, -88, -94, -95, and 2000) when no central bargain was reached and bargaining occurred at the industry level. Also, the share of unions that accept the central bargain has varied from year to year.

It is possible to construct measures that characterize the degree of centralization in the different bargaining rounds. Perhaps the most natural measure is the share of union members covered by the central agreement displayed in Figure 2. The degree of centralization varies across years because in some years no central agreement was reached, and because the number and size of the unions that do not accept the central agreement vary across years.

Naturally, the absence of a central agreement does not imply that there is no co-ordination in the wage agreements. In fact, many industry-level bargaining rounds do lead to somewhat similar bargaining results in different sectors. Typically, one of the larger unions reaches an agreement first and the subsequent agreements do not differ much from the first agreement. In the presence of such wage-wage -linkages between sectors, it is not clear whether industry-level agreements are substantially different from the centralized agreements. For example, Eriksson, Suvanto and Vartia (1990) note that decentralized settlements have not differed much across industries.

**Fig. 2.** Coverage of Central Bargains

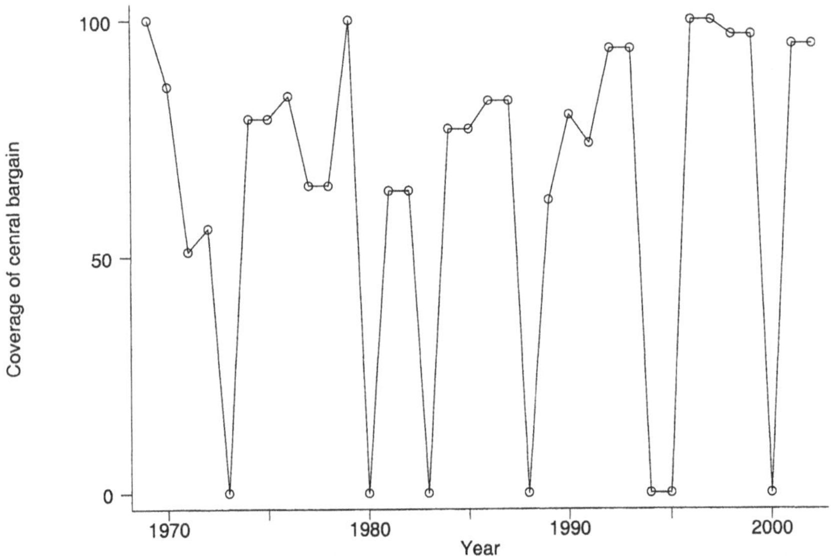


Notes: The figure shows the fraction of the union members covered by the central bargain calculated by Ruutu (1997). We updated the series using data from Marjanen (2002). Zero coverage implies that no central bargains were negotiated and that bargaining occurred at the industry level.

## 2 Empirical Results

The purpose of this paper is to analyse whether centralized agreements lead to smaller nominal wage increases than the industry-level bargains. An intuitive idea behind these calculations is that a centralized bargain is a co-operative solution where the unions internalise the effects of the wage increases on the aggregate inflation and unemployment.

I use data from the period from 1968 to 2002. The choice of period is mainly determined by the availability of data. In the empirical section, I rely heavily on the data collected by Marjanen (2002), which describes in detail each bargaining round between 1968 and 2002.

In this paper I do not derive the wage equation from an explicit theoretical framework. I neither attempt to control for a large group of potential explanatory variables nor adopt some general-to-specific modelling strategy. Instead, I simply compare the nominal wage increases between more and less centralized bargaining rounds. The only control variables included in this comparison are unemployment and inflation rates at the time of wage negotiations. The reasons for parsimonious specifications are obvious. The period 1969–2002 only includes 34 annual observations, so the inclusion of a large number of explanatory variables and the search for a suitable empirical specification are likely to lead to over-fitting of the model. In addition, several of the potential variables that could be included in the wage equation behave almost like linear time trends or are endogenous with respect to the outcomes of the bargaining process.[2]

**Fig. 3.** Bargained Wage Increases and Nominal Wage Growth from 1969 to 2002

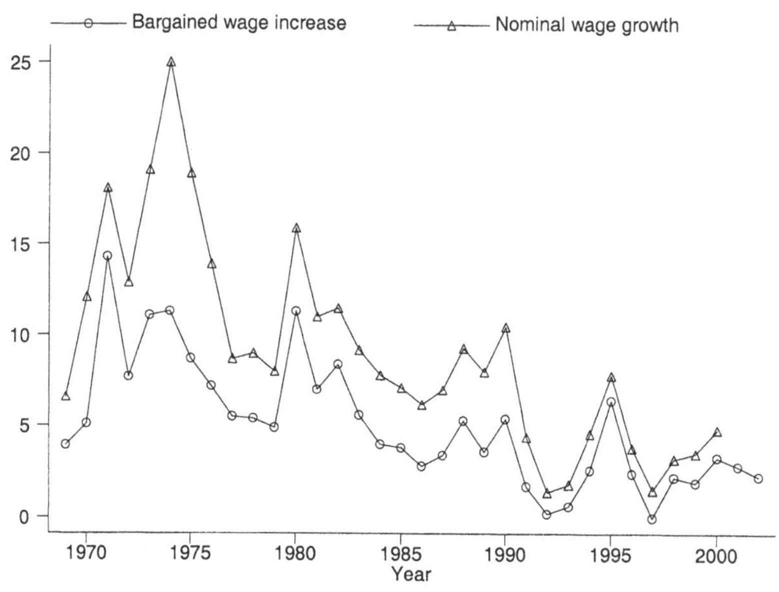


[2] A good example of such a variable is the tax wedge, which has increased almost linearly up to the late 1980s. In the 1990s the development is even more problematic. Taxes increased rapidly in the early 1990s and slowly decreased in the second half of the 1990s, closely tracking the developments in unemployment.

As a first illustration of the data, Figure 3 reports the time series of the average bargained wage increase and the change in nominal wages from 1968 to 2002. The figure clearly shows the decrease in wage inflation from the 1970s to the 1980s, and perhaps another structural shift after the recession of the 1990s. The figure also illustrates the fact that there is a substantial difference between the growth of average wages and the bargaining outcomes. This wage drift has been, on average, slightly below four per cent over the whole period. A decline in wage inflation has also reduced wage drift: while the average drift in the 1970s was over 6 per cent, it has been only 1.5 per cent since 1990.

Figure 4 shows the bargained wage increases separately in 13 major industries. The figure also provides a first glance at the potential effects of centralization by allowing a comparison between the industry-level and the national bargains. If one simply looks at the figure, it appears that the nominal wage increases during the decentralized bargaining rounds (marked with darker dots) are, on average, higher than the wage increases during the national bargaining rounds. However, perhaps unexpectedly, the differences across the sectors do not seem any larger in the industry-level bargains.

**Fig. 4.** Bargained Wage Increases by Year and Industry

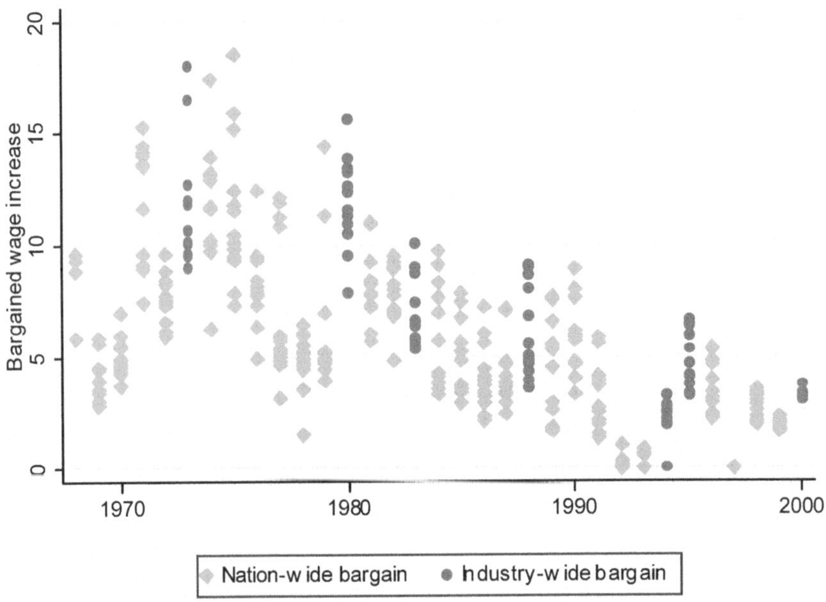


The numbers in Table 1 confirm the visual impression from Figure 4. Table 1 presents the (unweighted) mean, and the average across-industry standard deviation by the bargaining regime. According to the table, the average bargains have been 1.1 percentage points higher in the industry-level bargains than in the national bargains. The difference in the nominal wage growth is slightly smaller,

0.65 percentage points. There is no difference in the across-industry variance between the industry-level and the central bargains. The variance in the wage growth across industries (that includes wage drift) has been even slightly higher in the decentralized bargaining rounds.

**Table 1.** Average Wage Increases and Average Across-Industry Standard Deviation by the Bargaining Regime

| Bargained wage increase | Mean | Average standard deviation |
|---|---|---|
| Decentralized bargaining | 6.61 | 1.57 |
| Centralized bargaining (all) | 5.52 | 1.55 |
| Nominal wage growth | | |
| Decentralized bargaining | 9.69 | 1.83 |
| Centralized bargaining (all) | 9.04 | 2.04 |

**Fig. 5.** Wage Growth and Unemployment

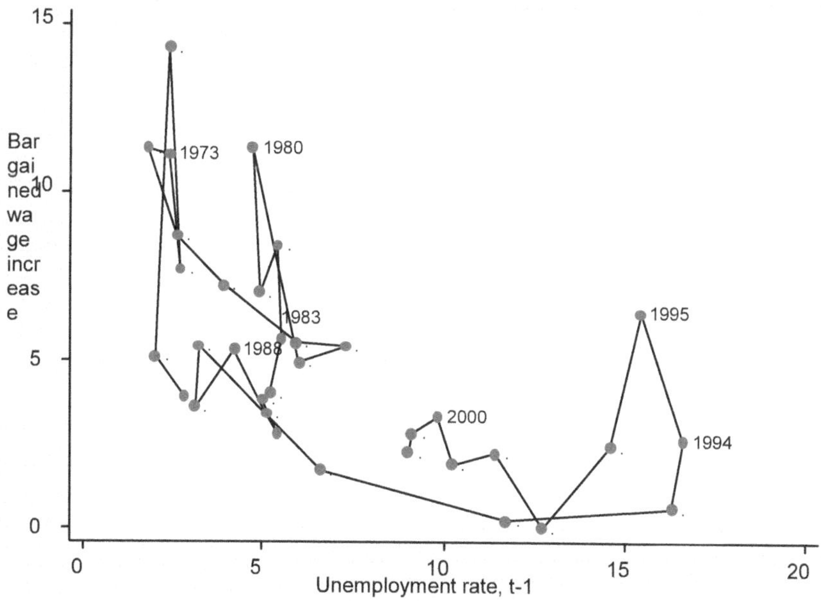


The differences in the wage increases across the bargaining regimes may naturally depend on the macroeconomic conditions at the time of the wage negotiations. Furthermore, if the level of bargaining depends on these conditions, the correlation between centralization and wage growth may be spurious, merely reflecting the fact that centralized bargains occur more often when unemployment is high. Lower wage increases could then depend on higher unemployment and could have nothing to do with the level of bargaining.

Figure 5 tries to shed some light on the issue by plotting the bargained wage increases against the unemployment rate prevailing at the time of the wage negotiations. The figure shows a clear Philips curve relationship between the wage increases and unemployment. Comparing the wage increases in the industry-level bargains of 1973, -80, -83, -88, -94, -95 and 2000 with the centralized bargains reveals that wage growth tends to be higher in industry-level bargaining than in the other years with similar unemployment rates.

The estimates of the wage equation reported in Table 2 also indicate that industry-level bargains lead to higher wage increases, even after controlling for unemployment and inflation. The results are based on a simple regression model where the percentage increases in bargained wages (columns 1–3) and the percentage increases of nominal wages (columns 4–6) are explained by the unemployment rate and the inflation rate at the end of the previous year, and with a dummy for industry-level bargains.

In column 1, only these three variables are included in the equation. According to the results, bargained wage increases are lower when unemployment is high, and higher when inflation is high (although the inflation effect is not significant). Industry-level bargaining leads, on average, to a 3.2 per cent increase in the bargained wage. After a time trend is added to the equation in column 2 the unemployment effect is no longer significant.[3] Also, the effect of the bargaining regime decreases but remains highly significant.

Column 3 stretches the data to its limits (and probably beyond) by adding an interaction between the bargaining regime and the unemployment rates. The purpose is to examine whether the wages are more responsive to the changes in unemployment in the centralized bargaining rounds. The point estimates are consistent with this hypothesis. The effect of a one-percentage point increase in the unemployment rates reduces the bargained wage increases by 0.45 percentage points in the centralized bargains. The coefficient of the interaction term is 0.15, implying that the effect of a one percentage point increase in unemployment is only 0.3 in the decentralized rounds. With a small data set it is hardly surprising that the effect is not significant.

The final three columns in Table 2 repeat the analysis for the nominal wage growth. The estimates are reasonably close to the estimates in the first three columns and indicate that the wage drift does not undo the effects of bargaining regimes. In particular, the effects of industry-level bargaining on nominal wage growth are no lower than the effects on the bargained wage increase.

[3] Large increases in unemployment from the 1970s to the 1980s and the 1990s make adding trends complicated. Now the time trend partly captures the effects of the increase in unemployment.

**Table 2.** Wage Equation

| | Bargained increase | | | Nominal wage growth | | |
|---|---|---|---|---|---|---|
| | (1) | (2) | (3) | (4) | (5) | (6) |
| Unemployment | -0.394<br>(2.88)** | -0.113<br>(0.74) | -0.453<br>(2.75)* | -0.699<br>(3.27)** | -0.261<br>(1.07) | -0.786<br>(3.03)** |
| Inflation | 0.153<br>(1.22) | 0.042<br>(0.36) | 0.138<br>(1.08) | 0.314<br>(1.60) | 0.163<br>(0.89) | 0.294<br>(1.46) |
| Industry-level bargain | 3.248<br>(2.82)** | 2.760<br>(2.68)* | 3.025<br>(2.49)* | 4.113<br>(2.26)* | 3.715<br>(2.28)* | 3.814<br>(2.00) |
| Year | | -0.202<br>(3.06)** | | | -0.328<br>(2.88)** | |
| Industry-level * Unemployment | | | 0.154<br>(0.65) | | | 0.224<br>(0.60) |
| Constant | 4.435<br>(8.73)** | 7.633<br>(6.72)** | 4.416<br>(8.59)** | 8.137<br>(9.83)** | 13.044<br>(7.03)** | 8.091<br>(9.62)** |
| Observations | 34 | 34 | 34 | 32 | 32 | 32 |
| R-squared | 0.46 | 0.59 | 0.47 | 0.53 | 0.64 | 0.53 |

Absolute value of t-statistics in parentheses, * significant at 5%; ** significant at 1%

Table 3 reproduces these results in a form that might be more transparent. It first reports the raw differences in the bargained wage outcomes and the nominal wage growth across the bargaining regimes. It then splits the central bargains into three groups, based on the coverage of the central bargains. In the lower section of the table the regression results from Table 2 are used to adjust the differences across to the bargaining regimes to the differences in inflation and unemployment by calculating the predicted values for the case when inflation and unemployment are on their average level calculated over the whole period.

As shown in Table 3, the average bargained wage increases have been 1.8 percentage points lower during the centralized bargaining rounds. If one looks at the differences between centralized bargains with wide coverage (almost all unions accepting the central agreement) and decentralized bargains the difference is even greater, 4%. Controlling for the differences in unemployment and inflation at the time of wage negotiations does not alter the picture. The difference between central bargains and industry-level bargains is 3.3% and the difference between centralized bargains with wide coverage and decentralized bargains is 4.1%.

**Table 3.** Nominal Wage Increases by the Level of Wage Bargaining

| Raw averages | Number of cases | Bargained wage increase | Nominal wage growth |
|---|---|---|---|
| Decentralized bargaining | 7 | 6.5 | 10.1 |
| Centralized bargaining (all) | 27 | 4.7 | 8.9 |
| Degree of centralization | | | |
| No coverage (decentralized) | 7 | 6.5 | 10.1 |
| Low coverage | 3 | 8.4 | 13.3 |
| Medium coverage | 10 | 6.6 | 12.0 |
| Wide coverage | 14 | 2.5 | 5.1 |
| **Controlling for unemployment and inflation** | **Number of cases** | **Bargained wage increase** | **Nominal wage growth** |
| Decentralized bargaining | 7 | 7.7 | 12.2 |
| Centralized bargaining (all) | 27 | 4.4 | 8.1 |
| Degree of centralization | | | |
| No coverage (decentralized) | 7 | 7.3 | 11.8 |
| Low coverage | 3 | 7.1 | 10.6 |
| Medium coverage | 10 | 5.5 | 9.5 |
| Wide coverage | 14 | 3.2 | 6.7 |

The numbers in the lower section of the table are based on a regression model of bargained wage increase (and nominal wage growth) on lagged unemployment and inflation rates and dummies for the different bargaining regimes. The estimation period is 1969–2002 for the bargained wage increases and 1969–2000 for the nominal wage growth. Data on the degree of centralization, the bargained wage increases and the nominal wage growth are from Marjanen (2002). The unemployment and inflation rates are from the Labour Force Survey and the Consumer Price Index of Statistics Finland. In all estimated equations unemployment had a significant negative effect, and inflation an insignificant positive effect, on both the bargained and the actual wage increases. The dummy variables for different bargaining regimes were highly significant in all estimated equations. Adding a time trend to the equations had only a small effect on the estimated differences across bargaining regimes but lowered the coefficient on the unemployment rate so that it was no longer significant at the 5 % level.

The last column of Table 3 repeats these calculations for the nominal wage growth. According to the results, nominal wage increases have exceeded bargained wage increases by 4 percentage points, on average, but the differences in the nominal wage increases between the centralized and the industry-level bargains are approximately as large as the differences in the bargained wage increases.

To conclude, the results using Finnish data conform with findings from cross-country data according to which centralized bargaining does moderate wage growth and, thereby, will decrease equilibrium unemployment. The prime examples from the 1990s include national bargains in the recession years of 1992 and

1993 when the nominal wages did not increase at all. On the other hand, different rates of economic recoveries across industries led to industry-level bargaining and somewhat higher wage increases in 1994 and 1995.

## 3 Discussion

This paper reports a simple relationship between the degree of centralization and the level of nominal wage increases. Though evidence is based on only 34 data points, it appears that more centralized rounds lead to lower average wage increases. The result seems robust to the inclusion of simple macroeconomic indicators describing the state of the business cycle at the time of wage negotiations. The result holds both for the bargained wage increases and nominal wage growth – wage drift does not undo the wage-moderating effects of centralization.

How should one interpret the results? Perhaps the most obvious explanation is that the centralized rounds, particularly those where government has played an active role, typically involve many qualitative aspects in addition to wage increases. Such non-wage agreements range from changes in religious holidays (1984) and reductions in working hours (1987) to the reallocation of social security contributions paid by the employer and the employee (1992). The employer associations routinely calculate the labour cost effects of such non-wage agreements, but the value of tax cuts or other government policies attempting to sweeten the deal is hard to calculate. Still, accounting for all the effects would probably lessen the difference in the labour cost increases between the centralized and decentralized rounds.

Another interpretation is that industry-level bargaining often takes place only after negotiations between central organizations have failed to reach a nationwide bargain. The offer that was on the table was rejected by at least one of the parties. When the negotiations then started again at the industry level, this rejected offer was used as a benchmark, and the first agreements typically contained somewhat higher wage increases. Other industries then followed the lead, and agreed on similar raises.

No matter what the reason is, the fact remains that, on average, the industry-level bargains have led to higher nominal increases. The key question is whether the level of bargaining had something to do with the difference or whether all of the difference can be explained by other factors. It is possible that the same factors that make a central agreement difficult to achieve also increase wage pressure and lead to higher wage increases in the decentralized rounds. The calculations in this paper only included the level of unemployment and inflation at the time of wage negotiations. In a related paper, Piekkola and Marjanen (2003) also include productivity and profits, noting that both the level and across-industry dispersion of profits has been higher during the industry-level bargaining rounds. None of this has much effect on the difference between wage increases in the industry-level and the national agreements.

## References

Barkbu, B., Nymoen R. and Roed, K. (2001): "Wage coordination and unemployment dynamics in Norway and Sweden", unpublished discussion paper.

Calmfors, L. and Driffil, J. (1988): "Bargaining structure, corporatism and macroeconomic performance" *Economic Policy* 6, 1361.

Ebbinghaus, B. and Visser J. (2000): "Trade unions in Western Europe since 1945". MacMillan.

Eriksson, T., Suvanto A. and Vartia, P. (1990): "Wage formation in Finland" in Lars Calmfors (ed.) "Wage formation and macroeconomic policies in the Nordic countries", SNS Förlag and Oxford University Press.

Flanagan, R. (1999): "Macroeconomic performance and collective bargaining: An international perspective", *Journal of Economic Literature* 37, 1150–1175.

Marjanen, R. (2002): "Palkkaratkaisujen sisältö ja toteutuminen tulopolitiikan aikakaudella", The Research Institute of the Finnish Economy (ETLA) B Series No. 188, Helsinki.

Nickel, S. and Layard, R. (1999): "Labor market institutions and economic performance", chap. 46 in Ashenfelter and Card (eds.) *Handbook of Labor Economics*, vol. 3. Elsevier.

OECD (1997): Employment Outlook. Paris OECD

Piekkola, H. and Marjanen, R. (2003): "Wage Settlements and Wage Drift: New Scene of Income Policy" (in Finnish), The Research Institute of the Finnish Economy (ETLA) B-Series No. 202.

Ruutu, J. (1997): "Suomalainen työehtosopimusjärjestelmä, palkat ja inflaatio". The Research Institute of the Finnish Economy (ETLA) Discussion Papers No. 611

# Finnish Wage Bargaining – Actual Behaviour and Preferences

Kenneth Snellman[1]

The Labour Institute for Economic Research
Helsinki, Finland

## Abstract

Wage changes at the industry level are examined and it is shown that differences in wage increases at the industry level are linked to the level at which bargaining on wages takes place. Non-participation in the centralised agreement has been associated with, on average, almost one per cent higher wage increases than participation. Wage drift has, to some extent, compensated employees in participating industries for lower bargained wage rises. In industry-level bargaining rounds there seem to have been fewer systematic variations both in bargained wages and in wage drift across industries. Survey responses do not indicate economically significant differences in opinions concerning the bargaining process corresponding to the differences in behaviour.

## 1 Introduction

The Finnish labour market is characterised by collective wage bargaining between representatives of employers and employees. Since the design of the bargaining system affects the parties' bargaining position, it indirectly affects both the wage structure inside firms and across firms and industries, the efficiency of allocations, as well as the inflation rate and unemployment. Because of this, the design of the bargaining process is of interest both for the bargaining parties and society as a whole. In this study we will examine the outcomes of the bargaining process in Finland as well as survey responses concerning the bargaining parties' opinions on it.

---

[1] This is part of the research project "Rules of the game in the labour market: Industrial relations, the bargaining system and income policies in the 2000s", financed by the Finnish Work Environment Fund, and carried out jointly by ETLA, The Research Institute of the Finnish Economy and the Labour Institute for Economic Research. I am grateful for helpful comments from Steinar Holden, Jukka Lassila, Hannu Piekkola, Ralf Ramm-Schmidt and Roope Uusitalo on an earlier draft.

The actors in the bargaining process differ in their bargaining power and they also give different weights to aggregate variables such as inflation and unemployment, since differences in, for example, demand elasticities and profitability mean that cost rises hit some firms (or industries) harder than others. A small trade union with a strong bargaining position is more likely to be able to push up the wages of its members without incurring costs that are too high. The small size may also prevent it from initiating higher inflation or equally high wage demands from other trade unions. The preferences of the employers also differ with respect to how important they consider wage dispersion and flexibility. Because of these differences in costs and benefits, players in the bargaining game sometimes have differing opinions on the appropriate level of bargaining. The costs and benefits of choosing a certain way of bargaining vary over time and therefore the preferences of the parties may change temporarily or permanently. In consequence, one can expect mixed and changing preferences about as well as actual behaviour in wage bargaining.

In the following section I provide a short overview of previous research on centralised and industry-level wage bargaining. In the third section I examine the actual behaviour of the parties in different industries in the Finnish economy during the latest decades. The fourth section includes an examination of survey responses concerning the bargaining process. The fifth section concludes.

## 2 The Choice of Bargaining Level

Wage bargaining can take place on a number of different levels in the economy, from being completely centralised at the economy-wide level to bargaining on the level of the individual.[2] Bargaining on different levels can be complements, and the outcome on a higher level can form a basis for further bargaining on lower levels. To what extent the bargaining on lower levels affects wage formation depends on what kinds of restrictions the agreements on higher levels and the institutions set on bargaining processes at lower levels.

If firms are not bound by collective agreements in wage setting, they set wages to maximise their profit. However, they do this under certain restrictions regarding the reactions of individual employees, which in the principal-agent literature are called the participation and the incentive compatibility constraints. The participation constraint requires that the pay offered should be high enough for the employee to hold on to the job. The incentive compatibility constraint implies that the payment scheme should induce the employee to do what is in the interests of the firm. The employee should thus put in the optimal amount of effort and allocate it correctly. When there is a continuum of effort levels, the incentive compatibility gives a set of combinations of the levels of effort and the lowest level of pay required to attain a certain level of effort from the employee.

[2] The wage changes may even be bargained on a European level, which means that the outcome is largely exogenous to a small economy.

Along with immediate pecuniary rewards employees may be concerned with their career. Career concerns produce additional incentives that affect the behaviour (Fama 1980, Holmström 1999). By working hard, the employee can get a better job in another firm (under the condition that his performance on the current job is observable to other employers), be promoted inside the firm (if there are appropriate jobs in the firm) or get a pay rise in his current job. These long-run incentives may often be more important than short-run rewards. By changing the pay in jobs on the career ladder, the firm also changes the employees' incentives. In consequence, in a firm with more than one job these incentives have to be taken into account when the pay is being set. In particular, a firm may raise the employees' productivity if it succeeds in getting them to aim at being promoted. This means that it is likely to be profitable to give entrants relatively low pay but higher pay and higher positions to older employees who have performed well. See Lazear (1995, 1998) as well as Gibbons and Waldman (1999) for overviews of how firms can use promotions to motivate employees.

Wage setting is also affected by employees' actions. Even in a firm without unions the owners may consider it best to give a share of high profits to employees to keep them satisfied. Such rent sharing can raise the pay of employees in profitable firms by several percentage points (Snellman 2002). Similarly, efficiency wage theories claim that it may be profitable for a firm, regardless of its profit level, to pay employees more than the market wage to motivate them, if productivity is imperfectly observable.

How collective bargaining affects wage formation depends on the bargaining positions and the level at which bargaining takes place. In Finland there is centralised bargaining on the economy-wide level, although the outcome is not strictly binding at the industry level. Bargaining on the industry level implies that the union can set its demands, taking the profitability of the industry into account. When bargaining takes place at the economy-wide level, or there is at least coordination at that level, the state of the economy as a whole and the effects on it are more likely to be considered, as has been emphasised by Holden and Raaum (1991). According to a number of empirical studies, inflation and unemployment in the economy are lower with centralised bargaining than with industry-level bargaining (Iversen, Pontusson and Soskice 2000, Iversen 1999, Calmfors and Driffil 1988). A study of Holden (1989) also indicates that central wage settlements can have persistent effects on wage formation that are not compensated by wage drift. See also Calmfors (1990) for a number of studies of the interaction between centralised wage settlements and wage drift. Centralised wage bargaining may thus internalise the effects on inflation and unemployment of the agreements.[3]

The analysis of the wage bargaining process builds on both microeconomics and macroeconomics. Each party maximises its payoff given the behaviour of other parties. Given the design of the wage bargaining system, there will be some expected payoffs for the parties. The parties determine their preferences, based on

[3] Coordinated bargaining at lower levels may clearly function as a substitute for centralised bargaining in internalising such effects. However, to simplify the analysis all potential coordination will be disregarded in this study.

these expectations, regarding at what level to bargain on wages. The wage bargaining process can thus be seen as a repeated two-stage game. For a given state of the world there is a Nash equilibrium in which no party has any interest to deviate. However, this does not mean that the game is stable over time, because the production processes, surpluses and bargaining power change over time.

Centralised bargaining may reduce wage dispersion. Teulings and Hartog (1998) have argued that more centralisation makes the income distribution more equal. According to them the origin of this effect is the positive effect of centralised bargaining on the wages of those with a weak bargaining position. However, this may also mean that centralised bargaining makes it difficult for wages to respond to changes in demand and supply.

Interests can also differ between employees within an industry. Unions, especially those of wage earners, have usually pressed for lower pay differentials. The trade unions' aim to compress wage differentials has been opposed by employers, partly because such wage compression has been very costly for firms employing low-wage employees and partly because firms have regarded a compression of the pay structure damaging for the incentives (Hibbs and Locking 2000, Marjanen 2002). If the lowest wages are raised, employers may strive to maintain incentives and raise the pay of high-wage employees, which implies wage drift. To limit the possibilities for wage drift, unions representing low-income earners may respond by demanding higher pay rises than would be in accordance with as high pay rises for everyone and a low inflation in the economy. Nevertheless, raising the pay of certain employees may increase profitability (Muysken and van Veen 1996). The firm is, therefore, likely to respond by raising the rewards of being promoted or getting pay rises on the initiative of the management, i.e. by restoring some of the wage differentials.

Differences in bargaining positions can make it difficult to reach an agreement that is acceptable to both parties in all industries. Players deviate from the coalition that is participating in centralised bargaining if it is in their interest. If those who would prefer centralised bargaining, given that other industries also participate, choose not to participate due to the deviations of others, there will be industry-level bargaining in that year. This is sometimes foreseen even before the negotiations start. When many others (are expected to) deviate there may be no point in attempting to hold pay rises down, because it means too large pay losses relative to the average pay rises in the economy.

To avoid the outcome that the unions always deviate from the centralised solution, there has to be some benefit from not deviating. In Holden and Raaum's study (1991) there is a multiperiod game and the benefit of participating in one period is that centralised bargaining that benefits everyone can also take place in the next period. Although for Finland there is some anecdotal evidence in Marjanen (2002) and Kahri (2001) that deviations have made it more difficult to bargain centrally and to hold wage changes at a sustainable level in the coming years, the effect is not very clear or immediate. In this study we implicitly assume, instead, that there are some benefits regarding bargaining costs from participating in the centralised solution, since it offers a "standardised" agreement. This reduces the negotiation costs of individual unions that are participating. The parties can also make the centralised agreement conditional on the requirement that a high enough share of the labour market participates in it. This is, in fact, a method that the parties in the Finnish labour market have used since the early 1990s to keep the participation rate in the centralised agreements high.

## 3 Actual Behaviour in Past Decades

In Finland wage bargaining has mostly been centralised since 1968 with a few interruptions for industry-level bargaining rounds. In the years with centralised bargaining the confederations of both employees and employers have made agreements on pay and other central issues that should be followed in the industry-level agreements. Sometimes the government has also participated by promising, for example, tax reductions or social reforms that have benefited the employees. Although there is also industry-level bargaining in the years of centralised bargaining, the central agreement has strongly influenced the contents of most agreements on the industry level. However, even in years with centralised bargaining some industries have chosen to stay outside the central agreement and signed agreements on pay changes that are not in accordance with the central agreement. Sometimes the reason for staying outside the centralised agreement has been disagreements concerning qualitative issues in the industry. Disagreements on qualitative issues have sometimes also been an important explanation to the occurrence of industry level bargaining rounds.

The usefulness of the Finnish collective bargaining system has been questioned in recent years and some, especially among the employers' representatives, have advocated a shift to more decentralised bargaining. To some extent there has also been a shift towards agreements on the local level. The local agreements have often been concerned with working conditions or working hours but sometimes also with the design of performance-related pay schemes or other issues concerning compensation. However, the collective agreements still set the limits of what can be agreed locally.

In this study we will concentrate on deviations and temporary changes rather than attempt to find a stable long-run equilibrium for the bargaining process. The different bargaining levels are not seen as mutually exclusive. Rather, they are seen as complementing parts in the development of the changing wage structure. Centralised bargaining in one year can be followed by industry-level bargaining in the next, with a return to centralisation in the following year. Industry-level bargaining then functions as a safety valve that enables a continuation of centralised bargaining.

The small number of observations means that a number of variables, which might strongly have influenced the bargaining processes and wage formation during the period, have to be disregarded. For example, the depression at the beginning of the 1990s, the slowdown of inflation, the joining of the EMU and the increasing international competition might all have influenced the bargaining process and the its outcomes. However, a division of the period into different subperiods would have reduced the number of observations to a number far below what is necessary for any observed difference of reasonable size to be significantly different from zero. Neither can all the institutional characteristics of the bargaining rounds be taken into account. There are certainly, for example, coordination mechanisms between industries other than centralised bargaining. As this study is the first one that attempts to examine differences across industries due to differences in bargaining levels, it seems acceptable to leave these issues to further studies in the future. However, conclusions should be drawn with the limitations in mind.

Marjanen (2002) provides an extensive overview of the development of wage bargaining in Finland in the years 1968–2002 and it has been further explored by Piekkola and Marjanen (2003). Uusitalo in this publication shows that during that period pay rises in years with centralised bargaining have been lower on average than in years when the pay rises were agreed on in industry-level bargaining rounds. According to Uusitalo, the differences in nominal average wage growth become even greater when differences between the years in unemployment and inflation are controlled for than when they are not. In their study, rather similar differences apply for the average bargained wage increase. The unions in Finland have, in general, been striving for lower pay differences and higher wage increases for persons with low pay (Marjanen 2002). This policy was particularly influential in the 1970s.

Bargaining on the industry level seems to have been inevitable in some years (Marjanen 2002). Occasionally, this seems to have been a consequence of industry-specific issues, e.g. working time and compensation for shift work in industries with much shift work. However, at least sometimes industry-level bargaining has rather been a result of differences in bargaining positions across industries. The dispersion of pay changes in years with centralised bargaining and years with industry-level bargaining is displayed in Tables 1 and 2.[4]

These tables show that there are rather small differences in the dispersion of wage increases between years with centralised and industry-level bargaining. This is remarkable, since the standard deviation, at least of the bargained wage changes, should be close to zero if there is the same proportional pay rise in all industries. Neither Uusitalo in this book finds nominal wage growth dispersion between industries to increase in the periods of industry-level bargaining. One reason for the high dispersion of wage increases in years with centralised bargaining may be that some industries have occasionally deviated from the centralised agreement. When only the years with high coverage are included in the calculation, the average pay rises and standard deviations fall, which is what can be expected, if non-participation in the centralised agreement is associated with differences in out-

[4] Marjanen (2002), on which the tables are based, lists wage changes only for those industries in which there is one corresponding union. A number of industries for which the boundaries of the unions do not correspond to those of the industry boundaries are, therefore, excluded. The industries included in this comparison are the graphic, clothing, textile, metal, sawmill and wood board, paper, food, shoe and leather, building construction, chemists', trade, hotel and restaurant, banking, and insurance industries. The standard deviation of the wage rises is calculated on the basis of the unweighted average of the wage changes in the industries according to Marjanen.

comes. Although the differences are small, the table gives some support to the claim that low participation in the centralised agreement is associated with larger differences in the wage changes.

**Table 1.** Unweighted Average Wage Rises (realised and bargained) and Wage Drift as Well as Standard Deviations for 14 Industries 1969–2000.

| Category of bargaining round | Total pay rise | | Bargained pay rise | | Wage drift | |
|---|---|---|---|---|---|---|
| | Mean | S.d. | Mean | S.d. | Mean | S.d. |
| Centralised | 8.8 | 2.0 | 5.4 | 1.6 | 3.4 | 1.8 |
| Centralised with high coverage | 8.0 | 1.8 | 4.8 | 1.4 | 3.2 | 1.6 |
| Centralised with very high coverage | 7.6 | 1.9 | 4.4 | 1.3 | 3.2 | 1.6 |
| Industry level | 9.6 | 2.0 | 6.7 | 1.7 | 2.9 | 1.6 |

The pay changes and the classification of bargaining rounds are taken from Marjanen (2002).

**Table 2.** Unweighted Average Wage Rises (realised and bargained) and Wage Drift as Well as Standard Deviations for 8 Manufacturing Industries in the Period 1969–2000.

| Category of bargaining round | Total pay rise | | Bargained pay rise | | Wage drift | |
|---|---|---|---|---|---|---|
| | Mean | S.d. | Mean | S.d. | Mean | S.d. |
| Centralised | 8.7 | 1.4 | 5.1 | 1.0 | 3.6 | 1.3 |
| Centralised with high coverage | 7.9 | 1.2 | 4.5 | 0.9 | 3.4 | 1.2 |
| Centralised with very high coverage | 7.5 | 1.2 | 4.1 | 0.9 | 3.4 | 1.2 |
| Industry level | 9.8 | 1.5 | 6.8 | 1.2 | 3.1 | 1.4 |

The pay changes and the classification of bargaining rounds are taken from Marjanen (2002).

Another source of variation in years with centralised bargaining rounds is solidaristic wage policies and the fact that agreements have often been made in absolute rather than proportional terms, leading to very high pay rises in low-wage industries when wage changes are measured as a percentage of pay. In addition, a part of the pay rises has been directed to specific groups such as women, low-paid workers or shift workers. That these issues have been important for the outcomes in pay changes is supported by the descriptions in Marjanen (2002) and Piekkola and Marjanen (2003). Another issue that might also have contributed to differences in wage changes across industries is the disappearance of low-wage jobs due to the high increases in wage costs.

**Table 3.** Deviations from Centralised Bargaining Agreements in the Period 1969–2002.[5]

| Year | Deviating industries | Reasons | Effects on wages |
|---|---|---|---|
| 1969–70 | None of importance | – | – |
| 1971 | Metal and construction inter alia | Demands for higher pay and schedule wages | Higher pay and schedule wages |
| 1972 | None of importance | – | – |
| 1973 | All | Disagreement on wages and taxes between unions, employers, and state | – |
| 1974–75 | None of importance | – | – |
| 1976 | Food, construction, hotel & restaurant | Disagreements on wage changes | – |
| 1977–79 | None of importance | – | – |
| 1980 | All | Disagreements on wage changes | |
| 1981–82 | Metal, food and graphic inter alia | Differences in preceding bargaining rounds | Higher in these industries |
| 1983 | All | Disagreements on wages, working hours and qualitative issues | – |
| 1984–85 | None of importance | – | – |
| 1986–87 | Food and building construction inter alia | Differing opinions of unions and employers | – |
| 1988 | All | Industry-specific issues | – |
| 1989 | Paper, sawmilling, food, construction, trade, hotel & restaurant | Disagreements on wage changes | Much higher pay rises in these industries, partly offset by index based compensations to others |
| 1990 | Paper, sawmilling, food, textile, clothing, banking, hotel & restaurant, chemists | Disagreements on wage changes | Much higher in these industries, partly offset by index based compensations to others |
| 1991 | Paper, sawmilling, food, banking, hotel & restaurant, chemists inter alia | Disagreements on wage changes | Slightly higher wage rises |
| 1992–93 | Food and building construction | Disagreements on wage changes | Small |
| 1994 | All | Industry differences in capability to pay | Some rises already in 1993, rises mostly in manufacturing |
| 1995 | All | Industry differences in capability to pay | Highest in manufacturing |
| 1996–97 | None of importance | – | – |
| 1998–99 | Some not examined here | – | – |
| 2000 | All | Qualitative issues | – |
| 2001–02 | Food and insurance | – | – |

[5] In the tables the sawmilling industry also includes the wood board industry.

A closer examination of the differences in wage changes across industries and types of bargaining rounds necessitates an investigation of the wage bargaining outcomes of the different industries. Below follows an investigation of the effects on the industry level. In many years with centralised bargaining some industries have not been able to come to an agreement within the boundaries set by the central agreement. The employers' federation and the union in these industries have, instead, agreed on a different contract, which in some respects has differed from what was agreed on among the others. Table 3 lists years and industries in which such deviations have occurred, based on Marjanen (2002). The reasons for and consequences of deviations from centralised bargaining are also listed if they are given by Marjanen.

Two issues that may explain the differences in behaviour are capital intensity and the importance of international competition. An important difference among the capital-intensive industries is that the food industry, as opposed to the export industries, was rather protected from foreign competition during a significant number of years. From Table 3 one easily sees that the food industry has rather infrequently participated in centralised bargaining. The Finnish Food Workers' Union was also known for being rather radical and for not accepting what was agreed

**Table 4.** Average Pay Rises 1969–2000 in Some Industries by Type of Bargaining Round and Differences to the Average Rise for All Industries.

| Industry / Type of bargaining round (Observations) | Total pay rise | | Bargained pay rise | | Wage drift | |
|---|---|---|---|---|---|---|
| | Mean | Differ. | Mean | Differ. | Mean | Differ. |
| Food | | | | | | |
| Centralised (15) | 9.5 | -0.2 | 5.7 | 0.3 | 3.8 | -0.5 |
| Deviating (10) | 8.0 | 0.4 | 4.8 | 0.8 | 3.2 | -0.3 |
| Industry-level (7) | 10.4 | 0.3 | 6.3 | -0.2 | 4.1 | 0.5 |
| Paper | | | | | | |
| Centralised (22) | 9.5 | 0.5 | 5.0 | 0.0 | 4.5 | 0.5 |
| Deviating (3) | 7.6 | -0.1 | 3.6 | 0.0 | 4.0 | -0.1 |
| Industry-level (7) | 10.2 | 0.1 | 6.3 | -0.2 | 3.9 | 0.3 |
| Sawmilling | | | | | | |
| Centralised (22) | 9.2 | 0.2 | 4.9 | -0.1 | 4.3 | 0.2 |
| Deviating (3) | 8.6 | 0.9 | 4.2 | 0.7 | 4.3 | 0.3 |
| Industry-level (7) | 10.4 | 0.3 | 6.5 | 0.0 | 3.9 | 0.3 |
| Building constr. | | | | | | |
| Centralised (19) | 9.1 | -0.1 | 3.9 | -1.3 | 5.2 | 1.2 |
| Deviating (6) | 4.5 | -1.9 | 2.2 | -0.7 | 2.2 | -1.2 |
| Industry-level (7) | 9.3 | -0.8 | 5.2 | -1.3 | 4.1 | 0.5 |
| Hotel & restaurant | | | | | | |
| Centralised (21) | 9.8 | 1.0 | 7.0 | 2.0 | 2.8 | -1.1 |
| Deviating (4) | 9.9 | 0.7 | 7.4 | 3.0 | 2.5 | -2.2 |
| Industry-level (7) | 9.1 | -1.0 | 7.1 | 0.6 | 2.0 | -1.6 |

centrally. Moreover, the protected home market may have allowed pay rises that were higher than what had been agreed on centrally. The forest industries have also deviated a number of times and have sometimes been the driving forces accomplishing industry-level bargaining rounds. One can also note that after the beginning of the 1990s all the largest industries have participated in the central agreements that have taken place, which reflects the fact that it has been a condition for them to be approved.

Table 4 lists the average wage changes in industries that have chosen not to participate in a centralised agreement at least three times.[6] Unions have often been the party forcing a deviation from the centralised agreement. The differences in pay rises relative to the average of all employees show that there have been higher payoffs in agreed wages from deviating from centralised bargaining than from bargaining rounds with only industry-level bargaining. The difference in wage changes has, on average, been somewhat less than one percentage point in favour

**Table 5.** Average Pay Rises in the Year After the Bargaining Round in Some Industries by Type of Bargaining Round and the Differences from the Average for All Industries.

| Industry / Type of bargaining round (Observations) | Total pay rise | | Bargained pay rise | | Wage drift | |
|---|---|---|---|---|---|---|
| | Mean | Differ. | Mean | Differ. | Mean | Differ. |
| Food | | | | | | |
| Centralised (15) | 10.1 | -0.2 | 6.1 | 0.1 | 4.0 | -0.3 |
| Deviating (10) | 7.1 | 0.3 | 4.7 | 0.9 | 2.4 | -0.6 |
| Industry-level (7) | 11.2 | 0.6 | 5.9 | 0.1 | 5.3 | 0.5 |
| Paper | | | | | | |
| Centralised (22) | 9.7 | 0.3 | 5.4 | -0.1 | 4.3 | 0.4 |
| Deviating (3) | 5.8 | 0.3 | 2.7 | 0.3 | 3.1 | 0.1 |
| Industry-level (7) | 11.2 | 0.6 | 5.8 | 0.0 | 5.4 | 0.6 |
| Sawmilling | | | | | | |
| Centralised (22) | 9.6 | 0.2 | 5.4 | -0.1 | 4.2 | 0.4 |
| Deviating (3) | 5.7 | 0.3 | 2.4 | 0.0 | 3.3 | 0.3 |
| Industry-level (7) | 10.6 | 0.0 | 6.2 | 0.4 | 4.4 | -0.4 |
| Building constr. | | | | | | |
| Centralised (19) | 8.6 | -0.4 | 4.3 | -1.0 | 4.3 | 0.6 |
| Deviating (6) | 4.6 | -2.4 | 2.4 | -1.4 | 2.1 | -1.0 |
| Industry-level (7) | 10.6 | 0.0 | 4.2 | -1.6 | 6.5 | 1.7 |
| Hotel & restaurant | | | | | | |
| Centralised (21) | 9.9 | 0.5 | 7.4 | 1.9 | 2.5 | -1.4 |
| Deviating (4) | 6.1 | -0.2 | 4.5 | 1.3 | 1.6 | -1.4 |
| Industry-level (7) | 11.3 | 0.8 | 7.9 | 2.2 | 3.4 | -1.4 |

[6] See Table 3 for information on when industries have not participated in centralised bargaining.

of opting out from centralised wage agreements.[7] A test of the significance of the difference also shows that the largest differences are significantly different from zero, although there are rather few observations. The case is strengthened by the fact that similar tendencies can be observed for several industries.

However, much of the gain from higher agreed wage increases seems to have been eroded by lower wage drift. To some extent, this may be a result of extraordinarily low wage drift in the years of the depression at the beginning of the 1990s. The high pay increases in the hotel and restaurant industry is probably a consequence of solidaristic wage policies and low pay in the industry.

A part of the pay changes may take place so late that they can be observed only in the pay of the following year.[8] To investigate this and to test for other significant lagged effects of the bargaining level, the pay changes for the year after the respective bargaining round were examined. The averages are listed in Table 5 but there are no significant and systematic differences in the pay changes that would correct for the changes in the preceding year.

The results support the claim that different ways of bargaining lead to different outcomes. However, the effects are mostly concentrated on the collectively bargained changes in pay. The wage drift compensates to some extent for differences in bargained wage increases. However, it is difficult to determine to what extent the results contradict or support earlier studies that claim that wage drift counterbalances differences in agreed wage changes.

## 4 Opinions on Bargaining and Their Relation to Earlier Behaviour

It is interesting to relate these findings to the opinions of the representatives of employers and employees about the bargaining system, including the preferred level of bargaining and structure of wage increases, expressed in a recent survey (Alho et al. 2003, Pekkarinen and Alho in this publication). The survey was directed at the CEOs, the shop stewards of wage earners, salaried employees and professionals as well as to the central organisations of employers and employees. In this section the opinions expressed in the responses and their relation to the actual behaviour described in the previous section are examined.

Under the condition that preferences are sufficiently stable, the preferred level of bargaining of industries according to the enquiry can be expected to reflect the differences observed in the past behaviour. Thus, opinions in favour of industry-level bargaining should be more common in industries that have stayed more frequently outside centralised bargaining. Similarly, it could be expected that basing

[7] The measures taken to reach these results such as strikes are disregarded in this study because of a lack of data. Sometimes the costs may have been larger than the benefit of higher pay.

[8] Postponing pay rises was a way of reaching agreements when representatives of employers and employees disagreed on the appropriate size of the change in pay. Postponed pay rises made it more difficult to compare agreements of different unions and allowed for "hiding" pay rises in the end of the contract periods (Kahri 2001, Marjanen 2002).

**Table 6.** The Average Ranking (1 is the highest and 5 is the lowest) of Bargaining Levels Made by Different Categories of Respondents as Averaged Over All Industries, the Employees' and Employers' Central Organisations, as Well as Separately in a Number of Industries.[9]

| Industry | Bargaining level | | | | | |
|---|---|---|---|---|---|---|
| Respondent category | Individual | Firm | Industry | Economy | Europe | N |
| All | | | | | | |
| CEO | 2.82 | 2.08 | 2.62 | 2.70 | 4.76 | 600 |
| Wage earners | 3.91 | 3.06 | 1.75 | 2.16 | 4.06 | 270 |
| Sal. employees | 3.41 | 2.77 | 1.99 | 2.36 | 4.44 | 283 |
| Professionals | 2.60 | 2.24 | 2.62 | 2.84 | 4.68 | 206 |
| Organisations | 3.33 | 2.52 | 2.09 | 2.33 | 4.71 | 147 |
| Services | | | | | | |
| CEO | 2.85 | 2.11 | 2.57 | 2.64 | 4.84 | 188 |
| Wage earners | 3.45 | 3.00 | 1.98 | 2.37 | 4.06 | 62 |
| Sal. employees | 3.27 | 2.66 | 1.93 | 2.56 | 4.54 | 71 |
| Professionals | 2.57 | 2.09 | 2.55 | 2.87 | 4.89 | 47 |
| Food | | | | | | |
| CEO | 3.04 | 2.15 | 2.78 | 2.70 | 4.33 | 27 |
| Wage earners | 4.38 | 2.62 | 1.62 | 2.38 | 3.88 | 16 |
| Sal. employees | 3.46 | 3.00 | 1.69 | 2.15 | 4.38 | 13 |
| Professionals | 1.64 | 2.18 | 3.18 | 3.18 | 4.82 | 11 |
| Forest | | | | | | |
| CEO | 2.95 | 1.55 | 2.68 | 2.92 | 4.89 | 38 |
| Wage earners | 4.36 | 3.05 | 1.41 | 2.09 | 4.09 | 22 |
| Sal. employees | 3.56 | 2.60 | 2.08 | 2.04 | 4.72 | 25 |
| Professionals | 2.42 | 2.00 | 2.67 | 3.25 | 4.67 | 12 |
| Mach. & equip. | | | | | | |
| CEO | 2.89 | 2.24 | 2.51 | 2.64 | 4.64 | 45 |
| Wage earners | 4.00 | 3.37 | 1.59 | 1.96 | 4.07 | 27 |
| Sal. employees | 3.42 | 2.84 | 1.89 | 2.00 | 4.84 | 19 |
| Professionals | 2.55 | 2.27 | 3.18 | 3.00 | 4.00 | 11 |

Based on responses to question 1B in Alho et al. (2003).

[9] There were very few responses from firms in the hotel and restaurant industry and the statistics for this industry are, therefore, not displayed. Services include all observations from firms that are members of the Employers´ Federation of Service Industries (as opposed to The Confederation of Finnish Industry and Employers). The forest industry includes the pulp, paper and wood industries.

pay rises on productivity changes in the industry is more popular in those industries. However, it can also be claimed that bargaining on the industry level and on an economy-wide level are rather close to each other and complement each other, since they have been alternating in recent decades. The institutions have allowed both bargaining levels, and the inflexibility of the centralised agreements to take industry-specific issues into account has been eased by the possibility to opt out from the centralised agreement. The centralised agreements have offered a natural alternative for those parties who have thought that they can withstand any industry-specific problem, including deterioration in the suitability of the wage level, for another year or two.

The preferences of the different parties inside firms may differ, depending on the experienced payoffs of the different forms of bargaining. As can be seen in Table 6 when compared to firm-level bargaining both centralised and industry-level bargaining are somewhat more popular among employees than among employers according to their answers to question B1 in the enquiry.[10] However, neither do employers advocate full decentralisation. One piece of evidence for this is that employers are not willing to abstain from the industrial peace on the firm level (see alternative E in Table 9). Somewhat surprisingly, industry-level bargaining is more popular in relation to centralised bargaining among wage earners. One explanation could be that employees have received higher wage rises when the industry has not participated in central agreements. However, in Table 6 one can see that the differences in preferences across industries with different bargaining records are small. This also applies to the food industry and other industries in which deviations have been frequent.

**Table 7.** Spearman's Rank Correlation for the CEOs' Ranking of the Attractiveness of the Bargaining Levels Displayed in Table 6 (600 observations).

| Bargaining level | Individual | Firm | Industry | Economy |
|---|---|---|---|---|
| Firm | 0.3141* | | | |
| Industry | -0.6096* | -0.3549* | | |
| Economy | -0.6716* | -0.5820* | 0.1585* | |
| Europe | -0.2847* | -0.3578* | -0.0202 | 0.1046* |

Significance at the 95% level is denoted by *.

Table 7 confirms that the employers see industry-level and centralised bargaining as rather close to each other. However, the correlation in the rankings of industry-level and centralised bargaining are negative for wage earners. One reason for this might be that wage earners more often rank either one as their most preferred bargaining level. The correlation is -0.2003* for wage earners, 0.1158 for salaried employees, 0.1724* for professionals, and 0.1917* in the answers

[10] The numbers of observations differ somewhat from those in Alho et al. and from table to table in this study, because not all respondents answered all the questions and Alho et al. deleted a number of responses in which the answers to some questions were missing.

from the central organisations of employees and employers. The employees' preferences seem to become more similar to those of the employers, the higher one goes in the hierarchy. This is in accordance with other results presented in Alho et al. (2003).

**Table 8.** The Average Ranking of the Criteria for Wage Rises Made by Different Categories of Respondents.[11]

| Industry | Criterion for wage rise | | | | | |
|---|---|---|---|---|---|---|
| Respondent category | A | B | C | D | E | N |
| All | | | | | | |
| CEO | 4.28 | 2.62 | 1.96 | 2.08 | 4.03 | 607 |
| Wage earners | 3.41 | 1.98 | 2.09 | 3.33 | 4.17 | 246 |
| Sal. employees | 3.82 | 1.97 | 2.08 | 2.97 | 4.15 | 272 |
| Professionals | 4.16 | 2.37 | 2.03 | 2.38 | 4.07 | 192 |
| Services | | | | | | |
| CEO | 4.35 | 2.50 | 2.03 | 2.21 | 3.89 | 191 |
| Wage earners | 3.28 | 1.92 | 2.51 | 3.25 | 4.03 | 61 |
| Sal. employees | 3.96 | 1.99 | 2.29 | 2.72 | 4.04 | 69 |
| Professionals | 4.27 | 2.30 | 1.98 | 2.52 | 3.89 | 44 |
| Food | | | | | | |
| CEO | 4.07 | 2.33 | 1.81 | 2.48 | 4.30 | 27 |
| Wage earners | 3.19 | 2.25 | 1.94 | 3.44 | 4.12 | 16 |
| Sal. employees | 3.46 | 1.77 | 2.00 | 3.38 | 4.31 | 13 |
| Professionals | 4.55 | 2.73 | 2.00 | 1.64 | 4.01 | 11 |
| Forest | | | | | | |
| CEO | 4.00 | 2.78 | 1.90 | 1.70 | 4.62 | 40 |
| Wage earners | 3.65 | 2.00 | 1.80 | 3.45 | 4.10 | 20 |
| Sal. employees | 4.04 | 2.07 | 1.78 | 2.63 | 4.48 | 27 |
| Professionals | 4.23 | 2.92 | 1.54 | 2.23 | 4.08 | 13 |
| Machinery and eq. | | | | | | |
| CEO | 4.28 | 2.68 | 1.86 | 2.11 | 4.07 | 44 |
| Wage earners | 3.38 | 2.29 | 1.75 | 3.29 | 4.29 | 24 |
| Sal. employees | 3.50 | 1.75 | 2.00 | 3.50 | 4.25 | 20 |
| Professionals | 4.00 | 2.20 | 2.10 | 2.70 | 4.00 | 11 |

[11] Alternative A represents "Pay rise should be the same in Finland as elsewhere in the Euro area", B "Pay should be raised according to the capability of the economy to pay wages, i.e. should follow the productivity development of the whole economy (adding the inflation target)", C "Pay should be raised according to the productivity rise of work in the industry (adding the inflation target)", D "Pay should be raised firm-wise according to how much the profitability of the firm allows" and E "Pay rise should be connected to the unemployment situation".

In order to analyse similarities in preferences and the possibilities of reaching agreements on the firm level more explicitly one can examine the rank correlation between the ranking of industry-level and centralised bargaining for employer and employee representatives in the same firms. Inside firms the correlation of rankings seems to be very weak. Rather, opinions are randomly distributed between firms. Also, when one examines how the preferences are related to the pay types (piece rate, time rate and different types of bonuses) the correlations seem to be weak. An examination of the correlation inside firms shows no evidence of any differences in correlation in rankings between industries and results indicate that there are few common opinions inside firms. In consequence, a change in the bargaining system is likely to meet resistance from some party in a firm. The low correlation between respondents in the same firms also points towards the notion that similarities in preferences across categories are a consequence of common interests rather than communication inside firms.

One could imagine a number of different criteria for wage rises. The actors are more likely to arrive at an agreement easily, if their opinions on these criteria are more similar. Question B3 in the questionnaire of Alho et al. (2003) asked the respondents to rank 5 different criteria according to how appropriate they are for determining wage rises in the agreements; see footnote 11. The responses are also likely to reflect the respondents' opinions concerning bargaining levels. According to the results in displayed in Table 8 and Alho et al. employers in general had a more negative attitude to alternatives A and B as well as a more positive attitude to D than employees.

Table 8 shows that C, the productivity increase in the industry, is, in general, the most popular criterion in all these industries. However, the differences between industries are small, although C is somewhat more popular in the food and forest industries, which have sometimes deviated in centralised bargaining rounds. It is also worth pointing out that the employers in the food industry are less positive to binding the wage rises to the profitability of the firms. Also note that wage earners in the service industries are less positive towards wage rises based on productivity change in the industry (alternative C) than wage earners in general, which is probably a consequence of lower productivity growth in the service sector.

The experiences in the different industries may also be reflected in the preferences concerning what an agreement concerning wages should include. Traditionally, it has included a general pay rise (minimum absolute and/or proportional rise) and changes in schedule wages, the minimum pay in different industries and occupations. For an examination of the differences in preferences the respondents were asked to rank five alternative ways of agreeing on pay changes, which are denoted A, B, C, D and E here; see footnote 12. The average rankings made by the respondents are displayed in Table 9.

According to Table 9, wage earners are very satisfied with the current situation while many employers and representatives of professionals would prefer agreements that are less binding with regard to the pay rises of individual employees (alternatives D and C). As can be seen in the table there seem to be rather small differences across industries.

**Table 9.** The Average Ranking of Bargaining Types Made by Different Categories of Respondents.[12]

| Industry | Bargaining type | | | | | |
|---|---|---|---|---|---|---|
| Respondent category | A | B | C | D | E | N |
| All | | | | | | |
| CEO | 2.80 | 3.19 | 2.85 | 2.23 | 3.92 | 591 |
| Wage earners | 1.28 | 3.29 | 3.03 | 2.83 | 4.63 | 220 |
| Sal. employees | 1.52 | 3.19 | 3.21 | 2.63 | 4.50 | 258 |
| Professionals | 2.18 | 3.35 | 3.18 | 2.08 | 4.22 | 181 |
| Services | | | | | | |
| CEO | 2.73 | 3.07 | 2.82 | 2.52 | 3.85 | 186 |
| Wage earners | 1.25 | 3.43 | 2.89 | 2.88 | 4.64 | 56 |
| Sal. employees | 1.73 | 3.23 | 3.34 | 2.36 | 4.34 | 64 |
| Professionals | 2.44 | 3.63 | 2.98 | 1.88 | 4.07 | 41 |
| Food | | | | | | |
| CEO | 2.52 | 3.44 | 2.93 | 2.07 | 4.04 | 27 |
| Wage earners | 1.33 | 3.07 | 2.87 | 3.13 | 4.80 | 15 |
| Sal. employees | 2.25 | 2.92 | 3.08 | 2.92 | 4.08 | 12 |
| Professionals | 2.81 | 3.72 | 3.36 | 1.45 | 3.64 | 11 |
| Forest | | | | | | |
| CEO | 3.33 | 3.56 | 2.72 | 2.10 | 3.28 | 39 |
| Wage earners | 1.16 | 3.11 | 3.26 | 2.63 | 4.84 | 19 |
| Sal. employees | 1.21 | 3.08 | 3.29 | 2.67 | 4.75 | 24 |
| Professionals | 2.08 | 3.25 | 3.75 | 1.75 | 4.08 | 12 |
| Machinery and eq. | | | | | | |
| CEO | 2.84 | 3.32 | 2.64 | 2.09 | 4.11 | 44 |
| Wage earners | 1.17 | 3.04 | 3.22 | 3.04 | 4.52 | 24 |
| Sal. employees | 1.50 | 2.85 | 3.10 | 2.95 | 4.60 | 20 |
| Professionals | 2.36 | 2.91 | 3.00 | 2.18 | 4.55 | 11 |

The respondents are rather satisfied with the current system in other respects as well. As far as there are wishes to make changes, the parties usually seem to have differing opinions on the appropriate direction of the changes. Generally, the responses show that the views of professionals are closest to those of employers,

[12] Alternative A is that "the bargaining system is kept approximately as it is", B that "one continues to agree on wage changes but abandons the scheduled wages", C that "one continues to agree on scheduled wages but abandons completely or partly the current use of wage raises that are binding for everyone", D that "instead of bargaining on a general wage rise one bargains on minimum wage rises and, in addition, local agreements on pay changes are made while work peace applies", E that "one abandons minimum wages, bargaining on wages and general wage rises, and moves decisions concerning industrial actions to the firm level".

whereas the views of wage earners differ most from those of the employers. A low correlation between the responses in the same firms mostly applies to issues on bargaining. This indicates that similarities and differences in opinions across categories are not a consequence of communication inside firms.

According to the results there are small differences across industries in their fundamental preferences concerning the bargaining system. In consequence, the observed differences in the actual behaviour of parties in different industries are likely to reflect temporary differences in bargaining positions and in what bargaining topics are regarded as important.

## 5 Conclusion

How bargaining on wages is organised is of great importance for the outcome. In the Finnish bargaining system, centralised and industry-level bargaining have alternated, and industries have usually also had the opportunity to opt out of centralised agreements. The choices made on the industry level concerning bargaining type have been related to differences in bargained wage changes. The bargained wage changes have been particularly favourable for the employees opting out of centralised agreements, disregarding the costs of industrial actions taken to attain the pay rises. When there is industry-level bargaining there seems to be much fewer systematic differences across industries. To limit the possibilities of employees in certain industries to get advantages from opting out of centralised bargaining, the centralised agreements in recent years have included a clause that requires a great majority of the employees to join the agreement.

There do not seem to be any fundamental and persistent differences in opinions across industries on the appropriate way of wage bargaining, as the behaviour in recent decades is not reflected in the responses to the enquiry. Despite the employees' high preference for industry-level bargaining, there are small differences across industries. The choices about whether or not to stick to centralised agreements probably reflect temporary variations in bargaining positions and the existence of important industry-specific issues, although the description in Marjanen (2002) supports the claim that there is a significant intertemporal elasticity in the need for handling industry-specific issues. The occasional occurrences of industry-level bargaining rounds are the system's inherent way of allowing flexibility across industries. On the other hand, there is no evidence of greater nominal wage growth dispersion between industries in the years with industry-level bargaining.

Finally, one can point out that there has been some decentralisation of wage setting in recent years, as, for example, performance-related pay and profit sharing schemes have become more common (Snellman, Vartiainen and Uusitalo 2003; Kauhanen and Piekkola 2002). This has been accompanied by an increase in the share of dispersion between industries in wage changes that is explained by wage drift (Piekkola and Marjanen 2003). This follows an international trend of allowing more industry- and firm-level factors to affect the wage level. The lower inflation level is likely to have meant an increased need for both coordination and flexibility, but there is too short a period of bargaining in a low-inflation and EMU environment to enable one to draw conclusions concerning changes in bargaining patterns in recent years that are based on statistically significant differences in wage changes. Nevertheless, there are changes in the bargaining institutions that are likely to continue to influence wage formation in the future.

## References

Alho, K., Heikkilä, A., Lassila, J., Pekkarinen, J., Piekkola, H. and Sund, R. (2003): *The Finnish wage bargaining – Views of the Social Partners* (in Finnish), Labour Institute for Economic Research / The Research Institute of the Finnish Economy (ETLA) Research Reports 89 / Series B No. 203. Helsinki.

Calmfors, L. (ed.) (1990): *Wage Formation and Macroeconomic Policy in the Nordic Countries.* Oxford: Oxford University Press.

Calmfors, L. and Driffil, J. (1988): Centralization of wage bargaining. *Economic Policy,* 6, 14–61.

Fama, E.F. (1980): Agency problems and the theory of the firm. *Journal of Political Economy,* 88, 288–307.

Gibbons, R. and Waldman, M. (1999): *Careers in Organizations: Theory and Evidence.* In Aschenfelter, O. C. and D. Card (eds), Handbook of Labor Economics Volume 3B, 2373–2437. Amsterdam: Elsevier Science B.V.

Hibbs, D.A. and Locking, H. (2000): Wage dispersion and productive efficiency. *Journal of Labor Economics,* 18, 755–782.

Holden, S. (1989): Wage drift and bargaining: evidence from Norway. *Economica,* 56, 419–432.

Holden, S. and Raaum, O. (1991): Wage moderation and union structure. *Oxford Economic Papers,* 43, 409–423.

Holmström, B. (1999): Managerial incentive problems: A dynamic Perspective. *Review of Economic Studies,* 66, 169–182.

Iversen, T. (1999): Contested Economic Institutions: *The Politics of Macroeconomics and Wage bargaining in Advanced Democracies.* Cambridge (UK): Cambridge University Press.

Iversen T., Pontusson, J. and Soskice, D. (eds) (2000): *Unions, Employers, and Central Banks: Macroeconomic Coordination and Institutional Change in Social Market Economies.* Cambridge (UK): Cambridge University Press.

Kahri, T. (2001): *Viheltääkö pilli? Työmarkkinamiehen muistelmat.* Helsinki: Otava.

Kauhanen, A. and Piekkola, H. (2002). *Profit Sharing in Finland: Earnings and Productivity Effects.* The Research Institute of The Finnish Economy (ETLA) Discussion Papers, No. 817, Helsinki.

Lazear, E.P. (1995): *Personnel Economics.* Cambridge (Mass.): MIT Press.

Lazear, E.P. (1998): *Personnel Economics for Managers.* New York: John Wiley & Sons.

Marjanen, R. (2002): *The Content and Realisation of Wage settlements in the period of Income Policy.* (in Finnish), The Research Institute of the Finnish Economy (ETLA) Series B No. 188. Helsinki.

Muysken J. and van Veen, T. (1996): Efficiency wages and local wage bargaining. *Scandinavian Journal of Economics,* 98, 119–27.

Piekkola, H. and Marjanen, R. (2003): *Wage Settlements and Wage Drift: New Scene of Income Policy* (in Finnish), The Research Institute of the Finnish Economy (ETLA) Series B No. 202. Helsinki.
Snellman, K. (2002): Why do More Profitable Firms Pay More? (in Swedish). *Journal of the Economic Society of Finland*, 55, 99–111.
Snellman, K., Vartiainen, J. and Uusitalo, R. (2003): *Profit sharing and changes in industrial wage setting*. (in Finnish), Helsinki: Edita / Sitra.
Teulings, C. and Hartog, J. (1998): *Corporatism or Competition? Labour Contracts, Institutions and Wage Structures in International Comparison*. Cambridge, UK: Cambridge University Press.
Uusitalo R. (2004): Do Centralized Bargains Lead to Wage Moderation? Time-series Evidence from Finland in Piekkola, H. and Snellman, K. (eds) *Collective Bargaining and Wage Formation – Performance and Challenges*. Springer-Verlag.

# Is the Labour Share Too Low in Finland?

Pekka Sauramo[1]

The Labour Institute for Economic Research, Helsinki, Finland

## Abstract

The paper discusses the drastic decline in the labour share which took place in Finland during the 1990s. It examines whether the low level of the labour share can be regarded as a new equilibrium level or whether it is an indication of macroeconomic disequilibrium. The concept of ELIS (equilibrium labour income share) employed by Draper and Huizinga (2000) is used in the characterisation of the level of the labour share. The paper emphasises that the low level of the labour share is, like the high level of the unemployment rate, an indication of disequilibrium. During the coming years the share can, therefore, increase without threatening the macroeconomic equilibrium.

## 1 Introduction

In Finnish economic history, the 1990s will remain as one of the most exceptional decades of the 20th century. The strong decline in the labour share is probably not the most important feature, but, anyway, it reflects the peculiarity of the decade (Figure 1). For the decline, the years 1992–94 were the most important. Since then the share has remained relatively steady. At the end of the 1990s the labour share was therefore at a much lower level than it was at the end of the 1980s.

Looking at Figure 1, one may ask whether the share has stabilised to a level which can be regarded as a new normal level. Alternatively, one may ask whether the share is too low in the sense that it cannot be regarded as a normal level. Obviously, the current level of the unemployment rate, about 9 per cent, is too high in the sense that it can become lower, or it can be lowered, without threatening positive economic developments. Similarly, it is possible that the labour share is too low in the sense that the share can become larger without threatening, for example, steady economic growth. If this is the case, the current level of the labour share is, like the level of the unemployment rate, an indication of disequilibrium.

---

[1] I owe special thanks to Mika Maliranta and Matti Pohjola for helpful comments on the Finnish version of the paper.

**Fig. 1.** The Labour Share in Finland 1975–2001, the Private Sector

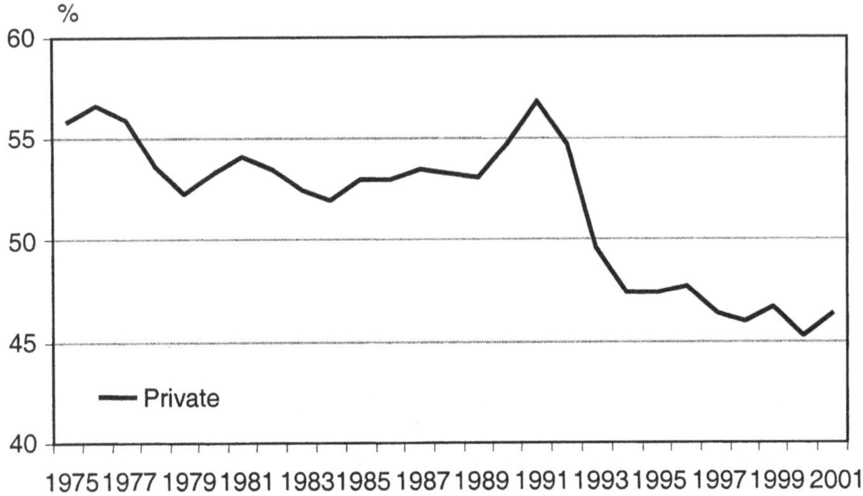


Source: Statistics Finland, National Accounts.
Note: The labour share is defined as the ratio of wages, salaries and employers' social contributions to gross value added.

It is important, for incomes policy, to analyse the current state of the functional distribution of income. If we think that the present level of the labour share reflects a new normal, i.e. desirable, level, new wage agreements, and wage claims, should be consistent with that kind of assessment. On the other hand, if we think that the current level is an indication of disequilibrium, future increases in wages may lead to an increase in the labour share without threatening steady economic growth.

In assessing the present level of the labour share we need a measure by which we can obtain information about the normal level of the labour share. By using the language of economic model building, we need an equilibrium concept which characterizes an equilibrium of the labour share.

It is not difficult to find related concepts. NAIRU may be most common one. Recent work on factor income distribution has employed models which utilize notions of the equilibrium labour share. Draper and Huizinga (2000) have introduced the concept ELIS (equilibrium labour income share). In their framework, which is based on the modern macroeconomic theory of imperfect competition, the ELIS and the NAIRU are closely related. Normally, when the framework has been utilized, emphasis has been on unemployment and not on the functional distribution of income.

It is a well-known fact that the NAIRU is a very vague concept and so is the ELIS. However, the use of an equilibrium concept like ELIS may provide a useful tool for analysing the developments of factor income distribution during the 1990s and also for considering its future developments. In this paper I utilize the same approach which Draper and Huizinga (2000) used in their study on the functional distribution of income in the Netherlands. In answer to the question "Is the labour share too low in Finland?" I compare changes in the labour share with changes in alternative estimates of the ELIS.

## 2 Equilibrium Labour Income Share (ELIS)

As an equilibrium concept, the ELIS is based on traditional neoclassical microeconomic theory on production and distribution. Macro theory is based on the assumption about a profit-maximizing (or cost-minimizing) representative firm. ELIS is defined as the value of labour income share which gives the representative firm a rate of return on physical capital equal to the required rate of return on the capital market. Because the theoretical base is neoclassical, changes in the profitability of the representative firm govern economic developments. If the actual labour share is below the equilibrium level given by the ELIS, the rate of return is higher than the required rate of return. This induces investment, and, accordingly, increases production and employment. Therefore, if unemployment is initially at a high level, the means of lowering unemployment is to encourage investment by keeping the labour share below the ELIS. On the other hand, if the labour income share exceeds the ELIS, the representative firm cannot realise the required rate of return. Low profitability results in a decline in investment and, consequently, in an increase in unemployment.

Because of the neoclassical foundations, functional distribution of income is largely determined by changes in relative prices and technology. In addition to these factors, the labour share is also affected by the nature of competition in the product and labour market. In this paper I assume that the production technology of the representative firm can be characterized by the following CES production function

$$Y = (\theta(\alpha L)^{(\sigma-1)/\sigma} + (1-\theta)(K^{(\sigma-1)/\sigma}))^{\sigma/(\sigma-1)}, \qquad (1)$$

where $Y$ denotes production, $L$ labour input and $K$ capital input. Parameter $\sigma$ is the elasticity of substitution and $\theta$ the distribution parameter. Parameter $\alpha$ is a technological parameter which characterizes the nature of technological progress. Changes in $\alpha$ describe labour-augmenting technical change.

If in equation (1) the elasticity of substitution equals unity, i.e. if $\sigma = 1$, the production function characterizes the Cobb-Douglas technology. It can be shown that, in the case of Cobb-Douglas technology, changes in relative prices do not cause changes in factor income shares (in a competitive economy consistent with the neoclassical theory of distribution). Consequently, if the relative price of capital increases by 10 per cent, the capital-labour ratio ($K/L$) decreases by 10 per cent, leaving the relative factor shares unchanged.

According to empirical studies, the elasticity of substitution has been below unity in Finland (Pohjola 1996, Kiander 1998, Dimitz 2001, Ripatti and Vilmunen 2001). Therefore, the investigation of this paper is based on the assumption that $\sigma$ is less than unity, and, accordingly, relative changes in the prices of inputs can affect the labour share under the standard neoclassical assumptions.

It is also important to notice that the labour-augmenting technical change specified as in equation (1) may cause changes in relative factor shares, because movements in parameter $\alpha$ affect the effective wage cost faced by the representative firm. With given relative prices, it is the production technology which determines relative factor shares in a world which is consistent with the traditional neoclassical theory of production and distribution. The traditional theory, which was already developed by Clark (1908) and others, is based on the assumption about the competitive product and labour markets.

It can be shown (Draper and Huizinga 2000) that profit maximization by the representative firm leads, in a competitive economy, to the following equilibrium labour income share:

$$WL/PY = 1 - (1-\theta)(pk/c)^{1-\sigma}. \tag{2}$$

In equation (2) $W$ denotes the nominal wage rate (per hour worked) and $P$ the price of the product produced by the representative firm. Variable $pk$ is the user cost of capital. Movements in the user cost are strongly affected by changes in the interest rate. The definition of user cost will be discussed more thoroughly later. Variable $c$ is defined as follows.

$$c = (\theta(W/\alpha)^{1-\sigma} + (1-\theta)pk^{1-\sigma})^{1/(1-\sigma)}. \tag{3}$$

It represents both the unit and marginal costs associated with the CES technology.

Equation (2) defines one equilibrium labour income share which is consistent with the traditional neoclassical theory of production. Therefore, we can also write

$$\text{ELIS1} = 1 - (1-\theta)(pk/c)^{1-\sigma}. \tag{4}$$

According to equation (4), the increase in the user cost of capital lowers the equilibrium labour share, if the elasticity of substitution is less than unity. If the user cost of capital increases, for example, because of an increase in the interest rate, maintaining the profitability of the representative firm requires that the labour share be lowered. Otherwise, the firm makes losses.

Equations (3) and (4) also show that, with given wages, an increase in parameter $\alpha$ decreases ELIS, if the elasticity of substitution is less than unity. This is one way of saying that increases in parameter $\alpha$ describe labour-saving technical change when the elasticity of substitution is less than unity.

The equations also show that the ELIS remains unchanged if increases in parameter $\alpha$ are matched with equal increases in wages. Even though equation (4) describes a static equilibrium, it can also be interpreted as a long-run equilibrium or as a steady state characterizing a situation in which both labour and capital are optimally allocated. In this paper, equation (4) is usually interpreted as a long-run equilibrium. Consequently, changes in wages over time are compared with technical change which is represented by changes in parameter $\alpha$.

The ELIS defined by equation (4) provides one equilibrium concept which can be utilized when developments of the labour share are analysed. It provides, of course, a highly idealized yardstick because it is based on the assumption about the competitive markets. However, it is a natural starting point, and the assumption about the nature of competition will be relaxed later. I utilize equation (4) in analysing the importance of relative prices and technical change for the developments of the labour share.

To obtain empirical estimates of the ELIS, one needs, in addition to data on relative prices, an empirical aggregate production function. In this paper, empirical analysis will mainly be based on calibration and not on estimation. Consequently, I utilize previous work on the estimation of aggregate production functions for the private sector of the Finnish economy. For the elasticity of substitution the most appropriate values are between 0.5 and 0.8 (Pohjola 1996, Kiander 1998, Dimitz 2001, Ripatti and Vilmunen 2001). The larger the value is, the smaller are the effects of the changes in relative prices. The calculations are based on the assumption that $\sigma = 0.5$. In addition, it is assumed that $\theta = 0.53$.

## 3 ELIS in Finland: The Importance of Relative Prices

According to equation (4), one reason for the decline in the labour share during the 1990s may have been an increase in the relative price of capital. In order to maintain the average profitability of the Finnish firms, the labour share had to decrease. This hypothesis can be examined by analysing movements in relative prices, and movements in pk/c in particular.

The characterisation of the user cost of capital is not straightforward because the construction of a long series reflecting all the relevant changes which affect the user cost of capital is not easy. The user cost is influenced, for example, by alterations to taxation (Koskenkylä 1986). Because of the difficulty of taking such changes into account, the definition of the user cost of capital is based only on the commonly used basic factors:

$$pk = q(r - g + d), \tag{5}$$

where

$q$ = price of investment goods,
$r$ = interest rate,
$g$ = expected rate of inflation and
$d$ = depreciation of capital.

Nor is the use of equation (5) straightforward, because it allows, for example, the use of various interest rates. In what follows, both short-term and long-term interest rates (on government bonds) are utilized. (For price indices of investment goods the corresponding data from the National Accounts were utilized. The expected rate of inflation was described by realized changes in the price if investment goods. Depreciation of capital was measured by consumption of fixed capital in the private sector.)

The use of equation (5) gives Figure 2, which depicts two alternative series on *pk/c*. The first one is based on the use of a short-term interest rate (corresponding to the three-month HELIBOR and EURIBOR) and the second on the use of a long-term interest rate (taxable government bond yield, approximately five years). Strong fluctuations in *pk/c* reflect both changes in interest rates and changes in price movements. Fluctuations could have been smoothed by averaging, but some exceptional periods can be neglected in the interpretation.

The series have been constructed under the assumption that no technological change has taken place. They therefore only reflect movements in relative prices. The main conclusion to be drawn from Figure 2 does not depend on which interest rate is used. The 1990s could be characterized as a period of cheap rather than expensive capital. The start of the decade was, of course, an exception.

The series in Figure 2 can be used in the construction of two alternative series of the ELIS. These series, in addition to the labour share, are shown in Figure 3. According to the ELIS estimates, the relative price of capital has not been the cause of the decline in the labour share. The relative price of capital has been low – not high. This would have resulted, in equilibrium, in an increase and not in a decline in the labour share.

**Fig. 2.** The Relative Price of Capital and Labour 1975–2001

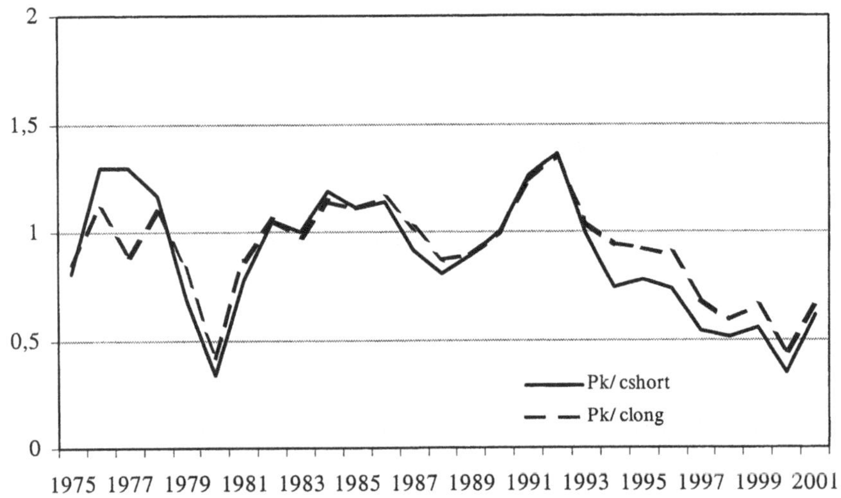


Source: Statistics, Finland; Bank of Finland; own calculations.
Note: The numbers are index numbers of which 1990=1.

Obviously, movements in relative prices do not explain movements in the labour share during the 1990s. According to the traditional neoclassical theory of distribution, the other factor, i.e. technical change, could have caused and maintained the decline in the labour share.

## 4 ELIS in Finland: The Importance of Labour-Saving Technical Change

In this paper technical change is represented by changes in parameter α. It is possible that all aspects of structural change which took place in Finland in the 1990s cannot be described by changes in the production technology of the representative firm. The years from 1992 until 1994, in particular, were exceptional. The strong growth in labour productivity was associated with restructuring of the economy (Maliranta 2003). However, the limitation of the model can, at least to some extent, be taken into account in the interpretation of the results. It is worth noticing that Ripatti and Vilmunen (2001), while analysing the stability of the parameters of their CES production function, concluded that the elasticity of substitution remained unchanged during the 1990s.

Within the framework of this paper the demand for labour can be expressed as

$$\log L = \log Y - \sigma \log(W/c) - (1-\sigma)\log\alpha + \sigma\log\theta \,. \tag{6}$$

With a given level of output, if parameter α increases, the demand for labour decreases when the elasticity of substitution is less than unity. This is one way of illustrating that increases in parameter α describe labour-saving technical progress when $0 < \sigma < 1$.

**Fig. 3.** The ELIS: Two Series without Technical Change

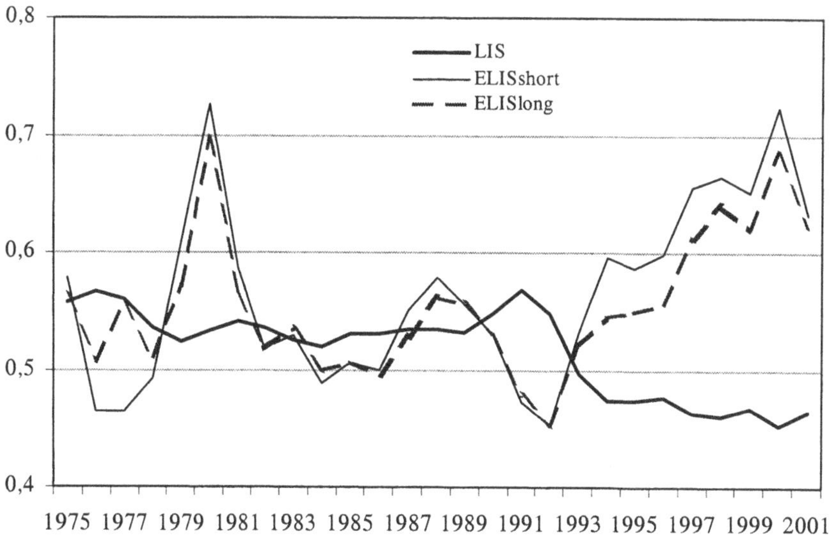


Source: Statistics, Finland; Bank of Finland; own calculations.

**Fig. 4.** The ELIS 1990–2001: The Importance of Technical Change

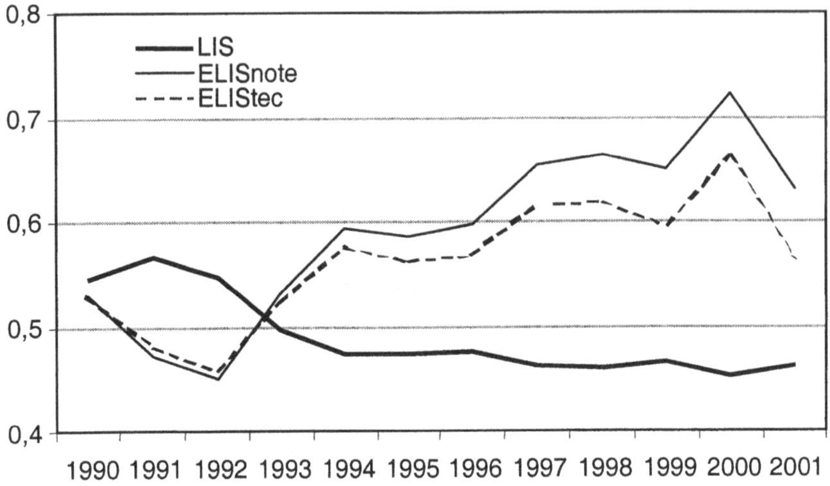


Source: Statistics, Finland; Bank of Finland; own calculations.
Note: The ELIS series are based on the short-term interest rate.

The construction of time series for parameter $\alpha$ is not straightforward. The method which is used in this paper resembles the way of computing the so-called Solow residual. Assuming that $\sigma = 0.5$ and $\theta = 0.53$ I construct the series for $\alpha$ as a residual series by utilizing realized values of output, labour and capital.

The importance of labour-saving technical change can be seen from Figure 4. It depicts, in addition to one series from Figure 3, a series which has been obtained by utilizing equation (4) and the series for $\alpha$. Labour-saving technical change has had a strong impact on the ELIS during the 1990s. It has lowered the ELIS by 7 percentage points. According to equation (3) this follows from wage increases which have been smaller than the increases in $\alpha$.

However, at the end of the 1990s the labour share was about 10 percentage points lower than the level indicated by the ELIS. The decline in the labour share can therefore not be explained as a change in the equilibrium level of the labour income share caused by the two basic factors, changes in relative prices and labour-saving technological change. With given wage developments, labour-saving technical change decreased the ELIS, while the cheapening of the relative price of capital had an opposite effect.

## 5 ELIS and Imperfect Competition in the Product Market

Because the decline of the labour share could not be explained by changes in relative prices and by labour-saving technical change, the explanation must be sought somewhere else. Within the traditional neoclassical theory of distribution, one of the basic assumptions is that the product and labour markets are competitive. The representative firm, therefore, maximizes profits by regarding prices and wages as given. The assumption is, of course, unrealistic. It can, however, be relaxed.

The assumption about imperfect competition in the product market leads to a new definition of ELIS. It can be shown (Draper and Huizinga 2000) that, under imperfect competition, the new equation for the ELIS is given by

$$\mathrm{ELIS2} = (1 - (1-\theta)(pk/c)^{1-\sigma})/M, \tag{7}$$

where $M$ is the mark-up parameter representing the market power of the representative firm. Under perfect competition $M = 1$, and the ELIS is defined by equation (4). Increases in pricing power are reflected in increases in $M$. Within the framework of this paper, the best way of interpreting $M$ is to associate it with a long-run equilibrium.

Obtaining empirical estimates of $M$ is a difficult task. In the literature, one traditional approach is based on the assumption that the economy is in equilibrium, and, consequently, equations describing equilibrium conditions can be utilised in the estimation. Ripatti and Vilmunen (2001), for example, proceed in this way. Their main result and conclusion is that the decline in the labour share has not been caused by technological change but by increased mark-ups, i.e. by decreased competition in the product market. Even though they do not utilise an equation identical to equation (7) their approach is similar to the use of that equation in the computation of $M$. Obviously, if it is assumed that the economy is in equilibrium, the simplest way of getting estimates of $M$ is to employ realized values of the labour share and utilise the equilibrium condition provided by equation (7).

**Fig. 5.** The Mark-up 1975–2001

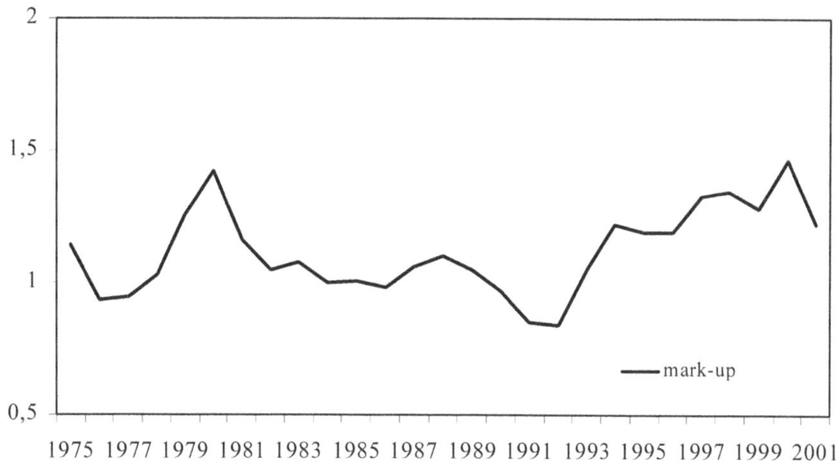


Source: Statistics, Finland; Bank of Finland; own calculations.

Because my aim is to analyse whether the current level of the labour share can be regarded as a new equilibrium or not, the use of equation (7) would be inept. However, the calculation of values of *M* by utilising equation (7) may still be useful, because they may also illustrate disequilibrium. Big increases in *M* may be an indication of disequilibrium, because it is natural to think that during the 1990s, when economic integration deepened, competition in the product market increased and did not decrease.

The use of equation (7) in the calculation of movements in *M* gives Figure 5. Changes in the mark-up have been strong in the 1990s, and the years of the late 1990s, especially, were exceptional. It is not easy to find reasons why the big increase in the mark-up should be interpreted as illustrating a new equilibrium. Rather, it can be argued that it only shows that, at the turn of the century, the economy was in disequilibrium.

The analysis has shown that, if the decline in the labour share illustrates a decline in the ELIS, it is mainly due to decreased competition in the product market. Changes in relative prices and labour-saving technical change, are not able to explain it. Because it is hard to believe that competition has decreased, a natural conclusion is that the labour share has not been in equilibrium. In comparison with the ELIS, it has been too low.

Even though this conclusion would be persuasive enough, it is too early for one important reason. The analysis has been partial in the sense that the determination of wages was not endogenized. Obviously, if one argues that the labour share is not in equilibrium one should base his or her view on an analysis which is not based on exogenously given wages. In what follows, I complement the investigation by endogenizing the determination of wages. The analysis of wage determination also makes for a more comprehensive illustration of the disequilibrium. The endogenization of wage determination can be based on the use of modern union models.

## 6 ELIS and NAIRU

When union models are used, the outcome of the negotiations between a representative union and a representative firm is normally represented by a wage curve, which describes a wage claim as a function of unemployment and some other factors like the tax wedge and the replacement ratio. Even though the wage claim is normally expressed as a real wage claim, the level of labour productivity can also be incorporated and the overall result of the bargaining can be expressed as a claim concerning the labour share (Broer et. al. 2000, Draper and Huizinga 2000, Nymoen and Rødseth 2003):

$$WL/PY = \mathrm{f}(U,Z), \qquad (8)$$

where *U* denotes the unemployment rate and vector *Z* other factors influencing the outcome. An increase in unemployment decreases the claim on the labour share.

The ELIS equation (4) (or (7)) and equation (8) characterise the labour share in two alternative ways. The ELIS equations reflect the behaviour of the representative firm while equation (8) represents the aim of the representative union. (It should be noticed that not all bargaining situations are consistent with equations (4) and (8). They are consistent with the situations typical of right-to-manage models, but they are not consistent with efficient bargaining. See Bentolila and Saint-Paul 1998, Blanchard and Giavazzi 2003.)

When the two ways are combined, the role of unemployment becomes important. It serves as a means of matching the two probably inconsistent claims on the division of factor income. According to equation (4) (or (7)) the exogenously given interest rate mainly determines the level of the labour share which ensures that the profitability of the representative firm is good enough, with given wages. But the representative union does not necessarily accept this level. However, according to equation (8) there exists such a level of the unemployment rate which makes the two claims compatible, with given vector $Z$.

This equilibrium unemployment rate is normally called NAIRU. It can be expressed as follows (Draper and Huizinga 2000).

$$\text{NAIRU} = g(\text{ELIS}, Z). \tag{9}$$

Equation (9) expresses the NAIRU as a function of the ELIS, because the ELIS, as an equilibrium, is not dependent on unemployment. This is illustrated by Figure 6, in which equation (4) (or (7)) is expressed as a horizontal curve. This curve can be regarded as a long-run and not as a short-run curve because it describes a situation in which both labour and capital have been optimally allocated. (One could add an upward-sloping short-run labour demand function into the figure illustrating a situation in which capital is not yet at its long-run level. See Rødseth 2000, Nymoen and Rødseth 2003.)

Figure 6 is one way of illustrating, within the framework of this paper, the importance of the interest rate, and monetary policy, as a determinant of functional distribution of income, and the NAIRU. The figure also shows that the location of the wage curve does not affect the equilibrium labour share but only the unemployment rate which makes the differing aspirations concerning the labour share compatible. Because the bargaining power of the representative union only affects the location of the wage curve, it affects only the NAIRU and not the ELIS.

In Figure 6, the equilibrium is depicted by point A. The equilibrium is somewhat peculiar. The ELIS corresponds to an equilibrium which is a result of optimal allocation of labour and capital with given relative prices. On the other hand, wages are negotiated under the assumption that labour and capital are given. If, initially, the economy is not at point A, it is natural to think that the equilibrium is not reached immediately but through a process which may take a lot of time. Adjustment of capital stock to changes in the interest rate takes time, and so do changes in wages.

During a dynamic process, wages, capital stock and unemployment change. Rødseth (2000), for example, illustrates this kind of process by a two-equation differential equation which describes movements in capital stock and wages (see also Rowthorn 1999a,b). The long-run equilibrium is reached when the rate of return on physical capital is consistent with the required rate of return on the capital market and when the representative union is satisfied with the division of the factor income. Points on the wage curve provide the potential points of equilibrium.

**Fig. 6.** ELIS and NAIRU

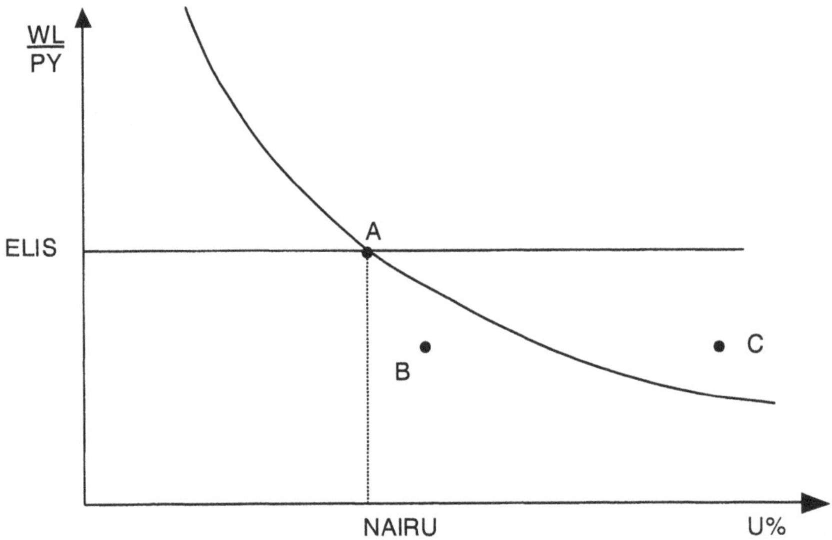


In Figure 6, point B represents a disequilibrium situation. At that point the level of labour share is below the equilibrium level, which means that the profitability of the representative firm is higher than at the equilibrium. Moreover, point B is on the left side of the wage curve, which means that, with a given level of unemployment, the representative union wants a larger than current share of the factor income. The equilibrium can therefore be reached through a process during which employment increases and profitability decreases.

One way of analysing recent developments of unemployment and functional distribution of income is to evaluate which point in Figure 6 corresponds to the situation prevailing at the turn of the century.

## 7 What Was the Situation in 2001?

According to the previous considerations, it is natural to think that the labour share was below the ELIS. For the purpose of this paper it is not of great importance to know how much below the ELIS the labour share was, for example, in 2001. Figure 4 can give an idea, even though the ELIS series are based on equation (4) and not on equation (7). In Figure 4, the ELIS estimate which contains the effects of technical change provides the upper limit of the gap between the ELIS level and the real level of the labour share. It should also be remembered that the ELIS is not a constant but a variable which is affected by fluctuations in the real interest rate, for example.

It is also natural to think that the unemployment rate has been above the NAIRU all through the 1990s. But which point, B or C, gives a better approximation about the situation in 2001? It is impossible to answer this question without using an empirical wage curve.

The simplest way of estimating such a curve is to estimate a curve which is based on equation (8), by regressing the labour share only on the unemployment rate and by assuming that the constant term of the regression equation captures the effects of vector Z well enough. This is, of course, an extremely simple way, by which, for example, the possible shifts of the curve cannot be properly described. However, it provides one means of assessing what the average location of the wage curve was during the estimation period, i.e. during the years from 1975 until 2001.

The simple way can be motivated by the fact that it is very difficult to get reliable estimates on the effects of the tax wedge or of the replacement ratio when aggregative data is used. Consequently, when the framework of this paper is employed in the estimation of the NAIRU, the results are bound to be unreliable (see also Alho 2002).

Because equation (9) should be regarded as a long-run equation, the relationship between the ELIS and the NAIRU can be modelled by employing a static model. The estimation of a simple static regression equation by using observations from the period 1975–2001 gives the following equation.

$$\text{LnLIS} = \underset{(30.0)}{-0.57} - \underset{(5.4)}{0.012}U\%, \tag{10}$$

where variable LnLIS denotes the natural logarithm of the labour share and $U\%$ the unemployment rate. (The numbers in brackets are t-values.)

Even though equation (10) is a very simple equation it can be regarded as a part of a dynamic model which has been estimated by the Engle-Granger two-step procedure and in which equation (10) is the error-correction term.

Equation (10) can be used in answering the question whether point B or C gives a better description of the economic situation in 2001. According to the equation, the representative union would accept the realized level of the labour share (46.4%) if the rate of unemployment were about 16%. Because it was much lower (9.1%), point B corresponds to the situation prevailing in 2001 better than point C does.

This is an essential piece of information, because by using it we can characterise both the past and potential future wage developments. Being at point B implies, with the assumption that the wage curve (10) is the error-correction term in a dynamic wage equation, that there are wage pressures. With a given unemployment rate, the representative union would like to get a larger share of the factor income. However, it is not easy to assess how big the pressures are. They may be smaller than equation (10) indicates if, for example, the bargaining power of the unions has weakened during the 1990s.

**Fig. 7.** The Realized and Required Rate of Return 1975–2001

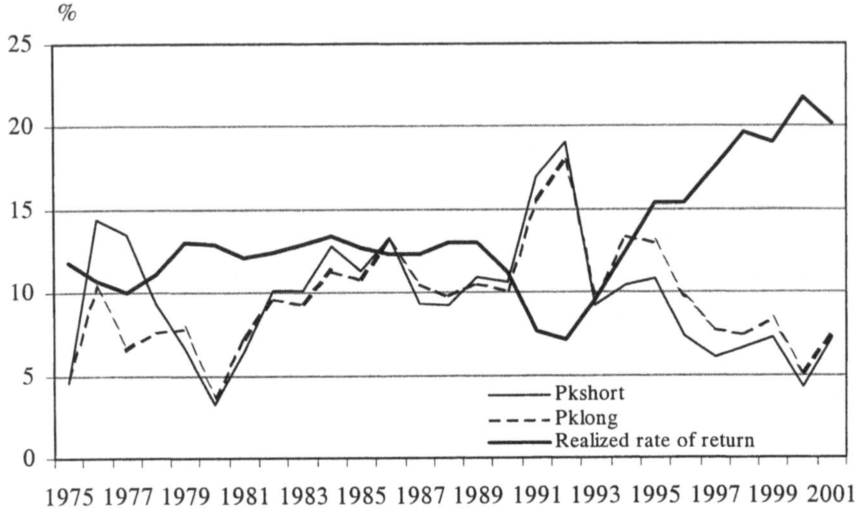


Source: Statistics, Finland; Bank of Finland; own calculations.

The endogenisation of wage formation confirms the view that neither the unemployment rate nor the labour share was in equilibrium at the turn of the century. The historically high unemployment rate has maintained the historically low labour share. It should be remembered that, within the framework of this paper, the labour share must be lower than the ELIS for unemployment to decrease. During the 1990s the unemployment rate has decreased from 16.6% to 9.1%, which is a considerable drop.

Because the labour share has been below the ELIS, the average profitability of Finnish firms has been abnormally high. This is illustrated by Figure 7 in which the realised rate of return has been compared with the required rate of return, because, in equilibrium,

$$\pi = r - g + d, \tag{11}$$

where $\pi$ denotes the rate of return on physical capital and where $r$,$g$ and $d$ are defined as in equation (5). (By using standard concepts of the National Accounts, the rate of return is defined as a ratio of operating surplus to the net capital stock at current prices.)

The high average level of profitability is mainly due to two factors which have already been discussed. The pace of wage inflation has been slower than the pace of technical change. Therefore, the 1990s can be regarded as a period of wage moderation. On the other hand, firms have not adjusted prices in accordance with movements in costs but have increased their mark-ups. In this paper, I argue that the best way of interpreting this increase is to regard it as a temporary and not as a permanent change.

## 8 Future Prospects

The considerations of future prospects and policy options are conditional on the prevailing state of the economy. For example, if the economy were at point A instead of point B (in Figure 6), the prospects and policy options would be different.

According to the analysis of this paper, the most accurate description of the state of the economy is that the economy is in the disequilibrium which is characterised by the low labour share and the high unemployment rate. The labour share is at such a low level that it is natural to expect that the share will start to rise even though the unemployment rate is higher than the NAIRU. Among the possible alternatives this is the most likely prospect because point B is on the left side of the wage curve.

If future developments were consistent with the model of this paper, employment would rise and the unemployment rate would decrease because the high level of profitability supports the growth of private investment and, accordingly, GDP. Simultaneously, the labour share would rise and the average profitability would decline, but this would not be an indication of a worsening disequilibrium but rather of a convergence towards the equilibrium. However, it must be remembered that some important aspects which are related to the openness of the economy cannot be described by the model. For example, the future role of foreign direct investment cannot be analysed by it.

Within the framework of the paper, the increase in the labour share should not automatically be interpreted as a worrisome sign of weakening economic developments. Maintaining the current level of the labour share in the future, too, is therefore not a necessary prerequisite for the decrease in the unemployment rate. This assessment can be taken as a starting point in future negotiations on incomes policy. However, it does not imply that the labour share, which is too low, could be restored overnight. As long as the unemployment rate is above the NAIRU, the labour share should be below the ELIS, within the framework of this paper.

For incomes policy it is important to recognise that the ELIS is not a constant but a variable. Because it is affected by changes in the real interest rate, it can be affected by monetary policy (i.e. by the European Central Bank) to the extent that real interest rates can be affected by monetary policy. The ELIS is also affected by the intensity of the competition in the product market. The more intense the competition is, the higher the ELIS is – and the lower the NAIRU is. Within the framework of this paper, all policy measures that increase competition in the product market are highly desirable.

According to Figure 5, the mark-up, instead of having decreased, increased during the 1990s. In this paper, I interpreted this as a temporary increase reflecting the disequilibrium of the economy. The basic reason for this interpretation is that the deepening of economic integration should enhance competition (see, however, López 2003). The interpretation is not, however, completely unproblematic because the decline in the labour share is due not only to the decline of the labour share in the manufacturing industry but also to those service industries which belong or have belonged to the sheltered sector of the economy and in which the lack of competition has traditionally been a problem. If the path towards the equilibrium resembles the path outlined above, the temporarily increased mark-ups should start to decrease. Even though the increase may turn out to be temporary, it provides a topic both for further research and for economic policy discussions.

## References


Alho, K.E.O. (2002): The Equilibrium Rate of Unemployment and Policies to Lower It: The Case of Finland, The Research Institute of the Finnish Economy (ETLA) Discussion papers No. 839. Helsinki.

Bentolila, S. and Saint-Paul, G. (1998): Explaining Movements in the Labour Share, CEPR Discussion Paper Series No. 1958, London.

Blanchard, O. and Giavazzi, F. (2003): Macroeconomic Effects of Regulation and Deregulation in Goods and Labour Markets, *The Quarterly Journal of Economics*, 118, 879–908.

Broer, D.P., Draper, D.A.G. and Huizinga, F.H. (2000): The Equilibrium Rate of Unemployment in the Netherlands, *De Economist*, 148, no. 3, 345–371.

Clark, J.B. (1908): *The Distribution of Wealth*, Macmillan, London.

Dimitz, M.A. (2001): Output Gaps and Technological Progress in the European Monetary Union, Bank of Finland Discussion papers 20/2001. Helsinki.

Draper, N. and Huizinga, F. (2000): ELIS: Equilibrium Labour Income Share, *De Economist*, 148, no. 5, 345–371.

Kiander, J. (1998): Työvoiman kysyntä ja yritysten hinnanasetanta (Demand for labour and price setting) in Pohjola, M.(ed.) Suomalainen työttömyys (Unemployment in Finland), Taloustieto Oy, Helsinki.

Koskenkylä, H. (1986): Koron ja muiden rahoitustekijöiden vaikutuksista investointeihin Suomessa (The importance of interest rate and other financial instruments for investment in Finland), in Suomen rahoitusmarkkinat (The Financial market in Finland), Bank of Finland Series A No. 64, Helsinki 1986.

López, M.C. (2003): Macroeconomic Effects of Oligopolistic Competition with Sectoral Wage Bargaining: What do we learn from deregulation? Mimeo.

Maliranta, M. (2003): Micro-Level Dynamics of Productivity Growth, Helsinki School of Economics, A–227, Helsinki.

Nymoen, R. and Rødseth, A. (2003): Explaining unemployment: Some lessons from Nordic wage formation, *Labour Economics*, 10, 1–29.

Pohjola, M. (1996): Tehoton pääoma (Inefficient capital), WSOY, Helsinki.

Ripatti, A. and Vilmunen, J. (2001): Declining labour share – Evidence of a change in the underlying production technology? Bank of Finland Discussion papers 10/2001, Helsinki.

Rowthorn, R. (1999a): Unemployment, wage bargaining and capital-labour substitution, *Cambridge Journal of Economics*, 23, 413–425.

Rowthorn, R. (1999b): Unemployment, Capital-Labor Substitution, and Economic Growth, IMF Working Paper 99/43, Washington D.C.

Rødseth, A. (2000): *Open Economy Macroeconomics*, Cambridge University Press, Cambridge.

# Bargaining on Pensions: The Finnish Pension Reform of 2001–2002

Jukka Lassila[1]

ETLA, The Research Institute of the Finnish Economy
Helsinki, Finland

## Abstract

A major reform of the Finnish private-sector earnings-related pension system was negotiated in 2001–2002 between central organisations of employers and trade unions and representatives of the central government. This paper describes the reform, views it in the light of previous reforms, and analyses the effects of the reform on the welfare of different cohorts and different educational groups. The analysis of the reform showed that current old workers generally kept their positions, and even improved them. Younger workers lost somewhat. Future workers will gain. Early retirement in general was punished, which on average will hit low-educated employees harder than more educated groups. The reform process also showed that the relative positions of trade unions and between-union comparisons were important.

## 1 Introduction

The social partners have had a very active role throughout the history of the Finnish pension system and in its numerous reforms. A major reform of the private-sector earnings-related pension system was agreed in 2001–2002. The reform was negotiated between employers' central organisations, central organisations of trade unions, and representatives of the central government. Thus it can be classified as centralized bargaining, which is different from that in countries like the Netherlands, where pension bargaining takes place at the industrial level, or the U.K. where the firm level is crucial. The Finnish reform has raised some international interest, mainly

[1] This paper is part of the research project "Rules of the game in the labour market: Industrial relations, the bargaining system and income policies in the 2000s", financed by the Finnish Work Environment Fund, and carried out jointly by ETLA, The Research Institute of the Finnish Economy, and the Labour Institute for Economic Research. I wish to thank Kari Alho, Eero Lehto, Ismo Risku and Eila Tuominen for comments.

because an agreement was found, whereas the social partners in Germany, France and Austria have recently been unable to agree on reforms. In those countries pension reforms have only been possible by government action.

This study describes the recent Finnish reform, views it in the light of previous reforms, and analyses the effects of the reform on the welfare of different cohorts and different educational groups. We hope that the study can provide information on the preferences of both employers and employees on long-term issues, especially the intergenerational issues that are inherent in all pension reforms. This kind of information will be important in view of the ageing of the population, which also means ageing of the labour force. It should also help us foresee the future changes and policy lines in pension issues.

Section 2 briefly describes the history of the Finnish pension system in its present form and the role of the social partners in it, and presents the pension system and the changes the reform will bring to it. Section 3 gives an assessment of the reform and its effects, including the winner-loser aspects. Concluding comments are in Section 4.

## 2 The Finnish Pension System and the Role of the Social Partners

### 2.1 A Brief History[2]

The Finnish pension system consists of two main parts. The earnings-related pension system aims to provide retirement income sufficient for consumption that is comparable both to that of working years and to current workers' consumption. It covers risks related to old age, disability, the long-term unemployment of ageing workers, and the death of family earners.

The national pension guarantees a minimum income in cases where the earnings-related pension is absent or insufficient. Both systems are mandatory. Voluntary pensions, whether employer-based or industry-wide supplementary pensions or personal pension arrangements, are becoming more common but are still of minor importance in Finland.

The earnings-related pension system covers almost all paid work, whereas the national pension is residence-based. There has been considerable rivalry between these two parts, with the former now the undisputed winner. The Finnish earnings-related system is statutory by law but largely privately run. It has collected substantial funds to smoothen the contribution increases due to population ageing in the future.

In the first comprehensive pension arrangement, the 1937 National Pension Law, the national pension was earnings-related. There were personal retirement accounts, which were fully funded. Contributions started in 1939. During the war, however, inflation ate half of the accounts, and unfunded but indexed supplementary benefits became dominant. What was left in the personal accounts was never

---

[2] This section is based on Lassila and Valkonen (2002).

paid to the contributors, but, instead, used as starting capital for a new system, enacted by the 1956 National Pension Law. The views of the rural population dominated then, and the national pension became a means-tested flat-rate pension.

The Employees' Pensions Act (TEL) came into force on 1 July 1962. It was created in negotiations between trade unions and employers' organizations, and supported politically by social democrats and conservative parties. To reduce political risks, administration was given to several private pension institutes. There were attempts during the '60s, in the form of law initiatives, to combine TEL with the national pension system, but they failed to get a majority. TEL is now by far the largest private sector pension system, and has served as a model for several other earnings-related systems in Finland.

After the 1960s, the growing importance of an increasingly united trade union movement was further reflected in the relative roles of the earnings-related and national pension systems (see Niemelä 1994). The former became the dominant pension arrangement, and plans to develop the national pension into a universal retirement provision, without means testing, were abolished.

The statutory earnings-related system was created in co-operation with labour market organisations, and they are represented in the administrative bodies. The administration is decentralised among several pension institutes. The largest of them are private pension insurance companies and the Local Government Pensions Institution. These institutes collect the contributions, pay the pensions and invest the retained funds. The Finnish Centre for Pensions maintains the central register, compiles statistics and redistributes between the institutions the pooled component of contributions collected in the private pension scheme.

The labour market organisations occupy at least half of the seats in the administrative bodies of the pension institutes. Together with the representatives of the central government, they also negotiate the future development of the pension scheme.

The earnings-related pensions in the public sector are very similar to those in the private sector described above. The amount of annual funding, however, is discretionary and not formally based on any formulae concerning accrued pension rights or future expenditures. The Local Government Pensions Institution, handling the earnings-related pensions for municipal employees, has funds amounting to 137% of the sector's annual wage bill in 1999, which is thus roughly comparable to the TEL system. The pension fund of the central government is still small, but it has been agreed to raise the funding rate to the same level as in the private sector by the year 2010.

There have been a large number of reforms in the pension rules. Until the severe recession at the beginning of the 1990s, the trend in reforms was to raise the benefit level and to loosen the rules for eligibility for early pensions. The recession created an urgent need to cut labour costs both in the private and in the public sectors and emphasized the problems of long-term sustainability of the pension system. In addition to the necessary expenditure cuts, the reforms during the 1990s were aimed at several other objectives such as a more stable ratio of pension expenditures to total wages during business cycles, a higher effective retirement age and a higher yield on pension funds.

## 2.2 Earnings-Related Pension System Before and After the 2001–2002 Reform

The 2001–2002 reform will mainly take effect from the beginning of 2005. Below we describe the current system in some detail and describe the changes due to the reform. The current system is sometimes referred to as "old" and the reformed as "new". For a more detailed description of the reform, see the web pages of The Finnish Pension Alliance at www.tela.fi.

Currently, every employment contract and self-employment period adds to the pension, after age 23. The pensionable wage is aggregated over the last 10 years of each contract. The accrued pension right is vested, even if the employer is changed or work is stopped. After the reform, accrual will start at the age of 18. Instead of using employment contracts and the pensionable wage concept, every year's earnings and accrual rates will directly affect the future pension (the career model).

The "target" level of benefits is currently 60% of wages. This accrues in about 40 years: 1.5 % per year between ages 23–59 and 2.5 % per year between 60 and 65. There is no upper absolute limit to benefits, but an upper percentage limit is 60% of the highest pensionable earnings. After the reform there will be no ceiling at all. The accrual rate will be 1.5% per year between ages 18–53, 1.9% per year between ages 53–62 and 4.5% per year between 63–68.

Pension rights and benefits are index-linked, with 50-50 weights on wages and consumer prices before age 65 and 20-80 weights after age 65. After the reform the change in indexation will take place at actual retirement, irrespective of age. The weights before retirement will be 80–20 on wages and consumer prices and 20–80 after retirement.

Contributions are collected from both employers (on average 16.8 % of wages in 2002) and employees (4.6 %). Future changes in contributions have been agreed to be shared equally between employers and employees. After the reform employees aged 53 and over will pay contributions that are about 1.27 times higher than the younger employees' rate, reflecting (but far from fully paying) their higher accrual.

The reform will bring the Swedish-type longevity adjustment coefficient to the pension system. It will start cutting monthly pensions for all cohorts reaching the age of 62 in 2010 or later.

The reform will bring major changes to the pre-retirement pensions. The unemployment pension will be abolished and the lower age limit for entitlement to continued unemployment allowance will be increased. Age limits for the part-time pension and the early old-age pension will also be increased and the individual early retirement pension will be abolished. There will be flexible retirement on an old-age pension between ages 62 and 68.

The private-sector earnings-related system is partially funded. Funding is collective but based on individual pension rights. Individual pension benefits do not depend on the existence or yield of funds. Funds only affect contributions. When a person receives pensions after the age of 65, his/her funds are used to pay that part of the pension benefit that was prefunded. The rest comes from the PAYG part, the so-called pooled component in the contribution rate. Some additional funding between 2003 and 2013 was decided in the reform, amounting to 7.5 % of the insured wage sum in 2013.

### 2.3 Why Do Social Partners Have Pension Power?

TEL is a statutory system, and the laws that govern it are decided upon in Parliament. Although trade unions and employers have been crucial in the creation of the system, it does not follow that their role should inevitably continue. Still, the very fact that they have been active can also be the reason for their influence in the future.

Béland (2001) compares the roles of trade unions in pension reforms in France and in the U.S. He uses the concept of 'veto player', meaning an actor whose agreement is required for a change in policy. Béland summarises that trade unions are 'veto players' in pension issues in France but not in the U.S[3]. The difference is, in his opinion, a result of the fact that the French trade unions are integrated in the management process of the pension system, whereas that is not the case in the U.S. In Finland the trade unions – if they agree with each other – are undoubtedly veto players.

## 3 Effects of the 2001–2002 Pension Reform

### 3.1 General Assessment of the Reform

The main aims of the 2001–2002 pension reform are to reward continued participation in working life and to postpone the average retirement age, to take increasing life expectancy into account and to curb the expected increases in the contribution rates, and to support ageing workers' ability to cope with their work. The initial targets of social partners and the state were not explicitly stated before the negotiations, but decreasing the expected future increases in contributions was certainly one target and postponing retirement was considered as the main instrument or sub-target in achieving it.

One initial and widely held target was to simplify the pension rules and make them both more transparent and more actuarial. This was not fully achieved; in particular, the different accrual rates in different ages blur the picture. Abandoning the pensionable wage concept, which depended on the number and length of employment contracts, does, however, simplify the system. It seems likely that this reform of private-sector pensions will lead to new decisions, gradually unifying different earnings-related pension systems in Finland.

Disagreements between different trade unions were the dominant feature that led to different accrual rates for employees in different ages. The current system favours those with both long employment contracts and rising wage-age profiles, typically white-collar workers with higher salaries. For them, the whole accrual percentage is applied to the last high wages of their careers. Moving to a system where each year of their career weighs the same would weaken their relative posi-

[3] Recent experiences in France seem to indicate that the veto player position of trade unions may have changed.

tion. The negotiated result was a compromise, where the latter years of the working career still matter more than the earlier years. The increase in the employee contribution rate for those over 53 years of age does not suffice to finance the increased accrual, which in the future will mean higher contributions for both employers and all employees. This will create a generational effect: those reaching 53 in 2005 or thereabouts will benefit from the higher accrual but retire before it really affects the contribution rates.

When the whole career wages affect the pension, the role of indexing becomes more significant. A move from 50–50 to 80–20 weights on wages and consumer prices is likely to overcompensate the effect that early career wages will be more important and late career wages less important than they are currently.

The changes in accrual rates, the move to the "career model" from the current model, and the changes in indexation are all included in Part I of the reform evaluation in the next section.

Part II of the reform consists of the longevity adjustment. The effects of such an adjustment in Finland had been previously considered in at least two studies (Lindell 1999, Lassila and Valkonen 2003). The latter study also includes generational effects. The only difference is that the measure takes effect later, from 2010 onwards, and thus its effects on pensions are also felt later. The effects depend on how much life expectancy will increase. Alho (2003) provides a predictive distribution of the adjustment, based mainly on previous errors in predicting future mortality declines.

Longevity adjustment is likely to be an important mechanism in cutting future pension costs. Rumour has it that it was thrown in during the latter phases of negotiations by the Ministry of Finance, to produce reductions in the long run that will offset the increases that the social partners had agreed upon in pensions in the form of accrual and index changes.

There has been some consensus among Finnish decision-makers that people should not retire as young as they do now [4]. The target of raising the age of retirement currently ranks high on the agenda of the debate amongst pension policy experts in all European countries. Unfortunately, however, this proposal is very unpopular amongst European citizens. A survey (European Commission, 2004) conducted in September–October 2001 showed that raising the retirement age is favoured by only 23%, whilst 69% express disagreement. (The rest do not know.) The Finnish numbers were very close to these EU averages. So even if this proposal seems attractive from an economic point of view, and with regard to the issue of intergenerational equity, it obviously faces big problems in public acceptance.

The average retirement age in Finland is currently somewhat below 60 years. For instance, the previous government aimed to increase the average age of exiting from the labour force by 2–3 years in the long term. There was a National Programme on

---

[4] The consensus does not extend to the role of social security in this issue. In a recent survey (Alho et al. 2003) 37–45% of private sector employers fully agreed and 34–50% partly agreed with the opinion that "social security and its financing have been developed so that leaving the labour market has become more lucrative". Only 3–20% of blue-collar workers' representatives fully agreed and 11–19 % partly agreed.

Ageing Workers for the years 1998–2002, organised by the Ministries of Social Affairs and Health, Labour, and Education, aiming to help older workers to stay in work. The measures included increasing the physical and mental condition of aged workers, designing specific services to be provided by employment agencies, and in general making attitudes more favourable to elderly workers.

Labour force participation rates of older people are likely to increase following the changes to the pre-retirement pensions in the pension reform. Also, the change in accrual rates for those over 62 provides better incentives to continue working for persons with short working careers and thus small accrued pension wealth before age 62. For those with long working careers the abolishment of the accrual ceiling may be important. Longevity adjustment will perhaps, for its part, postpone retirement, especially as it has been marketed and described in the form of the number of extra months each cohort needs to work longer in order to cancel the adjustment effect on pension. Other changes in the system will also affect the incentives to work or retire, if people know them and take them rationally into account, but there are opposing income and substitution effects so the net effects remain uncertain. All the effects of the reform that come in the form of postponed retirement are included in Part III in the next section.

Part IV of the reform evaluation considers the temporary increase in funding. It will take place in 2003–2013, and the use of these additions to funds will be decided later. Apparently, the trade unions demanded this measure, at least partly to prevent a situation where current pension rules would have resulted in contributions being temporarily lower, followed by a sharp increase.

Employer representatives have argued that funding should be lower, and existing funds should be run down to postpone increases in contributions or to actually lower them for some time. After the 2001–2002 pension reform the Confederation of Finnish Industry and Employers published a strategy paper, where the aim was to completely prevent increases in the employers' contribution rate. According to the paper, funds should be used as buffers, and pension benefits should be cut if other measures fail.

The main justification originally (40 years ago) presented for the partial prefunding was to alleviate the burden due to the baby-boom generations. The expressed aim was to use the funds to lower the projected peak in the contribution rate. The actual reason for funding was not necessarily, however, to serve as a precautionary tool for future ageing. Short-term tactical considerations may well have dominated. The employers' representatives could have favoured partial funding for two reasons. Firstly, it provided a way to have low actual contributions initially. Unions demanded higher pensions immediately, which would have meant high contributions. Funding allowed contributions to be raised with only small liquidity effects, as firms were entitled to borrow back most of the funded part of the contributions. Secondly, in the aftermath of the 1956 National Pension Law, there were fears of a political take-over of the earnings-related pension system. Employers thought that trade unions would be more willing to defend the TEL system when there was money in the funds. That turned out to be correct: even though socialists and communists in general favoured national pensions, in trade unions they, along with social democrats, supported TEL.

## 3.2 Winners and Losers

The between-cohorts or intergenerational effects of the pension reform are estimated with an overlapping-generations simulation model. The FOG model is an Auerbach-Kotlikoff type of dynamic general equilibrium model calibrated to the Finnish economy. A very brief description is in the Appendix; for a fuller description see Lassila and Valkonen (2003). The demographic scenario used is the non-stochastic path in Alho (2002).

As an intergenerational measure of the connection between benefits and contributions we define the following. The *actuarity ratio* is the ratio of a cohort's discounted benefits from the pension system to its discounted sum of payments to the pension system. The benefits include old-age pensions, disability and unemployment pensions and all other pensions from the earnings-related pension system. A ratio of 100 means that the cohort gets just what it pays, and a ratio below (above) 100 means that it gets less (more) than it pays.

Table 1 presents the changes in the actuarity rate, following from the different parts of the reform. The effects are calculated for three educational groups. The groups differ in the level and shape of career earnings, in ages when they enter the labour force, and in ages when they retire. Entering and exiting the labour force takes place gradually, with those with only basic education (and lowest earnings) entering and retiring younger and those with better education and higher earnings entering and exiting later. Differences in mortality rates between educational groups are not taken into account in the calculations.

Table 2 presents the welfare effects of the reform. In addition to the direct effect from the earnings-related pension system, these calculations take into account the general equilibrium effects on wages and prices that the pension reform has, according to the model. The changes in national pensions, which are means-tested on the earnings-related pensions, are also included here. The reactions of workers to these changes in the saving and labour supply decisions are also included. The utility measure shows relative compensated variations by generations. They are measured as logarithmic differences between the new discounted lifetime consumption expenditures and the consumption necessary to achieve the baseline utility at the new prices. Therefore, positive numbers express a welfare gain.

Actuarity effects and welfare effects may be very different. For cohorts who have mostly retired before the reform the actuarity effects are almost zero. Very small effects come via pension indexation, as wage and price developments are affected by the reform. But these wage and price changes may have important welfare consequences. Postponing retirement, especially, increases labour supply and reduces consumer prices, increasing the purchasing power of income and savings, and resulting in sizeable increases in welfare for the retired cohorts.

Future generations and the youngest current workers lose in welfare from Part I of the reform. Higher accruals mean higher pensions but also higher contributions. Part I means expanding a mostly pay-as-you-go system, and the gain of the initial winners is paid by future cohorts. Currently working generations, excluding the youngest, are the winners. Those already retired are little affected. Actuarity effects are broadly similar to welfare effects.

There are differences between educational groups. The gains are usually smallest and the losses largest (except for future cohorts) for those with only basic schooling. They retire earlier than other groups, and thus benefit less from the higher accrual rates for those in ages over 53 and 63. Instead they are hit hardest by the new timing of the index change: the 20–80 index takes effect immediately after retirement instead of at the age of 65 as in the current system. The index timing effect is smaller for better-educated groups, who retire later and thus also benefit from the higher accrual rates. In the long term, people with medium-level education lose the most. We have assumed that they, on average, have longer work relations than those with only basic education, and earnings that are relatively high at the late stages of the career. They lose, relatively speaking, when the work income affects the pension more evenly during the whole career. People with high education will also suffer from this feature in relative terms, but they will benefit more from the higher accrual rates because on average they have the highest effective retirement age.

The effects of the longevity adjustment are fairly clear-cut. Current working cohorts, whose pensions will be cut by the adjustment, lose in welfare because they do not benefit from the decline in contributions in the long run. The losses are largest for those born in the 1960s and 1970s. Generations born after the year 2000 will benefit from this part of the reform. Their pensions will be smaller but the decline in contributions more than compensates that. Actuarity effects are similar to welfare effects except that the gains seem to come later.

The actuarity losses from postponing retirement are larger for those with only basic schooling, because we assume that their retirement is postponed more than that of other groups. The postponement is assumed to be smallest among the highest education group. The cohorts born in the 1960s and 1970s who have acquired medium-level education also seem to be hit hard by the postponement effect. This is probably due to the assumption of the timing of the postponement and may be spurious.

The welfare effects that come from postponing retirement are the hardest to predict and evaluate. One crucial question is how much one's own retirement is postponed If it is not postponed, one certainly gains: when others work more, taxation, including pension contributions, is reduced. Postponing can be a voluntary decision, which should be welfare-increasing, or dictated by others, which is likely to reduce welfare as higher career earnings and higher pension may not compensate the loss of leisure. The reform will produce both types of postponement: flexible old-age retirement increases the scope of voluntary choice, and tightening the conditions for early retirement is an example of the other type. Table 2 presents one possible outcome. The welfare effects are estimated to be positive for current young cohorts and for all future cohorts.

Looking at the overall welfare effects we note that the winners are already retired cohorts, old workers especially with high education, and also future workers. The losers are young current workers and also old workers with only basic or medium-level education. Usually the losses are small.

Note that risk aspects are missing from the winner-loser analysis, because the current model does not include risks and uncertainties.

**Table 1.** Actuarity Rate Effects from the Pension Reform, by Cohort and Educational Group

| Birth year of cohort | 1930 | 1940 | 1950 | 1960 | 1970 | 1980 | 1990 | 2000 | 2010 | 2020 |
|---|---|---|---|---|---|---|---|---|---|---|
| Part I: Accrual and indexation | | | | | | | | | | |
| Basic schooling | 0.0 | 0.3 | 2.9 | 8.6 | 1.0 | -3.6 | -1.3 | -0.9 | -0.3 | 0.2 |
| Medium level | 0.0 | 0.4 | 6.7 | 6.7 | -1.2 | -4.9 | -3.0 | -2.5 | -1.9 | -1.3 |
| High education | -0.1 | 0.6 | 11.9 | 9.3 | 3.9 | -0.6 | -0.2 | 0.1 | 0.5 | 0.9 |
| Weighted | 0.0 | 0.4 | 6.5 | 7.7 | 0.7 | -3.1 | -1.6 | -1.2 | -0.7 | -0.2 |
| Part II: Longevity adjustment | | | | | | | | | | |
| Basic schooling | -0.1 | -0.1 | -0.2 | -4.4 | -5.0 | -4.6 | -4.0 | -2.9 | -1.2 | 0.4 |
| Medium level | -0.1 | -0.1 | -0.2 | -4.3 | -4.7 | -4.4 | -3.9 | -2.9 | -1.3 | 0.1 |
| High education | 0.0 | -0.1 | -0.1 | -4.0 | -4.5 | -4.2 | -3.7 | -2.8 | -1.5 | -0.3 |
| Weighted | -0.1 | -0.1 | -0.2 | -4.3 | -4.7 | -4.3 | -3.8 | -2.8 | -1.4 | -0.1 |
| Part III: Postponed retirement | | | | | | | | | | |
| Basic schooling | -0.1 | -0.5 | -4.3 | -6.8 | -3.9 | -1.3 | -0.5 | -1.3 | -2.2 | -2.2 |
| Medium level | -0.1 | -0.4 | -3.7 | -5.5 | -3.2 | -0.9 | -0.3 | -1.1 | -1.9 | -1.8 |
| High education | 0.0 | -0.2 | -1.5 | -0.8 | 1.5 | 3.1 | 3.1 | 1.9 | 1.4 | 1.4 |
| Weighted | -0.1 | -0.4 | -3.5 | -4.5 | -1.8 | 0.6 | 1.3 | 0.4 | -0.3 | -0.3 |
| Part IV: Temporary funding | | | | | | | | | | |
| Basic schooling | -0.1 | -0.1 | -1.0 | -1.1 | -0.1 | 0.7 | 0.9 | 0.6 | 0.3 | -0.1 |
| Medium level | -0.1 | -0.1 | -1.3 | -0.8 | 0.1 | 0.8 | 0.7 | 0.5 | 0.2 | -0.1 |
| High education | -0.1 | -0.1 | -1.6 | -0.6 | 0.3 | 0.7 | 0.7 | 0.5 | 0.1 | -0.1 |
| Weighted | -0.1 | -0.1 | -1.3 | -0.8 | 0.1 | 0.7 | 0.7 | 0.5 | 0.2 | -0.1 |
| Parts I-IV Combined | | | | | | | | | | |
| Basic schooling | -0.3 | -0.4 | -2.6 | -3.7 | -8.0 | -8.7 | -4.9 | -4.6 | -3.4 | -1.7 |
| Medium level | -0.2 | -0.2 | 1.5 | -4.0 | -9.0 | -9.5 | -6.4 | -6.0 | -4.9 | -3.1 |
| High education | -0.2 | 0.2 | 8.7 | 4.0 | 1.2 | -1.0 | -0.1 | -0.3 | 0.4 | 1.9 |
| Weighted | -0.3 | -0.2 | 1.6 | -1.9 | -5.7 | -6.0 | -3.4 | -3.1 | -2.2 | -0.6 |

**Table 2.** Welfare Effects from the Pension Reform, by Cohort and Educational Group

| Birth year of cohort | 1930 | 1940 | 1950 | 1960 | 1970 | 1980 | 1990 | 2000 | 2010 | 2020 |
|---|---|---|---|---|---|---|---|---|---|---|
| Part I: Accrual and indexation | | | | | | | | | | |
| Basic schooling | 0.28 | 0.46 | 0.31 | 0.53 | 0.11 | -0.06 | 0.03 | -0.04 | -0.08 | -0.07 |
| Medium level | 0.31 | 0.46 | 0.91 | 0.82 | 0.05 | -0.13 | -0.03 | -0.09 | -0.12 | -0.11 |
| High education | 0.69 | 1.19 | 2.81 | 1.50 | 0.45 | 0.05 | 0.04 | 0.01 | -0.01 | -0.02 |
| Weighted | 0.33 | 0.55 | 0.95 | 0.88 | 0.16 | -0.06 | 0.00 | -0.05 | -0.07 | -0.07 |
| Part II: Longevity adjustment | | | | | | | | | | |
| Basic schooling | -0.24 | -0.32 | -0.23 | -0.59 | -0.65 | -0.40 | -0.24 | -0.16 | 0.00 | 0.15 |
| Medium level | -0.27 | -0.32 | -0.23 | -0.74 | -0.52 | -0.28 | -0.12 | -0.05 | 0.06 | 0.16 |
| High education | -0.54 | -0.74 | -0.30 | -0.65 | -0.46 | -0.24 | -0.05 | -0.03 | 0.01 | 0.05 |
| Weighted | -0.28 | -0.37 | -0.24 | -0.69 | -0.52 | -0.28 | -0.10 | -0.05 | 0.04 | 0.11 |
| Part III: Postponed retirement | | | | | | | | | | |
| Basic schooling | 2.02 | 2.86 | 0.63 | -1.05 | -0.37 | 0.12 | 0.29 | 0.37 | 0.37 | 0.37 |
| Medium level | 2.39 | 2.73 | 0.93 | -1.07 | -0.78 | 0.03 | 0.20 | 0.27 | 0.28 | 0.28 |
| High education | 4.96 | 6.87 | 2.04 | -0.57 | 0.12 | 0.38 | 0.17 | 0.21 | 0.21 | 0.22 |
| Weighted | 2.43 | 3.29 | 0.97 | -0.97 | -0.49 | 0.15 | 0.19 | 0.25 | 0.25 | 0.26 |
| Part IV: Temporary funding | | | | | | | | | | |
| Basic schooling | -0.22 | -0.17 | -0.20 | -0.16 | -0.05 | 0.00 | 0.02 | 0.05 | 0.07 | 0.01 |
| Medium level | -0.22 | -0.17 | -0.26 | -0.15 | -0.03 | 0.00 | 0.01 | 0.04 | 0.06 | 0.01 |
| High education | -0.29 | -0.28 | -0.35 | -0.13 | -0.03 | -0.01 | -0.01 | 0.01 | 0.02 | 0.00 |
| Weighted | -0.23 | -0.18 | -0.25 | -0.15 | -0.03 | 0.00 | 0.00 | 0.03 | 0.04 | 0.01 |
| Parts I-IV Combined | | | | | | | | | | |
| Basic schooling | 1.84 | 2.82 | 0.51 | -1.26 | -0.96 | -0.34 | 0.10 | 0.22 | 0.36 | 0.46 |
| Medium level | 2.21 | 2.70 | 1.36 | -1.14 | -1.27 | -0.38 | 0.06 | 0.16 | 0.27 | 0.34 |
| High education | 4.82 | 7.05 | 4.20 | 0.15 | 0.08 | 0.18 | 0.15 | 0.21 | 0.23 | 0.25 |
| Weighted | 2.26 | 3.28 | 1.43 | -0.93 | -0.89 | -0.19 | 0.09 | 0.18 | 0.26 | 0.31 |

Welfare change as a percentage of consumption expenditure during the rest of life. Negative sign implies a welfare loss.

### 3.3 How Does the Pension Reform Affect Future Wage Bargaining?

Using the median voter approach in trade union decision-making in a computable general equilibrium model, Lassila (2000) studied how the pension system affects wage outcomes, when the trade union is a monopoly union that can set the wage unilaterally. If there were no trade union, each household would make its own decisions concerning leisure and consumption. In the model the trade union, in effect, makes the leisure-consumption choice for the households. Lassila showed that the key issue is the trade-off between leisure and consumption that the union faces in each period. The current period trade-off is affected by the previous choices, and the current choice will affect the trade-off of the future periods. There is a dynamic element that comes via the capital stock adjustment. By increasing the wage, the trade-off is better for the union today but worse tomorrow.

In Lassila's model, the higher the earnings-related PAYG pension benefit level is, the lower is the wage the median voter chooses, for two reasons. Firstly, if the voter claims high current wages, his lifetime wage income falls (because of capital stock adjustment), which will lead to lower pensions, and the advantage of lower pension contributions will go to future working generations. Secondly, the median voter has to pay higher pension contributions both because the current wage bill falls and because current pensions may increase due to indexation. Both these generational transfer effects lead the median voter to choose lower wages, which leads to higher employment.

If we assume that these general features apply to the Finnish pension reform and Finnish bargaining, we can draw some conclusions. Firstly, the size of the PAYG part of the pension system first slightly increases because of accrual and indexation changes, and then gradually falls, due to life expectancy adjustment. Thus the bargained wage levels are predicted to be lower at first and higher in the far future than would have been the case without the pension reform.

Another factor is the timing of the indexation change: after the reform the weaker index, with only a 20 per cent weight on average wages, will take effect after retirement, independent of the age of the retirees, whereas currently the index change takes place at the age of 65. Since retirement takes place, on average, well before the age of 65, this means that current wage increases will be passed on to current retirees to a lesser degree. This leads the median voter to choose higher wages than those without the reform.

The two above-mentioned factors are likely to be rather small. Bigger effects may come from the predicted and desired increase in the average effective retirement age. At least two features will emerge. Firstly, the median voter in the trade union will be older, as there will be more old people working and thus also taking part in trade union decision-making. Secondly, the dynamic element in the trade-off between leisure and consumption, mentioned at the start of this subsection, will count longer in the minds of each member of the trade union. The median worker, although older, will be further away from retirement than he was before the reform. The effects of these features are complicated and cannot be determined without proper analysis, which must be left as a topic for future research.

## 4 Concluding Remarks

The winner-loser analysis of the pension reform showed that current old workers generally kept their positions, and even improved it. Younger workers lost somewhat. Future workers will gain.

Early retirement in general was punished, which will hit lower-income employees harder than more educated groups. Higher accrual rates for workers in ages over 53 and 63 years also benefit higher-income employees more than lower-income employees, because the former retire later on average than the latter.

The results and the discussion above provide some ground for speculation. Workers seem to be more forward-looking with regard to the pension system than employers. Workers are in favour of funding, whereas employers are not. Although employers wanted funding when the pension system was created, their preferences seem to have been the same – as low contributions as possible. The theory (e.g. that behind the FOG model) says that workers pay the pensions in any case, in the form of lower wages, so why do employers care? One reason is that high pension contributions leave less room for firm-level wage policy. For workers, several reasons are possible. In general, a statutory pension system provides insurance for all, including myopic workers and those with hyperbolic utility function, and brings in potential free riders. The Finnish system also gives trade unions an opportunity to take part in the administration of funds and have decision power.

The size of the system is more important to employees than to employers. The latter are more willing to let the system decrease in relative size. The employers' attitude can be explained partly by tax issues, because contribution increases due to changes in population age structure can be seen as tax increases rather than part of the actuarial component. Reducing benefits can reduce this tax increase, if timing is right.

If workers prefer funding but not so much longevity adjustment, that may indicate that power aspects are important, and the pension system is a foothold whose role is not willingly reduced. Then the tax competition aspect may receive less attention than would be optimal for future workers.

The reform showed that between-union comparisons and the relative positions of trade unions are important. This may also be an important factor in future reforms.

Future research should ask how this pension reform will affect wage bargaining. Some comments were provided in Section 3, but a summary assessment requires a detailed analysis.

## References

Alho, J. M. (2002): The Population of Finland in 2050 and Beyond. The Research Institute of the Finnish Economy (ETLA) Discussion Papers No. 826. Helsinki.

Alho, J.M. (2003): Predictive Distribution of adjustment for Life Expectancy Change. Working Papers 3, Finnish Centre for Pensions, Helsinki.

Alho, K., Heikkilä, A., Lassila, J., Pekkarinen, J., Piekkola, H. and Sund, R. (2003): The Finnish wage bargaining system – views of the social partners (In Finnish). The Research Institute of the Finnish Economy (ETLA) Series B No. 203.

Béland, D. (2001): Does Labor Matter? Institutions, Labor Unions and Pension Reform in France and the United States. *Journal of Public Policy*, Volume 21, Number 2, 153–172.

European Commission (2004): Pension Policy and Pension Reform. Special Eurobarometer, January 2004.

Lassila, J. (2000): Wage Formation by Majority Voting and the Incentive Effects of Pensions and Taxation. *Finnish Economic Papers*, Vol. 13, Number 2, 89–115.

Lassila, J. and Valkonen, T. (2002): Prefunding in a Defined Benefit System - the Finnish Case. In M. Feldstein and H. Siebert (*editors*): *Social Security Pension Reform in Europe*. University of Chicago Press, 2002.

Lassila, J. and Valkonen, T. (2003): Ageing, demographic risks and pension reform. In M. Weale *(ed.): Social Security and Pension Reform*. NIESR, Occasional paper, No. 56.

Lindell, K. (1999): Life expectancy increases – what will happen to retirement age? (in Finnish). *Working group memorandum,* Finnish Centre for Pensions, Reports 1999:18. Helsinki.

Niemelä, H. (1994): *The development of Finland's overall pension system* (in Finnish, with an 18-page English summary). 2nd edition. Publications of the Social Insurance Institution, Helsinki.

# Appendix: FOG Model

FOG is an Auerbach-Kotlikoff type, perfect foresight numerical overlapping generations model. There are five sectors: households, enterprises, a government, a pension fund and a foreign sector. The labour, goods and capital markets are competitive and prices balance supply and demand period-by-period. There is no money or inflation in the model. Households and firms are forward-looking decision-makers.

## *Household Behaviour*

Households maximise the utility from consumption and leisure in different periods and the bequest that they give. The life-cycle plan for a household starting its work life at time $t = 1$ is the solution to the following maximisation problem subject to the periodic utility function (2), lifetime budget constraint (3) as well as the determination of gross labour incomes (4), the reference pension (5), old-age pensions (6) and the discount factor (7):

$$Max_{c,l,B} \quad \sum_{t=1}^{T} \frac{1}{1-\frac{1}{\gamma}} \frac{U_t^{1-\frac{1}{\gamma}}}{(1+\delta)^{t-1}} + \mu \frac{B_T^{1-\frac{1}{\gamma}}}{(1+\delta)^{T-1}} \; ; \tag{1}$$

$$U_t = \left( c_t^{1-\frac{1}{\rho}} + \alpha d_t^{1-\frac{1}{\rho}} \right)^{(1-\frac{1}{\rho})-1} \; ; \tag{2}$$

$$\sum_{t=1}^{T_W} g_t \left(1-\tau_t^e-\tau_t^W\right) R_t + \sum_{t=T_W+1}^{T} z_t (1-\tau_t^W) R_t + R_i B_i + \sum_{t=1}^{T} s_t + \sum_{t=1}^{T} s_t^Z \; ; \tag{3}$$
$$= \sum_{t=1}^{T} c_t p_t^C \left(1+\tau_t^C\right) R_t - R_T B_T$$

$$g_t = (1-l_t) e_t w_t \; ; \tag{4}$$

$$z^{ref} = \sum_{t=1}^{T_W} \theta_t b_t (1-\tau_t^e) g_t \left( \frac{(1-\tau_{T_W}^e) w_{T_W}}{(1-\tau_t^e) w_t} \right)^{\lambda_1} \left( \frac{p_{T_W}^C}{p_t^C} \right)^{1-\lambda_1} \; ; \tag{5}$$

$$z_t = z^{ref} \left( \frac{(1-\tau_t^e) w_t}{(1-\tau_{T_W}^e) w_{T_W}} \right)^{\lambda_2} \left( \frac{p_t^C}{p_{T_W}^C} \right)^{1-\lambda_2} \; ; \tag{6}$$

$$R_t = S_{1,1t} (1+r)^{1-t} . \tag{7}$$

Households consider the possibility of early death by discounting future consumption and incomes by a factor, which includes both the interest rate and the age-specific survival probability. The variable $c_t$ describes consumption, $p_t^C$ its price, $l_t$ is leisure, and of the constant parameters $\gamma$ is the elasticity of intertemporal substitution, $\delta$ is the rate of time preference and $\rho$ is the elasticity of substitution between consumption and leisure. Households receive a bequest $B_i$ at the age of $i$ and give a bequest $B_T$ before dying. The parameter $\mu$ determines the strength of the joy-of-giving bequest motive. The aggregate amount of the generation specific transfers $S_t$ is determined to balance the revenues and expenditures of the central government. A life-cycle plan is made at the age of 20, and people plan to retire at the age of $T_W + 1$. The budget constraint (3) says that discounted lifetime wage and pension income equals discounted consumption expenditure. The terms $\tau^{w}$ and $\tau^{C}$ are income tax and value added tax parameters. We have excluded the capital income taxes from this presentation to simplify the expressions.

The $\theta_t$ parameters depict the replacement rates of the current pension system. The $b_t$ parameters describe how the pension rights are related to career earnings. More weight is given to the last working years, because in practice the pensionable wage is aggregated over the last 10 years of each employment contract. As benefits depend on and contributions are paid from wages, there is an indirect connection between contributions and benefits at the individual level. This connection is not one-to-one, however, as not all career earnings are weighed equally. The indexing of accrued pension rights is different in working years and in retirement: in the current TEL index $\lambda_1$ is 0.5 and $\lambda_2$ is 0.2. The changes the reform means to the model's pension equations are not described here. The actual equations of the simulation model are the first-order conditions derived from the optimisation problem.

### *Decision Problem of the Firms*

Firms choose the optimal amount of investment and use of labour to maximise the price of their shares. The market value of the firm is determined as a discounted sum of future dividends. The problem can be presented as maximising, at the beginning of period $t$, the dividends $D_t$ distributed during the period plus the value of the firm $V_t$ at the end of the period, subject to the amount of initial capital stock, the cash-flow equation of the firm (9), the CES production function $F_t$ (10), the accumulation condition of the capital stock $K_t$ (11), the determination of the firm's debt $B_t^F$ (12) and the investment adjustment cost function $G_t$ (13).

$$Max_{L,I,K} \qquad D_t + V_t . \qquad \text{subject to:} \tag{8}$$

$$\begin{aligned} D_t = \Big[ p_t^F \left( F_t - G_t \right) - (1+\tau_t^l) w_t L_t^F - r_{t-1}^d B_{t-1}^F \Big], \\ + B_t^F - B_{t-1}^F - p_t^K I_t \end{aligned} \tag{9}$$

$$F_t = A^F \left[ \varepsilon K_{t-1}^{(1-1/\beta)} + (1-\varepsilon)\left( v^t L_t^F \right)^{(1-1/\beta)} \right]^{\frac{\beta}{\beta-1}}, \tag{10}$$

$$K_t = (1-d)K_{t-1} + I_t \quad , \tag{11}$$

$$B_t^F = bp_{t-1}^K K_{t-1} \qquad \text{and} \tag{12}$$

$$G_t = \xi \frac{I_t^2}{K_{t-1}} \quad . \tag{13}$$

Equations (8) and (9) have been simplified by leaving out the capital income tax terms. The price variables $p_t^F$ , $p_t^K$ describe the prices of value added and the capital unit. $r_{t-1}^d$ is the domestic interest rate, which generates interest flows to be distributed during period t. The typical CES production function parameters are as follows: $A^F$ is the scale parameter, $\varepsilon$ is the share parameter and $\beta$ is the substitution parameter. $\nu$ describes the rate of productivity growth of labour. The accumulation of capital $K_t$ is explained by using the depreciation rate $\lambda$ and the amount of new investments $I_t$ . The parameter $b$ describes the collateral value of the capital stock. In the last equation, the parameter $\xi$ determines the scaling of the investment adjustment costs.

Three of the four first-order conditions of the constrained optimisation are used as model equations, the fourth being the transversality condition.

### Markets

The model includes four markets, which clear every period. In the labour market, firms demand labour according to the marginal productivity of labour rule. Households' aggregate labour supply is divided between public and private employment. The wage rate is determined by equating supply and demand in the labour market.

Firms are sole suppliers in the market for the domestic good. The product is used by other firms as part of the composite intermediate and investment goods, by households as part of the composite consumption good and by foreign agents. The demand of domestic agents and the prices of the composite goods are determined by a cost-minimising procedure. Domestic demand for the fixed-price imported good is also determined by minimising the costs of the composite goods. The perfectly elastic supply adjusts to demand in this market. The fourth market is the capital market, in which saving and investment are balanced by the domestic interest rate $r_t^d$ . In the simulations we use a model version in which the interest rate is fixed to be the same as the rate in international capital markets. In this case, the total saving is the sum of domestic saving and foreign portfolio investments.

The presentation above describes only the relevant parts of the model. The actual model includes, for example, a government with an intertemporal budget constraint, and trade and capital flows with the rest of the world. The modelled pension system also includes prefunded disability and other early pensions.

### *Actuarity Ratio*

As an intergenerational measure of the connection between benefits and contributions we define the following. The actuarity ratio is the ratio of a cohort's discounted benefits from the pension system to its discounted sum of payments to the pension system. The benefits include old-age pensions, denoted by z, and, combined into $s^Z$, disability and unemployment pensions and all other pensions from the earnings-related pension system.

$$A^R = \left( \sum_{t=1}^{T} s_t^Z R_t + \sum_{t=T_W+1}^{T} z_t R_t \right) / \left( \sum_{t=1}^{T_W} \tau_t^l g_t R_t \right). \tag{14}$$

Printing and Binding: Strauss GmbH, Mörlenbach

The manufacturer's authorised representative in the EU is Springer Nature Customer Service Centre GmbH, Europaplatz 3, 69115 Heidelberg, Germany. If you have any concerns regarding our products, please contact ProductSafety@springernature.com

Printed and bound by CPI Group (UK) Ltd, Croydon, CR0 4YY
25/09/2026
02222857-0003